P9-CEY-880

MARRIED W8MEN WHO LOVE W8MEN

CARREN STROCK

alyson books
los angeles | new york

ALL OF THE NAMES ALONG WITH ANY IDENTIFYING CHARACTERISTICS OF THE WOMEN INTERVIEWED FOR THIS BOOK HAVE BEEN CHANGED TO PROTECT THEIR ANONYMITY.

© 1998 BY CARREN STROCK. ALL RIGHTS RESERVED.

MANUFACTURED IN THE UNITED STATES OF AMERICA.

THIS TRADE PAPERBACK IS PUBLISHED BY ALYSON PUBLICATIONS,
P.O. BOX 4371, LOS ANGELES, CALIFORNIA 90078-4371,
BY ARRANGEMENT WITH DOUBLEDAY, A DIVISION OF RANDOM HOUSE INC.

FIRST EDITION PUBLISHED BY DOUBLEDAY: JANUARY 1998
FIRST ALYSON EDITION: APRIL 2000

01 02 03 04 **a** 10 9 8 7 6 5 4 3 2

ISBN 1-55583-555-4
(PREVIOUSLY PUBLISHED WITH ISBN 0-385-48825-4 BY DOUBLEDAY.)

LIBRARY OF CONGRESS CATALOGING-IN-PUBLICATION DATA
STROCK, CARREN.
    MARRIED WOMEN WHO LOVE WOMEN / CARREN STROCK.
    ORIGINALLY PUBLISHED: NEW YORK : DOUBLEDAY, 1998.
    INCLUDES BIBLIOGRAPHICAL REFERENCES.
    ISBN 1-55583-555-4
    1. LESBIANS. 2. MARRIED WOMEN. 3. WIVES. I. TITLE.
HQ75.5.S77 2000
306.76'63—DC21   99-087155 CIP

COVER PHOTOGRAPH BY B. ZINDA.

This book is dedicated to

Noel,
Ian, and Laurie,
for their unconditional love and acceptance

"Whether women who love women are born or choose to be is not the issue. It is that we are."

—JOANNE LUELLEN

THE LIGHT

JEANNE FERG
July 13, 1940–February 11, 1990

in the plainness
of her words
i hear the echo
of women calling out
in their darkness
listening for answers
to questions never voiced
touched by feelings
newly felt
and i laugh in recognition
within myself, ah yes
!
the secret place
where i once lived alone
without answers
and only loud questions . . .

Contents

Foreword

I NEVER IMAGINED *Married Women Who Love Women* (hardcover, Doubleday, 1998) would touch so many women so deeply. Since its initial publication, I have received numerous letters and E-mails from across the United States and from as far away as South America, Australia, and Europe. They have come from women struggling with feelings of guilt, shame, and isolation as well as from women with long-unanswered questions.

Many have shared their own poignant stories. One woman, sobbing and clutching my book, approached me at a reading. "I came to thank you. I thought I was the only married woman ever to have fallen in love with another woman," she said, pausing often to regain her composure. Finally she told me, "I was so terrified, I decided to kill myself. Then I found your book, and it saved my life."

Married women who love women are not the only ones who have contacted me. I often receive mail from single lesbians thanking me for helping them gain a better understanding of the married women they love and from straight women thanking me for helping them to better understand what their sisters, daughters, mothers, or friends are going through.

While *Married Women Who Love Women* draws basically from women's perspectives, notes from husbands—also searching for answers and understanding—tell me I have only scraped the surface of this issue. Like their wives, they are grateful to learn they are not the only ones experiencing these surprising or shocking marital changes. One husband wrote, "My wife, feeling totally alienated by her newly discovered feelings, confided in me, and it was me who found and bought *Married Women Who Love Women* for her.... Ironically, now that she has come to terms with her sexuality, she absolutely exudes sexuality, and I find her more attractive than ever. But we are pretty realistic about everything and will just see what happens." Another husband wrote, "I still love my emerging-lesbian wife and am struggling to find a graceful way to let our relationship evolve into a friendship that will last longer than any union or marriage."

Since 59% of the women I interviewed for the book had no idea of their same-gender identification before they were married, I knew this topic would be an important one for everyone. *Newsweek* concurred, and published my related essay on their "My Turn" page (May 18, 1998). There were a few irate responses, such as, "How dare you deal with your own needs and happiness?" and "If you discover too late that you've made a mistake and should not have married a certain man or woman, you should keep your mouth shut and swallow it. Take it to the grave!" But more often, responses were in favor of bringing this frightening topic to light. "I now view the lesbian lifestyle with softer eyes," one reader wrote.

My original purpose in writing *Married Women Who Love Women* was to let other women going through their own discoveries know they were not alone and to help them by seeing how others have dealt with this issue. If I have also helped a few people to understand and be less judgmental, then I have accomplished a lot.

The following are quotes from letters and E-mails I have received in response to the book:

"After years of frustration, repression, denial, and therapy, I read your book and came out to myself. Thank you for making everything so clear."

"I felt like you were reading my mind, and feeling my heart.... I smiled, cried, and chuckled through all of your book.... I felt it was 'my' book.... I felt a part of every woman in there."

"I would well up every time I agonized over telling my husband. The secret was killing me. My 'gayness' was spilling out all over, and I was so frightened."

"I felt the pain of all the women that contributed to your book, and I realized there is no right and wrong. Everyone is an individual who has to live with her own actions and decisions. It is so very complicated."

"I derived so much strength from knowing that I was not alone. Thanks to you, that message rang loud and clear."

"Thank you for realizing how many of us are out there feeling that we are the only ones. Thank you for having the courage to write your book."

"I inhaled your book and painted it with a yellow highlighter as I read, related, and absorbed every last word."

For more information, or to contact me, please access my Web site at http://www.erols.com/carrens.

Introduction

MY WEIGHT PLUMMETED and my clothes hung sloppily over my body. I could not have cared less, but at the insistence of my family I found myself at Macy's. I had been instructed to buy some things that fit. Indifferently I pulled a blouse over my head. Suddenly I found myself sliding to the floor of the dressing room, choking back loud, anguished sobs. I sat with my back hunched over and my knees drawn to my chin, rocking back and forth, trying to muffle the cries I could not control.

These involuntary outbursts were coming more frequently. I had to find help. I had to find someone to tell. Where could I turn? Whom could I trust with this horrible secret?

In the space of six months my mind had become completely disordered. My value system had failed me. Suddenly I, who had been so sure about everything, knew nothing.

I had fallen in love with another woman!

My sister used to call me Pollyanna. I lived in a secure world protected by an invisible white picket fence. Mine was the "perfect" family.

My husband and I were married in 1964 after we had dated for three years. I was nineteen and he was twenty-one. We felt certain enough of our maturity to take on the responsibilities of raising a family. Our babies came as we had planned. Two and a half years after our wedding, our son arrived, and then two years after him, our daughter. We moved to our house in the suburbs.

Our door was open, and friends and neighbors dropped in all the time. I was great at stretching meals to accommodate unexpected guests. I was the one called when last-minute brownies were needed for the Girl Scout sale, or when a chairperson was needed for a charity drive. While my kids were growing up, I was active in the parent-teacher association, the Junior Women's Club, and Hadassah.

I was so preoccupied with my husband and children and their needs that I was oblivious to my own, or to what was happening in the larger world. Eventually, our children grew up and we moved to the city.

And then I met Toby.

With my new friend came the beginnings of my awareness of women's liberation. Toby had been divorced and raised two sons while putting herself through college and graduate school. She was a published author working on her second novel while supporting herself and her family. I was impressed by her accomplishments. I had always taken my own talents for granted, thinking that if *I* could paint and do craftwork, so could everyone else. But Toby was impressed with my abilities; she called me "the Renaissance woman."

We became fast friends and soon I couldn't imagine Toby not being a part of my life. We might phone each other five times a day to share some silly story or go for a week without talking. It didn't matter; each of us knew we were there for the other. We shared long walks and heavy conversations about intimate parts of our lives. We felt free in each other's kitchens and comfortable with each other's families.

One evening, while we were sitting and talking, I found myself looking, really looking, at Toby. She smiled at me from across the room and a strange and powerful feeling rushed through my body. My heart began to race. I realized I was in love with my best friend.

I didn't say anything at first, but my feelings grew daily. Each time I saw her, my stomach fluttered. Just being in her company, colors became brighter, sounds clearer. I had never felt like that before.

Toby and I had always hugged each other hello and good-bye,

but now these hugs took on new meaning. I couldn't wait to see her, and then I couldn't wait for her to leave for those brief moments when we would be in each other's arms.

Our friendship had always been based on honesty, and now, given the intensity of my new feelings, I felt compelled to share them with her. It felt so natural and so wonderful to love her as I did that it had to be all right. We arranged to meet for dinner and I picked her up at the station. Toby chatted animatedly about her week as we drove toward the shore. Her voice was comforting and it felt so good to be with her. Still, the pounding in my chest was growing louder. I swallowed several times and took a deep breath. Without taking my eyes from the road, I said, "Toby, I'm in love with you."

"I love you too, Carren," she said.

"No. You don't understand. I've fallen in love with you."

An uncomfortably long pause replaced Toby's laughter of minutes before. "Carren, you're in love with the idea of sisterhood, of feminism, I've opened your eyes to—"

"Toby," I cut her off. "I'm in love with you."

We drove on to the bay in silence and parked the car. I turned toward the dock where we usually walked before eating.

"I'd rather go right to the restaurant," she said. "I'm cold." The weather was mild and her coat was open, so I knew it was a different kind of cold she was feeling. Suddenly I was terrified. What had I done? I was filled with turmoil. What if my confession made her mad or she thought I was sick and never wanted to speak to me again? Could my being in love with Toby destroy our friendship? Then I thought no. That's absurd. We'll work it out. I ordered wine with my dinner, something I rarely did, then left my meal untouched, another thing I rarely did. I felt an awkwardness growing between us. I had never seen Toby at a loss for words, yet now she seemed to consider each one carefully before it left her mouth. Why had I been so insensitive? How could I have been such a fool? Why had I never anticipated her rejecting me?

Maybe it was the wine, I'm not sure, but by the end of dinner our customary way of bantering seemed to have returned. I drove her home, put the car in park, and we hugged as usual. After a brief second, however, I pulled away, suddenly shy.

For a while we continued to speak several times a week. Only now I found myself fumbling over words and having trouble keeping my voice steady. Toby was guarded and spoke only in generalities. Each time I lifted the receiver to call her, my hands trembled and I began to hyperventilate. Our conversations lost their fun and spontaneity. Their main theme became my obsession with her. I could talk of little else. Out of fairness to Toby, I must say that she did try to remain my friend. She listened kindly, but over the following months the frequency of her phone calls dwindled until she stopped calling altogether. She didn't feel toward me as I did toward her, and she had had enough of the crazed woman I had become. Our friendship ended.

At home, with great difficulty I functioned as though nothing had happened. After all, I was the nurturer and the caregiver— others depended on me. I had to be strong. If my husband or children saw any changes in my behavior, they never acknowledged them. Privately in great pain, I mourned the loss of my best friend. There was no one to offer comfort, no one with whom to share my sorrow. I lay awake night after night, replaying all that had happened, thinking of Toby. I began walking for hours at a time, needing to force myself into exhausted sleep.

I remember Toby asking me during one of our last visits if it was sex with her that I wanted. I had been shocked at her question. I realize now that I had no frame of reference for such an idea. I'd never thought of having sex with her, only about being with her, holding her, having her hold me. Sex was something I had with my husband. It had nothing to do with this passion I was feeling for her.

While I mourned, the question she had put into my head kept repeating itself. Was it sex with her that I wanted? Did I want to have sex with a woman? Did that make me a lesbian? I could hardly even say the word at first, but the more I thought about it, the less absurd it seemed. I began to wonder. Although my husband was always considerate about satisfying me, I had never had a strong sex drive with him.

Now I had to contend not only with the loss of my best friend, but the shock of discovering my possible new sexuality. I searched but found no reading material, no affirmation that I wasn't insane or that other women had had the same experience; the more alone I felt, the more terrified I became.

Eventually, without telling my family, secretly skimming money off the food budget to pay for it, I went into therapy. I had no idea of how it could help me, but I knew that I desperately needed to find someone I could talk to. I would not understand for several years that I had been going through a process of discovery. It is only now, looking back, that I can appreciate the strength it took as well as the courage to move forward, accept myself, and, eventually, come out to my family. Along the way I have also come to learn that my story is not unique.

Through the self-help groups I sought out during my transition period, I met numerous other married women who had also discovered their previously hidden sexuality, or were trying to come to terms with long-denied feelings of being different. They were trying to make sense of their lives, to preserve their marriages and families and, in some cases, their very sanity. Finally, I had connected with women who were like me. We talked on and on until everything began to make sense.

According to *The Hite Report*, 87 percent of all married women have their deepest emotional attachments with other women, usually their best friends. While it doesn't happen to every woman, sometimes these friendships unexpectedly burst into passionate romantic and physical love.

Due to the clandestine way in which married women who love women often live, few people have been aware that we even exist. Consequently, it is understandable that researchers might conclude that these women tend to divorce immediately upon learning about their sexuality. And who would contradict them? Nonetheless, I knew that not all married women who love women leave their marriages, and I set out to explore all the ways in which women who love women lead their lives.

Having accepted their culturally sanctioned roles as caregivers and nurturers, some women believe they have no choice other than to remain in their marriages and keep their feelings and needs repressed. Fear of repercussions—having their children taken from them, being shunned by family and friends, even becoming destitute—makes other women decide to stay married. All these women silently endure the guilt and anguish brought on by the frightening discovery of their new sexuality. At the same time, many have affairs outside marriage to discover who they are and what they crave. For the first time in their lives, they do what they need to do for themselves.

Married Women Who Love Women is the result of open and truthful dialogues with more than one hundred women who have had the courage to acknowledge their same-sex preferences. It addresses issues that have never been freely discussed before: Why do women turn to other women for emotional fulfillment? What would make a married woman cross that invisible line that turns her best friend into her lover? Why do some women struggle with identity while others easily embrace their sexuality? What do married women do when they realize that a large part of themselves has been missing? Why might they choose to remain in a marriage after having discovered their sexual preference? What kind of men are they married to? Why would men remain with wives who love women? How are these women and their husbands redefining their marriages? How are children, parents, and friends affected? And finally, where do straight women fit into the picture?

It will also answer intimate questions that have crossed the minds of all women, although few have had the courage to say so. What is it like for a woman who has believed herself heterosexual to come together physically with a woman for the first time? How is making love with a woman different from making love with a man? How does a woman know whether she is a lesbian or bisexual? What are the distinctions and why do they matter?

I have compiled my evidence from the courageous women who have stepped forward to speak with me. Their stories present an eye-opening picture of a growing population that has been silent too long.

In my search, I found married women who love women (MWLW) at women's groups and gathering places. Sharing my story made others comfortable enough to share their own. Consequently, while many women had never told even their therapists about their sexual preference, for me, finding MWLW to interview was relatively easy. The women I spoke to referred me to their friends. Others identified friends but, because of the sensitivity of the subject matter, were hesitant to give me their phone numbers. I gave them fliers to pass along instead.

Although the fliers specifically requested married women for the book, divorced women—who had discovered their lesbianism either before or after their divorces—also came forward to share their stories. In addition, I placed ads in lesbian publications and in newsletters that served lesbian communities. And, knowing that not all MWLW have access to those papers or are even aware of their existence, I placed an ad in *National NOW*, the newspaper of the National Organization for Women. In the NOW ad I revealed my same-sex feelings. This brought a response from women who lived in rural areas and had felt especially cut off.

I mailed fliers to feminist bookstores across the country and to women's centers at colleges and universities. I posted fliers on supermarket bulletin boards and left them in the ladies' rooms of restaurants and theaters.

I have received calls from women who said they had picked up my fliers in places I was unfamiliar with and later learned that other women had taken it upon themselves to make additional copies and further circulate the fliers.

Women told me things they said they had never been able to tell anyone else before. They expressed relief at being able to share their feelings openly and honestly. Long-pent-up frustrations spilled out along with angry or sad feelings about their husbands, marriages, families, and lives in general. At times it was difficult for me to hear about their pain and isolation without reliving my own. Many of the women I interviewed thanked me, saying that for the first time they didn't feel alone. One woman echoed the feelings of many when she said, "Your ad jumped off the page for me. Until now no one had seemed to care about married women who must live with their secret."

Through the course of my research, which grew to include both husbands and children of MWLW, the majority of people, both men and women, responded to the subject matter with a mixture of relief and gratitude.

The married women who love women interviewed ranged in age from twenty-one to seventy. Thirty percent were thirty-five or younger, 60 percent were between the ages of thirty-six and fifty-five, and 10 percent were over fifty-five.

Because the subject of lesbianism is no longer as taboo as it once was, and the average age at which women marry has risen from 20.3 in 1950 to twenty-four by 1990, younger women in general are growing up with an increased awareness and, having more time to explore, a better understanding of their own sexuality and available life choices. Yet some young women, aware of their preference for women, still elect to marry men. Their reasons may be as basic as medical coverage, or fear of rejection by family and friends, since societal pressures still restrict many young women, especially those outside of urban areas.

The majority of women interviewed, however, were in their mid-thirties through mid-fifties when their same-sex feelings became apparent. For the most part, middle-aged women grew up knowing that they were supposed to marry a nice man who would be a good provider and a good father. The unspoken message was: "A woman cannot take care of herself." Furthermore, sex outside marriage was considered taboo, and so nice girls married. The single career woman was still an anomaly.

Only 23 percent of the MWLW interviewed knew or had a feeling about their same-sex orientation before they were married. Twelve percent realized in hindsight that they had same-sex orientation, and 6 percent couldn't recall exactly when they made the discovery. However, the majority, 59 percent, had no idea of their same-sex orientation before they were married.

Married women discovering or reawakening their dormant sexual awareness generally fall into four categories. The first consists of women who, as young girls, sensed a difference between themselves and their peers but didn't have the words to describe their differences. They had no knowledge that there was any such thing as lesbianism. The second consists of women who knew positively, early in life, that they had lesbian tendencies. However, because they had been indoctrinated by society's teachings into believing that lesbianism was a sickness or evil, or because they simply wanted to fit into mainstream society, they tried to conform. The third is women who knew what lesbianism was, did not deny their feelings, and had even been involved with other women, but thought they were different. They were in such strong states of denial that they never characterized themselves as lesbians. And the fourth consists of women who totally believed they were heterosexual . . . until they fell in love with another woman.

Apparently, not all married women are happy. According to Carol Botwin's book, *Tempted Women*, "twenty-one million women in America—forty percent of the married population—are having affairs." Other current books such as *The Erotic Silence of the American Wife* by Dalma Heyn, and *Secret Loves* by Sonya Friedman, also discuss the extramarital affairs women have, though all three mainly focus on heterosexual affairs, thereby missing a very large slice of the issue.

This book fills that gap. And in so doing, I hope, sheds both light and understanding for MWLW, their families, and friends.

PART ONE

The Discovery

1

Awakening

UNTIL I WAS forty-three I would have said with absolute certainty, "I am not, nor could I ever become, a lesbian. I know exactly who and what I am."

One year later I fell in love with another woman. I was to experience more passion, pain, isolation, and turmoil than I had ever thought possible. Through it all, my life was to become clearer and brighter . . . and I was to grow wiser from my experience.

Although I felt totally alone at the time, I am not the only woman who has stumbled onto the path of sexual discovery and growth. My experience is not uncommon. Some women make a sudden discovery as I did. For others, it's a compilation of occurrences and a slow realization and awakening. This new awareness, brought on by the gradual synthesis of ongoing incidents and old recollections, can change an entire life.

Is there any woman, heterosexual or homosexual, who can truly say that she cannot remember having been especially fond of a particular woman in her life, maybe a teacher she admired, a girlhood friend, a special family friend? Women who knew or sensed that their sexual preference leaned toward women easily recalled crushes on schoolmates and female teachers. For me, it wasn't so simple.

When I finally had the courage to talk about my same-sex feelings, most women asked if I had ever suspected or had an inkling that I was attracted to other women. Some simply wanted to satisfy their curiosity, others wanted to reinforce in their own minds that they were not like me and they were, therefore, safe from any possibility of ever becoming lesbians.

Sometimes the questions felt like accusations. "How could you not have known?" And I felt forced to deny any knowledge, as if there must be blame and I am not to blame. I would answer, "No. Definitely not. Not me. I never felt attracted to another woman." What I was saying was: I'm innocent. I had no idea. It's not my fault. All of which was true.

It was not that I consciously lied about any feelings I might have had for women. The specific incidents I recalled seemed insignificant and innocent. I remember the older girl in Hebrew school, assigned to be my "buddy" when we went on a class trip: I must have been seven at the time, and I remember thinking that she was beautiful and feeling glad that the teacher had chosen her to team up with me. Then there was my camp counselor when I was nine. She was so pretty that I would rush to the front of the line so she would hold my hand when we took nature walks. But hadn't all of the girls in my group done the same thing?

Did having these feelings as a young girl mean I was destined to walk a different path? Not necessarily. Appreciating beauty in others is natural. Forming attachments to older women, wanting to emulate them, is also a natural process of growing up. Besides, I never went looking for a woman to fall in love with. At first I felt only anger. Why me? I didn't want things to change. I was married, had a husband, a family. I hadn't even known feelings like this existed.

The anger was followed by a period of deep grief. Initially, I thought I was mourning the loss of my best friend because she withdrew from me and our friendship dissolved. The pain of not having her as a part of my life was excruciating. We had shared everything. She had been my confidante. Now she was not there to help me through the most difficult road I had ever traveled. I realized I was also mourning the changes in myself. This newly acquired knowledge about my sexuality could never be forgotten. I would no longer be content, naive . . . or innocent.

There was also blame. I had to blame someone. It had to be someone's fault that all of this was happening to me. So I blamed my husband: He should have been more understanding, more perceptive, more supportive. I lost sight of the fact that there were other issues we had never dealt with, issues having nothing to do with my sexuality.

All of this was going on in my head, and he had no idea I was harboring these thoughts. I was living my life on a seesaw. On one side, with family and friends, I felt forced to go on as though nothing had changed. And I was a good actress, keeping everything inside until the last person had left the house in the morning; then I would collapse, sobbing, against the nearest piece of furniture. Or, when the family was home and my feelings became overwhelming, I'd run out on some fictitious errand, get in the car, and bawl. I spent many hours walking. Only when I was with women who knew about me did my vulnerability surface. Someone need only ask "How are you doing?" and the tears would flow. This went on for more than a year.

Slowly, these steps did lead to acceptance and growth. But these were not clear-cut periods in my life. My feelings vacillated between denial, grief, and anger. Although I visited old friends and extended family, until I began therapy and started connecting with women I could talk to, I felt as though I were living in total isolation.

SHARI

Shari, a forty-year-old wife and mother, says, "I'd pulled the van over because I was crying too hard to drive. . . . I thought I was crying about my intense physical and emotional feelings for a new friend (who I knew was a lesbian), when 'it' very suddenly hit me—right in the middle of my forehead, like a hammer.

"I was crying about myself, not about my friend and the fact that she was in love with someone else. I became aware that I was absolutely starving in a place I'd never known existed, and starving in a way I'd never known before: the need to be with others of my own kind.

"The next awareness, coming minutes later, was the revelation: 'I'm gay!'

"The sensation that immediately followed was falling backward into a bottomless pit: forever lost to an alien and yet completely known 'other life'. . . . I was taking in, all at once, the complete awareness that I was gay and that this was going to totally change the rest of my life.

"I simultaneously felt terror (What does this mean for me and my family?) and the purest euphoria of total relief. For the first time in my life, 'I' filled me from my core to the outer edges of my skin."

Shari is an educated woman, yet she was totally confused at the intensity of her emotional feelings for another woman. The only way she could explain her feelings was by deciding that on an emotional level, she must be bisexual. She wanted that to be the answer.

"That felt like the answer for about a day and a half," Shari says. "But when I pictured myself telling my longtime best friend that I was bisexual, the imaginary conversation was always interrupted by this inner voice that said, 'You're a fuckin' dyke.'

"I replayed this 'conversation' of voices for a couple more days—and on that night, in the van, somehow was able to let the last of whatever was holding me back go . . . and now, here all of me is!"

Shari had never questioned her sexuality, although she admits to thinking of herself as "strangely unique." She identified her uniqueness only as "I'm clumsy, clunky, not feminine." But what woman can't identify with having those same feelings at some time in her life?

Today's youth can turn on a television and find a talk show on any kind of sexuality, or go to a school counselor or the library to obtain information. Women raised prior to the late 1960s often had limited sex education. Although they may have sensed differences between themselves and their friends, they often had no understanding of these differences.

Most of the women, like Shari, never understood the significance of their feelings. Those who did have questions had no place to go for answers. They put their feelings on hold and did what society expected them to do: marry and have children.

MARTHA

Martha went to an all-girl Catholic high school. She had a large circle of friends and found herself caring about them emotionally

. . . and physically. When she realized that none of her friends seemed to feel the way she did, she began to feel "unusual."

In her senior year Martha and Roxanne became very close. Martha says, "We started hanging out together and going places together. It was incredible. It felt so natural. When we sat together in the movie theater and our elbows touched, it was wonderful.

"All we did was kiss. We were both young and naive. We knew we weren't satisfied with just kissing each other, but we didn't know what else to do. Anything else would have felt dirty. We were extremely Catholic. Roxanne was going into a convent. She was consecrated to God."

The day that Roxanne entered the convent, Martha was there for the ceremony. "I watched my friend walk down the aisle in a white dress and wanted to die. Roxanne went behind a door and came back in her habit." Martha remembers fighting back her tears because she was with Roxanne's family and it wouldn't be right to show how disappointed she was.

Both girls were so inexperienced that they were incapable of understanding their feelings, much less putting them into words. At the time, neither girl knew what a homosexual was. Even after Martha fell in love with Roxanne, she thought they were unique, that what happened to them didn't happen to other girls. Never did she identify herself as a lesbian.

"I remember a joke I heard at sixteen," Martha says. " 'Let's be lesbo and go homo.' I laughed because everyone else did, but I had no idea what it meant. If I knew at all, I wasn't sure that it had anything to do with women."

Since all of her friends had married, she realized it was time for her to do the same. She dated halfheartedly, and when the man she had been dating asked her to marry him, she rushed home to call her girlfriends before giving him her answer. "Should I feel a tingling when he touches me, or see skyrockets going off when he kisses me?" she asked.

"No," her friends assured her. "That only happens in the movies." How could she tell anyone she had experienced those feelings with her friend Roxanne?

It wasn't until she was in her early forties that Martha realized she was a lesbian. Meanwhile, Roxanne had died in the convent at thirty-three. Martha still grieves for the untried chance at happiness she and Roxanne might have had had they understood what their feelings were all about.

RIFKA

"Since I was four years old, I would identify more with women than with men. . . . I had crushes on boys and girls through my adolescence and adulthood, but I knew where I would go. I would get married. I would have babies. At twenty-one, I did.

"My sexuality could be satisfied with my husband because I wanted it to be. But emotionally there was always something missing. There was nobody in my life who could fill that. I had dozens of friends, but that didn't help. When I tried to talk to my husband about my needs, he said, 'Physically I can give you anything, but don't ask for anything emotionally.' "

Rifka was teaching a mental health course at a college and her students came to her and told her how their lives were changing. She says, "I listened to them and at forty, decided it was time to take care of me. Prior to that I was in a consciousness-raising group.

"That had helped me to realize I could make my life not my mother's, my husband's, or my children's, but entirely my own."

Rifka didn't know how she was going to take back her life. "I was not making a conscious decision at forty to become a lesbian," she says. "I was very homophobic, so when I fell in love with Fran, the shit hit the fan. The best and worst time of my life. My internalized homophobia was externalized as well. I'm grateful to Fran because she wasn't homophobic and her patience as a friend helped me."

ROBERTA

Roberta, on the other hand, had been sexually abused by her father from the time she was a little girl until he died when she was twenty-three years old, and felt a tremendous distaste for men from early on. She could have left home but she believed that by being there, she was saving her younger siblings the same fate with their father. Years later she found out that they were being abused despite her sacrifice.

Whether or not Roberta would have had same-sex tendencies

had she not been sexually abused by her father we can't tell, but psychotherapist Arlene DiMarco believes that women who have been incest victims and have had "no bonding with the father, the person they were supposed to be able to trust, would be more apt to try to find a constant with another woman. . . . Women view other women as being kinder and gentler, sensitive and more understanding than men."

Had she been aware that lesbians existed, Roberta would probably have made other life choices early on. Unfortunately, even with the abhorrence she had for men, she knew of no alternative.

Roberta says, "I lived in West Virginia and all of the women I worked with were always looking for men, so I would go with them on their outings. I wasn't interested but I had to do that. First of all, I couldn't let any of them know about my father . . . or that I even knew about sex. So I had to be this totally naive virgin. I pretended I didn't know anything about anything. We went to Myrtle Beach, South Carolina. They would be picking up guys. I remember thinking, 'I don't want to pick up anyone so I'm going to eat onions.' Then this cute guy came over. He was in the army, so he used to hitchhike three hundred miles every other weekend just to see me. I would sort of lead him on, but I wasn't about to have sex with him. I was scared to death to have sex.

"Still, I knew I had to get married. I didn't know what else a woman could or would do.

"Then, at a club, I met a much older man, a traveling salesman. He came over and wanted to dance with me. He started courting me and eventually I agreed to go to bed with him. I was twenty-five. So that was my first real sexual experience, not counting what happened with my father. I had sex with this man for about a year until I found out he had lied to me. He was married, not divorced as he had told me.

"At twenty-eight I met Jay, my husband-to-be. I actually met four other men before I met him at sort of a pickup place. They were all awful, absolute beasts. My friend was supposed to go with me that night, but she changed her mind. I had said to her, 'I'm going by myself and if I don't meet a nice man here I'm through with men forever.' And I went and I met those four awful men and I was raped and I thought I was pregnant, so when I met Jay and he was really nice and he seemed different . . . I felt, 'Jay would be a nice man to marry.'

"When I went into labor I couldn't give birth. I didn't know if my daughter was Jay's or one of the other men's. It was absolute terror. They had to do a cesarean. But I never told Jay. I carried the secret on my own, like everything. Everything was a secret. In the meantime, I tried to be the best mother and the best wife in the whole world, and I did that for twenty-four years."

Roberta sighed. "When I listen to my life, it sounds so awful.

"Probably about fourteen years ago I started struggling to claim myself. I started going to therapy and women's support groups."

Roberta fell in love with one of the first women she shared her story with. "When it happened I was startled, but that lasted for about five seconds, then I began to remember that I had always been in love with women.

"I could remember this little girl, Ann, we were in the first grade. I don't remember an erotic aspect to it, but I loved her madly. Then I remember working at the telephone company and there was a woman working there. I was really in love with her and I'd have these erotic thoughts and I'd say to myself, 'Cut that out. You're not supposed to be thinking that. She's a woman.' "

Other women knew positively, early in life, that they had lesbian tendencies. But because they had been told that to love a person of the same sex was wrong, they feared being ostracized by their families and peers and tried to conform to society's accepted standards. It was very natural for these women to do everything possible to put their feelings to rest. They made themselves "well" through therapy and by choosing the traditional roles of wives in heterosexual marriages.

HELEN

Helen, a sixty-four-year-old grandmother, was reunited with Bernice four years ago at their fortieth college reunion. Bernice had recently left the convent she'd been in since college. When the two old friends met, the forty years they had spent apart slid away. The women, then sixty, were immediately drawn back to each other.

"I had plenty of best friends when I was growing up. I was very attracted to one in particular but didn't know I was gay. I just thought I loved her.

"Then I went away to college. I found out I was gay when Bernice, the girl I roomed with, started making love to me.

"We were together for two years. After graduation Bernice went on to become a nun and I went out to find someone to marry. I was engaged three times before I did because I just never felt anything."

Why hadn't the two women remained together after college? Helen says, "Bernice wanted to be normal and I wanted to be normal. We did what we were supposed to do back then. We didn't talk about it. It was make love every night and then just kind of act like nothing was going on. We hated to leave one another, but we felt like in society that was the thing we should do.

"Before Bernice reappeared, every time I'd be attracted to somebody I'd run away from them. It was a part of how I lived my life. I'd just try to ignore it and hide it since I had four children and all these grandchildren. When we got together [after the reunion] we were running back and forth from her city to mine.

"I was going to get a divorce, but with the state laws, I would end up without anything and I wasn't willing to have that happen. I'm too old to do that."

Had Helen and Bernice met in college in the nineties instead of in the fifties, they would have known that more than one lifestyle option existed and might not have chosen to hide their natural sexual inclinations. They made their decisions based on the limited knowledge of their day.

ESTELLE

"I was always painfully aware that being a lesbian was sick," Estelle says. "During my twenties I played the part of the single heterosexual woman in every phase. The only place it wasn't true was in my heart and gut. I didn't come out, but when I saw a movie or was in a social situation, I knew where my preference was. It wasn't toward the men onscreen, but toward the women. I was very unhappy. After college I went into therapy, both individual and group, for several years. I picked a male father figure as my therapist to make me right. I believed that my therapist was going to cure me of my disease. When I was twenty-eight I met Jim. It was the therapist who encouraged me to see him because he said it sounded like wonderful therapy for me.

"I listened because I had paid him to get rid of my disease. I dated Jim and became infatuated with him. He was one of the first males I met who knew what to do sexually and did satisfy me and that was it for me. I thought that meant I was in love. I was thirty and Jim was thirty-four when we married.

"In the beginning I felt that I was cured. So for quite a few years I put my lesbianism—which I'd never really experienced—in remission.

"I never had a maternal desire and Jim called the shots. I was just very content to be his wife. To support him, follow him, and let him make every decision. For the first time in my life I felt normal. I became his slave as repayment.

"The first ten years he satisfied me sexually, but then, as problems crept into our marriage, I realized my husband was not really fulfilling me emotionally in terms of conversation or interaction with problems. I found, in the last few years, that my urges started coming back.

"I began wandering the streets of Greenwich Village, watching people. My parents had died when I was young and I was used to living on the periphery of life, so wandering the streets and looking at bookstores was not something I found lonely. It was a natural state. I was very curious, seeing how this world lived. I remember wandering into a mixed bar [gay and lesbian] and being absolutely thrilled. I was like a kid being let loose in a candy store." Estelle never took a phone number. "Just talking to gay women was thrilling after so many years of denial."

Estelle was almost fifty before she shared her lifelong secret at a twelve-step program for overeaters. Glenda, also attending the Overeaters Anonymous meeting for her own issue with food, heard Estelle speak.

GLENDA

"The things Estelle shared brought flashbacks of my own private sexual torments. For the first time, I was able to talk to another woman who had gone through what I had been going through.

Finally I told someone who I really was and what had been plaguing me for years."

Estelle and Glenda connected, becoming friends, and then lovers.

Glenda, like Estelle, thought she was attracted to women when she was a young girl but she could find no information to help her explain her feelings, so she put them aside, opting for a traditional marriage. She is now in her mid-fifties and has two grown children who are on their own.

"My very best friend was beautiful and I had a crush on her. My emotional attachment to women was always stronger. I knew, but I was ashamed of it.

"When I was little I remember adults didn't talk to children. But I would listen and I would hear them saying things. I heard that it was very normal to have a crush on a teacher or a girlfriend. 'Kids outgrow it.' But I kept thinking about my girlfriend and I didn't outgrow my feelings.

"As a child, nobody talked about it [lesbianism]. It was an embarrassment. So I looked in all the books I could find. I couldn't even find the word in the dictionary. I didn't know how to spell it. At the same time, having my hormones raging, boys certainly did the trick. And there was a certain satisfaction, but I went to therapy. In the fifties, if you went to therapy, you got out of it [lesbianism].

"I dated a lot of guys. In 1961 I got married. I was physically attracted to my husband and thoughts of women went by the wayside, but I never felt quite right.

"I lived a fantasy life after I got married. In the fantasy I was in love with a very good friend but I was a good girl and I would never say anything to her. She was just a darling person. It was a whole complicated matrix of friendships.

"I wanted to tell her everything, be with her, touch her, kiss her. Anyway, I was very busy with my children for years. Children, careers. But on my fiftieth birthday and going into menopause I think the urge—I don't know if it was my hormones changing—but it became an unbearable problem. I got to the point where I felt I was going to die from this and I had this middle-aged urgency pushing me along and I had no children at home and financial matters had eased up.

"When you hit fifty-one, fifty-two, you see that time is short and there are all the things you still want to do, so I started to think about me for a change. I started to do things independently. It just became imperative. I had made my mark and what was next? My emotional life. I couldn't put it on hold anymore. I couldn't sublimate with smoking. I couldn't sublimate with food. The desire to have an experience became intense."

SUSAN

"As a little kid I liked both boys and girls. I'm sure it was as sexual and emotional as a child could feel at eight or nine. But I felt freer to have a little girl hug me. I saw women hugging and kissing all the time and I got the message from my family that that was all right. I also got the message from them that it was not acceptable for me to have boys touch me, so I fantasized about having boys hug me or kiss me and I thought it would be very romantic. I made a very strong association of being swept off my feet by a male person. So my sexual identity as it continued was definitely toward men.

"I realized, however, at fifteen or sixteen that there was a constant thread of having an eye for women. I looked at them, sometimes I felt a little turned on by them. It felt strange, but I didn't know I was excited—it was not clearly identified for me. But I was aware that I had crushes on other women my own age. I felt romantic about them. If anyone hugged me, I would push away those feelings of pleasure. I found this distressing and disturbing. . . . I repressed all my sexual feelings. That's what part of my upbringing was. A lot of denial. I didn't know what these feelings were called, but I hoped I'd get over them real quick.

"I was spending a lot of time denying whatever sexual feelings I was having. 'I have to get home,' I'd say when I dated. I couldn't let them touch me in any way. It felt inappropriate. I was frightened of losing myself.

"When I turned twenty-one, I made up my mind that I had been a virgin long enough. Now I decided it was inappropriate not to have an experience. And I wanted to know what my sexuality was all about. I was walking around feeling pretty passionate most of the time, a state of having hot pants.

"My husband happened along at that time. I went on a trip and I was not looking for a husband and my husband was not looking for a wife, so we both clicked. In a short span of time it got very serious. He was kind and not pushy. I allowed myself to feel things and it was pretty good and I thought that was wonderful. He said he loved me, so we married."

For Susan, it was the simple brush of an arm by a close friend that triggered an electric current and forced her female-focused sexuality to surface.

Both women were living in suburbia, where they met as young marrieds. Each had small children and they became fast friends. Susan remembers: "Cynthia said something and I touched her arm, in a very innocent way, I thought. She pulled away and asked me not to touch her again because she had a funny reaction. I realized I had also had a feeling from her of a particular pleasure."

Susan laughs. "I thought this would be a good time for shock treatment. One time in my house, the babies were napping and we were sitting on the couch and watching television and she did that thing that boys sometimes do in the movies. She draped her arm around my shoulder and then kissed me. And we were both stunned. I don't know which of us was more surprised."

Most of the women who knew about their feelings for other women believed that if they kept active, the feelings would go away. Marriage did serve as a temporary antidote. Children, school, homework, dance lessons, Little League, parent-teacher associations, and weddings were wonderful distractions . . . until eventually their pent-up frustrations drove them to find a recipient for their love, or that special someone came along, making it impossible to deny their true selves any longer.

Yet, not every woman who loves women knows automatically whether or not she is a lesbian. Having experimented physically with another woman does not necessarily make one a lesbian, nor does the converse, never having an intimate encounter, discount her from being one. Then there are the women who remained in total denial, so terrifying was the thought of same-sex love. Although many were familiar with the term and may have been intimately involved with other women to some degree, these women chose to see no connection to themselves and lesbianism.

Maggie was one of these women. The mother of four, she says

she never loved sex with a man but accepted the fact that it was part of life. Still, she had never identified her sexuality.

MAGGIE

"For a long time I had wondered, was it normal to check out women? I was always noticing wonderful things about them. She looks nice. She looks soft. I like the way she speaks. But I had no idea this was homosexuality. I had thought you were born knowing and I didn't know therefore I was not. I was in a good state of denial.

"As a matter of fact, I was in a two-year relationship with my friend and I never put a name to it. It was sensual but we never actually had sex. Although close. We would make out, caress, dress each other, but I was still straight. I was in love with her but I thought as long as I didn't . . .

"Then I got a new job and I clicked with the person I was working with. She had a son in the service and so did I. One day, it was past closing and she was on the phone with her son. She hung up and said, 'My son is gay.' I said 'So?' She said, 'So am I. I knew my son was gay from the time he was a little fellow, but I didn't realize my own sexuality until I was twenty-nine.'

"It was like a ton of bricks hit me when she said that. I thought, oh, my God, so that's what's wrong with me. That's what it is. I said, 'I have to leave now.' Abruptly in the middle of her talking I got up and left and went to my car and hyperventilated for fifteen minutes. My body shook and thoughts went racing through my mind and everything became so clear. Hindsight is always twenty-twenty. I had been a lesbian all my life and never knew!"

SYLVIA

Even though she was physically active with a close girlfriend, Sylvia says, "We never really went to bed. We just kind of fooled around. I wasn't particularly attracted to her, but she was to me and I didn't mind." And even when she found herself being drawn to the lesbian and gay crowd at college, and spending all her free time with them, she says, "I guess because I never stopped being attracted to boys or dating boys, even though I knew about my sexuality, I never felt that I was . . . you know.

"I got married quite young [in college]. On some unconscious level I must have realized that if I didn't get into a 'safe place,' I might end up getting more involved with a woman than I was comfortable with. I think I was flirting with the whole thing and I was scared. Anyway, my girlfriend got married too, and we continued being friends, typical couples going out for dinner. . . . Every now and then she and I would just get together and do our thing: necking, cuddling. We didn't actually go to bed together. Then, finally we did. It was a long time coming."

Her denial was so strong that still, at that point in her life, Sylvia had no idea she might be a lesbian.

"Then," she says, "I became very attracted to another close friend. I thought she would be horrified if I told her what I had done [with my other friend] but I took the chance. . . . She wasn't horrified . . . and we just started. We were so happy. Our intimacy enhanced our relationship. I was married and she had this guy in her life, but we had this great thing and it was wonderful.

"Here I've had two relationships with two good friends that have become physical and I still was not saying that makes me anything. I'm saying I'm still just a married woman with a child but I continued to be fascinated by gay life and gay people.

"Five years ago I went to a [work-related] conference. It was the kind of conference where you really did a lot of soul searching and stuff and at one point I had to stop and say . . . my marriage isn't doing well. We're not meeting each other's needs. We're going in opposite directions.

"At the conference there were a bunch of gay people and I found myself hanging out with them a lot." It was there that Sylvia acknowledged this part of herself for the first time. "I guess I'd been too afraid to really look at this part of me. So I sort of came out to the woman I was at the conference with."

While she had been in therapy previously, it was only after the conference that Sylvia decided to explore her gender preference. "Although my marriage had not caused this [sexual confusion], the fact that it was dissolving enabled me to take a look at the sexual part of me."

Sylvia has finally been able to admit to herself who she is. She has also chosen to leave her marriage.

LYNN

Lynn had been married twice, the second time for twelve years. "I was very much in love with my husbands, especially my second husband. The first seven years were wonderful, but then we started having some trouble. I have to be honest. I had an affair with a man.

"Then I met her. In the beginning I wasn't consciously aware that we were dating. It was like, 'I can handle this. It's fun. I'm just flirting.' But we did go to bed."

Even after she had been going to bed with her womanfriend for six months, the denial part was so strong that Lynn was still saying, "I'm not a lesbian."

Lynn was studying to be a therapist, and for her, like Sylvia, the realization hit while she was away at a training course, seven months after her affair had begun.

"There was a lot of recovery stuff going on: AA, drug, and alcohol. As they announced all the different workshops, they announced a gay and lesbian meeting. I thought, no one knows me here. I could walk into this room.

"That was the first time I experienced a panic that maybe I was a lesbian. I went late and left early so I didn't get to talk to anyone but I said to myself, okay, everyone looks kind of normal. I went back the next day.

"For those two weeks I made friends. And now I was afraid that they would reject me for not being a real lesbian. 'You're married. You don't even call yourself a lesbian. You're just dabbling.' I had thought that being a lesbian meant you grew up being one.

"Then I got up and told my story and so many women stood up and said, 'I was married' or 'I am married.' And I realized that every lesbian doesn't start at thirteen.

"Even when my husband and I walked together and I'd look at women and say doesn't she have nice hair, or breasts, or legs, I never thought I was a lesbian. I thought all women looked at other women.

"My dearest girlfriend was a lesbian. She never told me she was, but she dated only women. I loved being around her. I had this dream that maybe she'd invite me to a gay bar. I had always dated boys and I wasn't a lesbian but I wouldn't mind seeing this. She never did.

Lynn says, "My husband said it came as no surprise to him when I told him, although I had never thought of myself as a lesbian ever, ever, ever."

CYNTHIA

Cynthia was a young bride in the early 1950s. She had never heard lesbianism discussed and had no idea that a woman could love other women like a man and a woman could love each other. She especially had no idea she could love another woman, until Susan set off feelings of passion in her that she never knew existed.

"I remember when I was a youngster, my girlfriends were very important to me. There was nothing sexual about it except that we all had a common frame of reference. There was a thread of understanding that didn't seem to exist in boy-girl relationships. I did date very extensively. I was engaged once before I got married. Somehow as I look back I see the relationship didn't have the same validity as my feelings with girlfriends.

"I'm not sure if I was in love with my husband when I married him. As I think back, I think maybe I was performing as I was supposed to. At that time I may have thought I was in love with him. I remember evaluating him in a way that was rather cruel—as someone who seemed like he would be reliable to earn a living. That was a serious consideration in 1954, because at that time it was pretty standard that women who were married did their work in the home, and their husbands earned the living.

"I met Susan shortly after we were both married. At that time I was living in a Long Island suburb. We became acquaintances when she and her husband moved to our development. My sister and Susan had worked together and she introduced us.

"We were together a lot during our first pregnancies. I had stopped working. She was also not working. We were together a lot with our children. It seemed perfectly natural seeing how close in age they were. We had so much in common.

"We didn't socialize much as couples though. Our husbands' interests were very different. I remember it happening a couple of times. More often than not, Susan invited me and my children to have dinner at her house and I would invite her and her children to have dinner at my house.

"My husband got sick when I was pregnant with my third child. At the time I didn't have a driver's license but I had been driving him and sometimes Susan drove." Then he had to be hospitalized. "While he was in the hospital I gave birth to my third child.

"Meanwhile Susan was very caring for him as well as for me. Every time there was a crisis where I would need help, I would turn around and she would be helping. And I became more and more fond of her. I don't know exactly what happened, but I did know it was very important for me to touch her. If I touched her arm I felt a particular pleasure, different from the pleasure I felt when I touched a baby."

These feelings that neither woman knew what to do with caused a great deal of stress on their friendship. They tried to have a physical relationship but at the time couldn't handle it and wound up in therapy.

"Still," Cynthia says, "there was no way I was going to let go of Susan if I had that choice. I found her adorable then, and I do now. We were both thoroughly wacky. I was very abrasive, very angry a lot of the time. She was very timid, unsure of herself, demanding, and obsessive. As time went on, the relationship continued to blossom. We are not the same people now that we were then."

It took several years before Susan and Cynthia, once realizing they were in love with each other, came to understand their differences, learn to accept themselves, and live with their alternative sexuality. That was when they became sexually intimate. They have remained best friends and discreet lovers for more than twenty-five years.

JACKIE

"I thought I was in love with my husband. I thought we had the perfect marriage. My husband was absolutely wonderful and I loved my family." Yet Jackie admits, "I don't remember my sexual life with him at all. I have no memory of it.

"Then he had an affair with my girlfriend. I don't know why, but he told me about it. It was one of the lowest points of my life.

I had had no idea. Up until that time he was my best friend and lover . . . though infrequently. And I trusted him with every single thing in the world. I never didn't trust him. . . ."

Jackie's husband's affair was a turning point for her. "It didn't mean I loved him less, but why it's important is, up until that point, I didn't look at people sexually at all. That part of me was closed down.

"This whole life opened up. It was so weird. I don't understand what happened. After he told me, I started to look at people differently, in a sexual way. Men and women. That's all I did, and I went on with my life. I noticed that I was looking at women more than at men, but I couldn't talk to anyone about it.

"For years I didn't do anything with these feelings. I just sat and looked at people.

"Several years before I realized what I was, I was visiting a friend who was a lesbian. She had a magazine with letters from married lesbians. I remember being surprised. I had never known that women who were married could love other women. I was so stupid. I never knew that people could change. I thought someone was a lesbian or not.

"Anyway, I went to college for a semester to take a teaching course and I fell in love with my teacher. In the beginning I had no idea I was falling in love with her. I remember the first night of class being shocked that the teacher was my age, smart, interesting, and had a good sense of humor. I had avoided education courses in college, finding them boring. Now I was taking the history of education and really loving the course.

"There was some attraction on her part too, although she wasn't a lesbian. Neither of us knew what to do with this. I thought it was that she was this really great teacher. At one point I got a very short haircut. She put her hand on my head to feel it like you would do with a kid and I was amazed. There was an electric charge. I didn't understand it at all. I had no idea where it came from. Neither of us knew what was happening.

"During the course we both found reasons to stay with each other . . . in a professional manner. We went for coffee, always with other students. When the course ended we arranged to go to a state park for the day. It was raining, but we went and sat in the car and suddenly we were making out like two teenagers. That was our beginning."

ANNA

Anna learned more from college than she ever imagined she would. A wife and the mother of an eight-year-old, she was taking a course and became friendly with the woman sitting next to her. One day while waiting for the class to begin, the woman shared with Anna that she was bisexual.

"Somehow that knowledge freaked me out. I couldn't believe what I was thinking. I was shocked, terrified. It made thoughts I must have been harboring subconsciously jump into my consciousness. It was like she was me, only more honest."

Anna's classmate's words had served as the catalyst, triggering an awareness of something that had been buried.

Many MWLW did not discover their attraction to women until they reached mid-life. When their children were grown or almost grown and their hectic lives revolving around children's schedules had slowed, they felt a sense of loss. They turned to their husbands for the companionship and communication they desired, only to find the men emotionally unavailable.

To fill the void, they returned to school or to the workplace, or joined organizations. There they connected with other women who were able to offer the warmth and understanding denied them at home.

A powerful emotional love can emerge from these feelings of being nurtured and cared for after years of doing the nurturing for others. Sexuality, not generally planned, becomes a natural extension of that love.

GRACIE

Married for thirty-two years and the mother of five, Gracie was active in her church and community and never felt an attraction for women until Fern set off feelings of passion she never knew existed. "In no way would I ever have believed that I could be enticed by or interested in a woman. I thought I was in love with my husband.

"When I met Fern, I knew she was a lesbian. We live in a small, artsy town, and she was out. She'd never made any bones about it. I have many gay friends and many straight friends. There are a tremendous number of women that I am in contact with. There are probably at least sixteen women whom I associate with weekly, and I'm very close to them, but not in a way that I would ever consider any kind of sexual behavior. And to this day I am not turned on by just anybody. So I didn't think about her sexuality. I liked her as a person.

"I had seen Fern on the street; she was in a wheelchair. I asked her if she'd like to come into my shop. I'd heard about her reputation for being a spunky, free-spirited woman, and I liked that.

"In fact, the first time she came into my shop she made a funny little remark. I said, 'I left the door open hoping you'd come in. I'm freezing.' "

Fern said, 'Well, I'll warm you up.' She chuckled and winked. Then she blushed and said, 'I can't believe I said that.' "

Gracie says, "I didn't know what to say, but I knew where she was coming from and I just thought it was kind of funny, and we laughed. That's the first time we really spoke. She became my very good friend. We talked and we compared our lives: They paralleled each other in so many ways. The more we talked, the more we realized how much we had in common. Soon I was just so eager to see her and talk to her.

"Then there was a town party. I went with my husband and Fern was at the party. There was a lot of dancing and a lot of loud music. I danced and danced for about two or three hours straight. I started out dancing with my husband and then he was tired and I danced with other people and then by myself and I danced across the room over to where Fern was and I asked her to dance and she danced wonderfully in her wheelchair. She was all over the place and I was laughing and smiling and I just felt so free and my arms were in the air and I was having a wonderful time.

"At three in the morning my husband and I went home, and in bed that night I couldn't stop thinking about dancing and the music and Fern in her chair. It was that night that I sort of dreamt about maybe snuggling up to her. Smelling her hair was the thing I wanted to do more than anything else. The next day when she came into the store we chatted. I wrote her a little note. She had a way with words, four-letter words in particular. I'm sort of strait-laced and proper and I think my note said something like 'you fucking knocked me off my feet' and she laughed and roared and we talked some more."

□   □   □   □

Like Gracie, I too felt as though I had been knocked off my feet. For a few brief weeks after I fell in love with Toby, my initial feelings were so overwhelming as to nullify any other thoughts. I walked around apart from the rest of the world. I might have been from another galaxy. Before entering a room I'd have to remember to clear my face of the huge grin that kept appearing involuntary. At the beginning, while I believed that her being a woman had little to do with my feelings for Toby, I soon realized I was deluding myself. I was attracted to her womanliness and I did love the woman in her. What did that mean? What did that make me?

2

What Am I?

INITIALLY, upon the discovery of my true sexual identification, I felt like a leaf on a current, flowing along, being tossed about, and then being trapped in a whirlpool and swirling in circles. Why didn't I know about myself before? Was it my environment? Genetics? Both? My feelings were of total desperation and, at the same time, overwhelming longing. An act as simple as sitting in a café and watching other women laughing, or walking together, arm in arm, brought excruciating pain.

Yet, when asked, "If you had it to do over, would you choose the kind of anguish you went through, or would you prefer your old life?" I would have to say, "I couldn't *not* do it again. To not know who I really am would be worse."

Still, MWLW, feeling forced to balance the roles society imposes on them, remain one of the most clandestine groups in our society. The total secrecy within which the phenomenon exists prevents researchers not only from finding MWLW who are willing to talk about their lives, but from knowing how widespread their presence actually is.

Citing the lack of studies on the subject of homosexual women in heterosexual marriages, and the unavailability of appropriate subjects to interview, Dr. Eli Coleman turned to bisexual, divorced bisexual, and single lesbian women to complete his research paper, "The Married Lesbian." Of the forty-five participants involved in his research, only four were currently married.

Amity Pierce Buxton, Ph.D., writes that the general under-standing seems to be, "once they [married lesbians] discover and admit their homosexuality [to themselves], most seem to come out to their husbands quickly."

To assume, as Dr. Buxton did, that *most* women who discover their female sexual orientation come out quickly, or, as Dr. Cole-man did, that married women who discover their lesbianism sim-ply leave their marriages, is misleading.

As one woman wrote in response to my ad, "I will make the assumption that your phrasing of 'we' is an indicator that you have experienced what it is like to be married, lesbian, and in the closet. . . ."

After receiving my assurance, she felt comfortable enough to write, "I just celebrated my twenty-fifth anniversary, five years after I finally admitted to myself I was in the closet. Probably some fifteen years of knowing, but just compartmentalizing it for a long time . . ."

She ended with, "You are certainly right about the loneliness . . . even during the periods when I've tried to be in *both* worlds. Now I stay in one [the heterosexual one], but it is so hard."

While 20 percent of the MWLW surveyed did leave their mar-riages and 8 percent separated, as in many heterosexual marriages, it was the general incompatibility between husband and wife that finally brought about the divorce or separation. Those women who had contemplated divorce before learning about their gender preference, but did not have the courage to take that first step, did note that it was the personal growth they experienced while com-ing to terms with their own sexuality that gave them the confi-dence to act on their previous desire to leave.

Seventy-two percent of the women I interviewed were cur-rently married. Like all minorities, married women who love women come from all ethnic and religious groups and from a large cross-section of the United States and other countries as well. They come from low-income city housing projects and sprawling suburban homes set on manicured lawns. They have attended public and private schools, day and boarding schools, coed and all-girl schools. They can be found at supermarkets and grocery stores, the cleaners, Little League games, and PTA meet-ings. Besides being wives and mothers, they are daughters, sisters, classmates, friends, and neighbors. MWLW are students, clerks, and lawyers. They are blue collar and white collar workers, executives with large corporations, artisans, and actresses struggling to survive. They are members of the workforce and educators in the schools.

The diversity of MWLW interviewed reflects that of any heterosexual group of women in our society. The most common experience recounted by those women consciously aware of their true sexual inclinations through their youth was dating boys despite being uncomfortable, so no one would know they were different, and drinking heavily or abusing drugs to get through evenings out with friends they couldn't confide in.

All MWLW related the initial feelings of stress, isolation, and despondency they secretly lived with once they acknowledged themselves. "Imagine having a secret and never being able to share it with even your best friend," one woman said. "I grew up trying to be who I was 'supposed' to be, always acting a part. Sometimes I lost sight of who the real me was—both of me were so unhappy."

Of course the idea of women loving women is not new. In contrast, though, while same-sex love between women was not viewed as the equal of heterosexual love, it was not always viewed in the same negative light as today.

In the seventeenth and eighteenth centuries, "romantic friendships" (the term used to describe the love relationships between two women) were considered noble and virtuous. Lillian Faderman, in *Surpassing the Love of Men*, says that by the nineteenth century, terms such as "sentimental friends," "the love of kindred spirits," and "Boston marriage" had replaced "romantic friendships" to describe the love relationships between two women.

"Boston marriage" described long-term monogamous relationships between two unmarried women, generally financially independent of men. They were usually feminists and often involved with culture and social betterment. These shared values formed a strong basis for their lives together. Mark DeWolfe Howe, the nineteenth-century *Atlantic Monthly* editor, who had contact with many of these women in the New England area, described their involvement as "a union—there is no truer word for it."

According to Faderman, "What surprised me most about these

romantic friendships was that society appeared to condone them rather than view them as disruptive of the social structure."

Such relationships were considered threatening to society only in a specific instance. If a woman dressed in attire that was termed masculine, she acted masculine because she was a man trapped in a woman's body and all her instincts were inverted, including her sexual instinct. "If she dressed in clothes suitable for her sex, it might be assumed that she was not sexually aggressive, and two unaggressive females together would do nothing to violate men's presumptive property rights to women's bodies."

Although she might be one, a woman dressed in feminine attire was often excluded from the category of lesbian, while a straight woman wearing men's work clothes was suspect. Nevertheless, in the early 1950s, significant numbers of lesbians were coming together and searching for a social identity. Since there were few lesbian models to follow, the community adopted the heterosexual patterns of masculine and feminine roles within marriage and assumed the parts of butch (the male version of a lesbian), and femme (the female counterpart), mandating appropriate masculine and feminine dress and role behavior for each partner.

Women who are turning to other women now, especially MWLW, have little desire to emulate the heterosexual relationships that didn't work for them. They are choosing to create more equal types of relationships instead.

As early as the 1800s, when women's colleges began to multiply, conservative writers, interested in what they believed to be the proper functioning of society, feared "race suicide" and prophesied the decline of the country. Their rationale was that since the best [female] blood of American stock went off to college and probably would not marry, the mothers of America would eventually all be from the lower orders of society. Worse, some writers came to fear that higher education for females, especially in all-woman colleges, not only "masculinized" women but also made men dispensable to them and rendered women more attractive to one another.

Statistics confirm "that those who were interested in maintaining women in the narrow prison of heterosexuality as it was experienced by females in the nineteenth century were quite right in fearing the spread of higher education." In *Odd Girls and Twilight*

Lovers, Faderman points out that females who attended college (with newfound opportunities in education and the professions) were far less likely to marry than their uneducated counterparts.

Today, as in other eras, as long as feelings for women by women are nonthreatening to men, the significance of their relationships are trivialized.

When asked why so little data could be found on married women who love women, one male psychologist, who preferred not to be named, responded, "because we live in a patriarchal, or male-oriented, country, female homosexuality is not as threatening to the male ego as is male homosexuality. Therefore, the subject of women who love each other is viewed as not terribly important."

Even as far back as the Bible, intimate relationships between women were not considered seriously. "Homosexual intercourse is not labeled *tebel* (improper) mixing, but the extreme prohibition of homosexuality by the death penalty (Leviticus 29:13 *[sic]*, cf. 18:22) . . . is best explained as a desire to keep categories of 'male' and 'female' intact. . . . *Lesbian interaction, however, is not mentioned possibly because it did not result in true physical 'union' (by male entry)."* (Emphasis added.)

"Samuel Tissot, a Swiss doctor whose work *Onania: A Treatise Upon the Disorders Produced by Masturbation* (1758) was translated into English in 1766, was one of the few writers who recognized the possibility of manual clitoral stimulation in female/female sex. 'The act,' he says, 'is even worse than masturbation because it sometimes causes women to love other women with as much fondness and jealousy as they did men.' "

In the earliest societies, families were composed of extended groups, with everyone sharing equally in the upbringing of the child; the mother did not particularly "own" the child, and there was no concept of "father" as we know it today. According to Shere Hite in *The Hite Report*, "The male role in reproduction was not understood for quite a long time, and intercourse and male orgasm were not connected with pregnancy."

When the connection was made as to the man's part in reproduction, men like Aristotle used their misogyny, parading as science, to elevate the importance of the father. According to Shari

L. Thurer, author of *The Myths of Motherhood*, Aristotle in his treatise *Generation of Animals*, was aware of the role the male seed played in reproduction by "cooking" the female residue and thus converting it into a new being. While he credited the male with having an active role, he decided that the female blood had a passive one. Aristotle then used this female passivity in reproduction to justify her social inferiority.

Nancy Marval, in a paper printed by The Feminists, says that while under normal circumstances, a man was needed to provide sperm for the conception of the baby, it was practically impossible to determine which man had done so. As individuals, a man's claim to any particular child could never be as clear as that of the mother, who demonstrably gave birth to that child. With the changeover to a patrilineal or patriarchal society, sexuality became a crucial issue. The sex act, beyond all of the aspects symbolizing the male's dominance, manipulation, and control over the female, assumed an overwhelming practical importance. A man could prove with absolutely certainty that he was the one to have contributed the sperm only if he took control of the sexual conduct of the woman.

Religious and civil laws gave men the authority to control the sexuality of the woman. This was done by keeping them monogamous. In the Middle Ages, women were made to wear chastity belts, straplike devices of leather or metal fastened on a woman to prevent sexual intercourse with men other than their husbands. Women were taught to believe in purity above all else. In the 1930s, writer Margaret Mitchell, who was considered radical for her time, would not allow *Gone With the Wind*'s Scarlett O'Hara to make love with any of the men she loved until she had married them. In her earliest book, *Lost Laysen* (the manuscript was found among Mitchell's papers sixty years after her death), the heroine commits suicide rather than allow herself to be dishonored.

There are African and Arab countries today that sanction genital mutilation to lessen a woman's sexual desires, and in the heterosexual United States today, according to Marval, the most commonly used method for controlling a woman's sexual conduct is to "convince her that sex is the same thing as love and if she has sexual relations with anyone else, she is violating the sacred ethics of love."

Male sexual dominance continues to be very strongly felt, especially by women who were brought up to feel that marriage validates their worth as women and that their life work should be serving their husbands and children. These women will go to almost any length to make their marriages work.

Before the nineteenth century, homosexuality may have been viewed as a misdeed, but those who "committed the crime" were not categorized as criminals. "This changed in the nineteenth century, when modern medicine and particularly the science of psychiatry came to view homosexuality as a form of mental illness. By the 1940s, homosexuality was discussed as an aspect of psychopathic, paranoid, and schizoid personality disorders.

"James Harrison, a psychologist who produced the 1992 documentary film *Changing Our Minds*, notes that the medical profession viewed homosexuality with such abhorrence that virtually any proposed treatment seemed defensible. Lesbians were forced to submit to hysterectomies and estrogen injections, although it became clear that neither of these had any effect on their sexual orientation."

In 1969 the gay community took a stand and fought for their recognition and rights at the Stonewall bar in New York City's Greenwich Village. "By the late sixties . . . human sexuality became a respectable subject for academic study, trade publications and individual therapy. . . . In 1974, the American Psychiatric Association voted to remove homosexuality from the list of pathological diseases, lessening the stigma attached to gay persons and activities."

Eighty-six percent of the women interviewed have been married only once, and 14 percent twice. Still, being raised to believe what our patriarchal society has presented as doctrine, many women had less difficulty giving up their marriages, or becoming involved in affairs with men, than giving up their heterosexuality, even when they knew it wasn't working for them.

While the majority of women had only been with their husbands until they became aware of their need for women, one woman told of having gone through six extramarital heterosexual affairs before acknowledging to herself that no man could give her what she was missing and had been searching for.

When Nicole, gloriously happy for the first time in years, confided to her friend Sandra that she was involved with another woman, Sandra was horrified. "You're married," she said. "How could you do this to your husband?"

"What about you," Nicole asked. "You've had two extramarital relationships with married men!"

"That's different," Sandra said, "they were men."

"The origins of human sexuality, and of homosexuality in particular, have puzzled philosophers, theologians, and ordinary people for thousands of years. In a few scattered cultures, homosexuality has been regarded as a normal part of life or even as a special talent or gift from the gods."

Many psychotherapists believe that gender preference is something we're born with. "Wilhelm Stekel, a co-worker with Freud, stated in his book *Bisexual Love* 'All persons originally are bisexual in their predisposition. There are no exceptions.' . . . At the age of puberty, however, the heterosexual represses his homosexuality, sublimating it to the more acceptable proprieties of friendship, nationalism, social endeavors and gatherings. The homosexual, on the other hand, somehow pushes the 'wrong' button and represses his or her heterosexuality instead. . . ."

Still, the debate of nurture versus nature continues. Psychiatrist Richard Pillard points out that "as fetuses, human beings of both sexes start out with complete male and female 'anlages,' precursors of the basic interior sexual equipment—vagina, uterus, and fallopian tubes for women, and vas deferens, seminal vesicles, and ejaculatory ducts for men. At conception an embryo is given its chromosomal sex, which determines whether it will develop testes or ovaries. In females, the female structures simply develop, without any help from hormones and the male parts will shrivel up. . . ."

Dr. Dean Hamer, a molecular geneticist, and a team of scientific colleagues, in a study done in 1993, reported finding a genetic link to homosexuality among men. He says, "We didn't isolate a 'gay gene'; we only detected its presence through linkage."

Dr. Hamer and his colleagues found a high rate of homosexuality among men on the mother's side of the family. This pattern showed consistency with the transmission of a gene through the X chromosome. Unfortunately, unlike eye or hair color, which can be readily seen and categorized, the only way to know a person's sexual identification is to ask about his or her behavior. Since people come out at different ages, their responses can differ from one year to the next, causing carefully researched data to go askew.

Hamer believes that female sexual orientation is as likely to be inherited as male sexual orientation, but narrowing the role of individual genes will require more effort than did the male project. "A complicating factor was that even if the X chromosome were involved in female sexual orientation, the expected pattern would not necessarily show an excess of either paternal or maternal gay relatives, because the woman inherits one X chromosome from her mother and one from her father.

"There is no way to be sure yet," Dr. Hamer concludes, "but it is unlikely the same version of Xq28 associated with male homosexuality also is associated with lesbianism."

"Research on the population percentages for homosexuality has begun only recently, and the figures are still extremely inexact since political, social, and religious pressure has always dissuaded homosexuals from identifying their sexual orientation."

The genetic concept of expression for the trait sexual orientation could be posed as the following question: If a homosexual is homosexual, just how homosexual is that homosexual? It turns out that the answer is different for men and women. For men, the answer is usually completely. For women the answer is sometimes not as homosexual as homosexual men. And straight women are not as straight as straight men either.

Molecular geneticist Angela Pattatucci "confirmed in the end that women do something men virtually never do: They move among straight, bisexual, and lesbian."

"While most women are stable in their orientation, Pattatucci determined that it is not unusual for a small portion of women to report feeling themselves to be straight at age sixteen, perhaps lesbian at age twenty-four, maybe bisexual at age thirty-eight, and straight again at fifty-five. With men, Hamer says flatly, 'This sort of movement is very, very rare. It's pretty much a phenomenon we see exclusively in women.' "

Pattatucci goes on to explain that if you ask men, gay or straight, if they have ever wondered about their sexual orientation, they almost always say no. It's not at all rare for women to say they've wondered. "A large number of straight women and almost as large a percentage of lesbians have wondered about their sexual orientations." She adds, "I think few people want to say what the real answers are because it's too politically sensitive."

Psychotherapist Gwenn A. Nusbaum, board certified diplomate in clinical social work with certification in psychotherapy and psychoanalysis, also believes that while there may be a genetic predisposition, family environment plays a significant role in the development of homosexual choices and lifestyles. She says, "If a genetic component exists, it tends to interact with and be further influenced by family dynamics and attachment patterns, though other contributing factors may be operative as well."

Lillian Faderman, who characterizes herself as "primarily a social constructionist," considers heredity theories too simplistic. "They don't account for the fact, as Kinsey pointed out, that people often move in and out of sexualities; they could be heterosexual for one period of their lives and homosexual for another. They don't account for the fact that in other cultures, same-sex relationships are ubiquitous. If they're given up, it's in order to procreate, and very often they are carried on even while one is married. It seems to me," she concludes, "the essentialists don't deal with the complexity of human sexuality."

Society, through the family, communicates the norms and values for all its members. Thus, it is understandable that even a woman with a predisposition toward other women, not wanting to be seen as an anomaly, might consciously or unconsciously deny anything that would keep her from slipping quietly into the role of a "normal" heterosexual female.

CHERRY

Cherry is one of these women whose actions contradict her true feelings. She is very definite about what is lacking from her life, but negative stereotyping of lesbians and fear have kept her from searching for the missing piece.

"When I first dreamed about romance with boys," Cherry says, "I saw them as gentle, but sex never entered my mind. Then, when I started going out with boys, I found them forceful, clumsy, slobbery. In general, they just didn't meet my expectations. I wanted to have a partner who was soft, cuddly, close to my size and reactive."

Still, Cherry ruled women out of her life. She says, "When I was in high school I heard bad things, and I'd get a funny feeling about the word *lesbian.*"

Knowing there was something missing, she married anyway, thinking she would be able to satisfy her longings through fantasies of women.

During her first two years of marriage, Cherry had been searching for an identity. "Eventually," she says, "by the process of elimination, I came to regard myself as bisexual. I am married to a man but secretly yearn to love women—what should I call myself? I wouldn't know where to put myself on a Kinsey scale because I consider myself in the closet and latent, and I am still not totally sure of my identity. I am not willing to call myself lesbian until the time comes that it is my lifestyle one hundred percent."

The declaration of lesbianism is so difficult for some women that they choose to adopt a bisexual tag instead, or use one as a transitory stopping point, to help them to avoid that initial, frightening lesbian identity. Declaring oneself bisexual also offers a person a chance to resist categorization, or to avoid making decisions.

"Because lesbianism is itself inevitably a value-weighted categorization," Beverly Burch, author of *On Intimate Terms,* says "individual lesbians and the communal norms of lesbianism could make either designation more desirable to one woman, less desirable to another, depending on her own political and emotional biases. For example, some lesbians do not consider bisexual women or women with heterosexual histories 'real lesbians' regardless of what they call themselves. Therefore, some women might hesitate to name themselves bisexual. Others may feel that being a lifelong lesbian is admitting to some limitation, or that being a 'real lesbian' is more stigmatizing than being a lesbian with bisexual potential."

"Are people essentially either straight or gay, with bisexuality being merely the unnatural by-product of confusion and repression among some homosexuals? Or is bisexuality a third distinct orientation? Is sexuality governed by biology or culture? Is it fixed, an identity that is set early and endures through life? Or is it fluid, shifting with time and temptation?" asks Anastasia Toufexis, author of *Bisexuality: What Is It?*

According to Toufexis, "Avowed lesbians sometimes sleep with men, and men who describe themselves as straight engage in sex with other men. In many Latin societies, men do not consider themselves bisexual or gay unless they take the passive-receptive role during sex. Moreover, sexuality is as much a state of mind as an act of body. People may be attracted to someone but unwilling to act on their desires out of guilt or shame; conversely, others may act contrary to their true feelings." Whether straight or gay, discovering our true sexual identity and feeling comfortable in our skin is a challenge.

But sexual identity is not set in stone and may not remain fixed throughout our lives. Patterns of sexual behavior evolve according to personal circumstances. Some women describe their marriages as always having been empty of emotional attachment. Others describe them as once having been a positive experience. Some women talked of previously feeling "in love" with their husbands, although they no longer felt an attraction to men.

One woman considers herself to be bisexual, not because she's married, but because she remembers how it once was with her husband. "When we first got married, there was definitely a sexual attraction for each other and we had a great sex life.

"Right now I'm not enjoying the physical aspect of being with my husband because I'm not in love with him. For me, sexual pleasure has to do with my being in love with another individual."

Another woman considers herself sexual rather than bisexual, but, as she says, "in this society, at this time, bisexual is what would be applied to me. I'm attracted to women and men. The gender doesn't matter much to me, rather who they are, how comfortable I am with them, etc. I've aligned myself with lesbians, but I've never ruled out the possibility of attraction to a man. Loving a man, as I do currently, does not, equally, rule out my loving a woman again, or a purple creature from outer space, for that matter. It's who they are and not what they are."

Constrained monosexual environments such as prison or the military can lead to same-sex liaisons, yet the participants continue to think of themselves as being heterosexual. Also, since it is possible to love someone of the opposite sex, then fall in love with someone of the same gender, and then, years later, to fall for someone of the opposite sex again, assigning labels or categories to individuals solely on behavior at one period in a lifetime can be difficult.

Still, "We as a society seem to have a need to stereotype people and their behavior. This is as true of sexual behavior as anything else. When we put people in carefully defined boxes, we feel we create a kind of order, that the acceptable and the unacceptable are codified.

"In the case of sexuality, we think that we are either heterosexual or homosexual, straight or gay. We may resist new scientific findings for fear that they will disturb our comfortable preconceptions."

While there are people who resist the idea of labeling, feeling that a label constricts them, for some having a sexual identity can be stabilizing. If you can fit into a category, you can find a support group with others who identify themselves the same way.

At a discussion titled "Married and Wondering," several women who attended spoke of being in celibate marriages and having same-sex relationships, yet they referred to themselves as bisexual. When asked to explain, one woman said, "I needed to find a support group. I tried going to a lesbian gathering but was shunned because of my marital status. Then I found a bisexual group. This group welcomed me. They were open and accepting. So I stayed. I may never be interested in men again, but by using the term bisexual, I am keeping my options open."

LAUREN

Lauren attended an all-female high school, where she fell in love with a classmate a couple of years her senior. Her love was unreturned. At the same time, she answered an ad in *The Village Voice.* "It wasn't that I was looking for a man but I happened to see his ad and I liked it," she says. "It was charming, with a quote from *The Merchant of Venice.*" After high school Lauren married the writer of the ad.

She describes her husband, twelve years older than she, as her soul mate. "I guess we're so much alike that there isn't a lot of sexual passion. I think that passion sometimes comes from tension, and we don't have any tension.

"My husband knew about me when we married and it was okay. I think it sort of fascinated him. And he's sort of interested. He always asks me who I'm going out with and he's very supportive."

Lauren continues to think of herself as bisexual and has had very intense friendships with men, both gay and straight, but believes that, at this time, if she had not met her husband, she would probably be with women exclusively. Still, she says, "There is no way I am going to leave my husband. That is not an option. I want a relationship where I can spend a lot of time with my husband and I don't know where I can find a woman who could put up with this."

Although not presently in an intimate same-sex relationship, Lauren belongs to a support group for bisexual women.

MIRIAM

Miriam and her husband had decided early in their marriage that their commitment to each other would not be based on sex. "I had been burned with romantic love and wanted a relationship that worked. . . . Sex was just not that important—and we kept hoping it would get better."

In the beginning, Miriam's only clue to her latent bisexuality was feeling heartbroken when her best friend got married, but she had no idea why she felt that way for some time.

Then the stress of her husband's graduate school studies created a rupture in their marriage. The terms under which they had gotten married were no longer working, yet it never occurred to either Miriam or her husband to break the commitments they had made to each other. After much dialogue, Miriam convinced her husband of the intellectual integrity of an open marriage, although it wasn't something he wanted. "It hasn't worked out great," she concedes. "But my husband is very good at intellectual abstractions. On some feeling level, he doesn't like it at all, but he doesn't discuss it with me."

Eventually, it became clear that Miriam was attracted to women. Still she says, "For a long time, I was bi in my head but not in my living. I had no desire to move in lesbian circles. To the extent that I went to women's dances, I felt biphobia. It was too much to explain that I had a husband and all this stuff. People acted like I had the plague.

"I had a strong need. Something was missing or empty. I knew I really wanted it but I was tied down at home with a small child and a career and I went to school full-time.

"I went to a group for bi women but they were different than me," Miriam says. "They were leading secret lives, cheating on their husbands, not telling them. This was not how my spouse and I were dealing with this thing. It seemed to me," Miriam initially said, "that their married lives were completely hollow. I was in an open relationship which was very different from sneaking around."

Eventually Miriam broke down as she further described her life. "I'm lonesome, sexually unfulfilled. My husband is resentful and angry. I feel like I'm living someone else's life. Sometimes I think if I didn't have a kid, I might try out another lifestyle, but now I don't see anything changing.

"After ten years of nothing, walking around with a strong bi identity, I finally had an ongoing relationship. I went to a national bisexual conference in San Francisco in 1990. I went expecting to be an anomaly and I fit fine. It wasn't weird that I was married, that I was non-monogamous. It wasn't weird that I identified positively in a Jewish way. None of it was weird. There were people with sexual experience and people without."

Miriam says, "Now I have a clear and overwhelming sense of just how much easier and more natural sex is for me with a woman. I've done a lot of wrestling with myself once I realized that was true. I think it's common within bi women to have different kinds of sexual feelings with different people. You don't have to have the same sexual response to both men and women to be bi. They can be qualitatively different responses."

While Miriam identifies herself as being sexually attracted to both men and women, she rejects most of the physical attributes of men. She says, "In no way do I enjoy as much the taste, the smell, the sight, the touches. When I reach out to touch or taste a man's body, it can't hold a candle to how I feel in relating to a woman's body. No contest." Still she says, "I actually like intercourse, standard, plain vanilla vaginal intercourse, and I enjoy receiving oral sex. But it's absolutely beyond me to enjoy giving oral sex to a man. And I don't really like holding a penis in my hand. I don't like how it looks or how it feels, and I hate how it tastes. I don't like how the whole area smells, even on someone who practices good hygiene.

"I have no particular desire to grapple with their genitals. I don't really have any interest." Still, with all these negatives, Miriam is equally clear about what she likes in a man. "I enjoy a man's physical strength and size. I love being picked up and carried, Clark Gable–style, up the stairs. I like a lot of things about the male energy. Nonverbal stuff that comes across. Their humor, their comfort; when they have comfort in their bodies I respond to that. I still think a lot of guys are cute and I can have some satisfying, although limited, sex with a man. I can have very nice kisses and embraces and intercourse.

"Still, I'm not interested enough in the male body to get off on just the sex. It has to have all sorts of other trappings associated with it. Whereas, with a woman, I think I could have all different kinds of sex: passionate, romantic, fuck-buddy, but I'm still not much of a casual sex person, even with a woman. I guess my feeling is that it's still important to me to be drawn to a person's mind.

"I have a friend that I'm occasionally lovers with and the sex has become a texture in our friendship. It feels real good, and nice on the friendship plane, a nice sharing."

Miriam says, "I think bi women are more honest about what sex is about. Bisexual women seem to be less conservative about sex than heterosexual women or lesbians, willing to celebrate sex for sex and to feel that it's not dirty even when you're doing it and not madly in love with somebody. I think it's a wonderful energy to share with other people and it can be valid even if you're not preparing to move in together. That's why I identify with the bi world and will continue to do so even if I end up engaging in nothing but lesbian sex."

LOUISA

The general consensus among the women I interviewed was that men are not as capable of having as intimate a relationship as women are. Louisa sees this inability as something positive. Now involved again with Pattie, her first love, but otherwise in a monogamous relationship with her husband, Louisa says, "It's so different, being with men and being with women. There are things I get from men that I wouldn't expect to get from women. There is a certain kind of distance that I always have with men. I really like that distance.

"I tend to always want my space. Men can't come into me the way a woman can, especially Pattie. We just read each other so fast. For me, if Pattie and I lived together, it would almost be too much. Right now, the space that's there works very well for me.

"My very closest friends are in lesbian relationships. What works for them is that they're very close, very together. They share everything. That doesn't work so well for me. So that's one of the things I like about being with a man."

Still, Louisa says, "If I didn't have a woman who could read me, I would miss that terribly. I really missed it when I was only with my husband. Being with my husband and being with Pattie, it's like they're two separate experiences. I certainly have gone back and forth and thought, 'Well, am I really more gay or am I really more straight?' and that's when I finally came to say I'm really bisexual."

At twenty-five, Louisa had been involved with Pattie. When that didn't work out, Louisa felt herself drawn to other women. "But I always knew I had a very strong attraction to men and wanted men in my life. I never identified myself as a lesbian, although my feminism was very radical. I felt that my sex life had to be bisexual. That's been incredibly hard." When she met her husband, the first thing Louisa told him was that she was bisexual.

Now forty, Louisa is struggling to sort out what has been going on. She had been married to her husband for six and a half years when Pattie came back into her life. That was almost two years ago.

According to Louisa: "If you want your life to be more in synch and you want to avoid dealing with a lot of conflict, it is easier to bring it all together."

MARYANN

"Looking back, I realize that women have always been an important part of my life, but I hadn't recognized it. During college, I started admitting to those feelings. My husband knew before we were married and he has no problems with my being bisexual. It is a turn-on to him to some degree, but not an overwhelming thing.

"I had a real problem in the beginning, trying to sort through how I wanted to define myself; how we, as a couple, wanted to define our relationship. There really was a whole process of trying to work out, 'Well, maybe what culture has to say about monogamy really isn't right for me as a person or us as a couple.'

"When I first came to the realization that I was bi and was interested in having a relationship with someone else, I wasn't the one who wanted to pursue that. I thought it wouldn't be fair to my husband. I'm not sure if I have a need to be with two people, but it's a need to not stifle the part of me that loves women. My husband actually encouraged me because, I think, he didn't want to deny me a part of myself.

"Sex is a big part of my relationship with my husband, but it's nowhere near the most important part of our relationship. I identify as a bi because there really isn't any other label. That's the best of it. Most of my activities are very feminist in nature, and while I'm in a wonderful relationship with this man, I've never found any other men who interest me.

"So, at this time, it's necessary to satisfy both sides: the need to be with my husband and not deny the fact that I also have the desire to be with women. I think one of the things society tries to convince people of is that you can love only one person. I don't believe that that's true . . . in some ways, being in two relationships is easier than being dependent on one person for all your needs."

According to early investigations by Alfred Kinsey, people exhibit a range of sexualities. Still, those who are not exclusively heterosexual in their sexual feelings and behavior have usually been considered homosexual, say Martin S. Weinberg, Colin J. Williams, and Douglas W. Pryor, authors of *Dual Attraction: Understanding Bisexuality*. As a result, a great deal of attention has been paid to explaining the differences between heterosexuals and homosexuals. This tendency has reinforced the belief that "there are two natural classes of people whose sexual desire is fixed. Bisexuals, who do not fit either category, have generally been seen as confused, dishonest, or in transition to becoming homosexual."

Another common perception that Anastasia Toufexis, author of the article "Bisexuality: What Is It?" brings up is that "bisexuals are basically straights with a taste for exotic adventure or essentially gays who are unable or unwilling to acknowledge their true orientation. To growing numbers of bisexuals, however, as well as therapists and researchers, this is nonsense. They insist that bisexuality is not a walk on the wild side or a run from reality but has a legitimate identity of its own."

Masters and Johnson argue that "*all* people initially learn the desirable aspects of both genders and can produce gendered pleasure in both directions. Becoming conventionally heterosexual, however, mandates that people unlearn or repress the attractiveness of their own gender.

"Following this line of thought, bisexuality emerges as the result of the failure to repress (or as the result of rediscovering) same-sex pleasures; those pleasures are then added onto opposite-sex attractions. Instead of connecting sexuality with gender in the conventional way, bisexuals seem to untangle gender and sexual preference, so that the direction of sexual desire—be it toward the same or the opposite sex—operates independently of a person's own gender."

Bisexuals, more open and accepting than heterosexuals or homosexuals, break down cultural rigidities about sexual and emotional closeness. The complexity of human sexuality makes trying to come to any conclusions or put labels on people a temporary measure at best. "Instead of learning *directly* to eroticize one gender or the other," say Martin Weinberg, Colin Williams, and Douglas Pryor, "we learn to act as a woman or to act as a man. A woman learns that to be an adequate woman in our society, her sexual feelings and behaviors should be directed toward men, because this is 'what women do.' Gender, not sexuality, is the encompassing framework through which we learn and process this information."

A majority of the women I spoke with initially labeled themselves bisexual, and yet many also agreed that if their husbands were no longer a part of their lives, it was unlikely that they would be intimate with another man. Given a choice, these women would now prefer to be exclusively with women. While some still enjoyed the sexual intimacy they shared with their husbands, and could therefore be labeled as bisexual, others felt no physical attraction toward men. They were being intimate only to maintain their marriages, having sex with their husbands either as an accommodation or because "it is easier to give in to his demands." For this reason, many women had mistakenly defined themselves as bisexual. Eventually they recognized that by choice they would be lesbian and redefined themselves accordingly.

Of the women I interviewed, 78 percent identified themselves as lesbians, while only 22 percent identified themselves as bisexuals. The major difference between the women drawn only to women and those drawn to both men and women seemed to be their initial reactions. Almost all women who classified themselves as lesbians said they initially felt an emotional attraction to the other women, which eventually led to a physical one. The majority of women who classified themselves as bisexual most often talked about being physically attracted to that other woman and then developing an emotional attachment later on.

Ten years ago I would have said, "I have no doubt. I am a heterosexual woman," yet when I discovered my true gender identity several years later, the label was so frightening that I could not have said, although it was true, "I have no doubt, I am a lesbian." Today, while I can comfortably say "I am a lesbian," I no longer have the need for a label. I see myself as a whole. Still, my journey was a frightening one and I kept asking myself, "What now?"

3

What Now?

IT TAKES a tremendous amount of strength for a married woman who discovers she loves women to explore what is happening to her and even more courage to acknowledge that she does have options and begin her search for them.

Some women seek self-help groups or therapy. Others secretly devour every book on lesbianism in the library, or apprehensively cross the threshold into their first "women's bookstore," once the only place to find the kind of information MWLW were searching for. Now, however, gay and lesbian titles are more readily available in all bookstores.

I will never forget the anxiety I experienced as I journeyed to my first women's bookstore. Initially I had scoured the libraries. The catalogue listed books about lesbianism but they were not to be found on the shelves. I could not bring myself to ask the librarian for help, so I searched through all the local libraries. I returned often, for several weeks, hoping the books would magically reappear.

Finally, someone told me about a woman's bookstore uptown. It took me more than an hour on the subway to reach the store. All the while, sitting on the train, I wondered if the other passengers could read my discomfort. It took every ounce of strength I possessed to enter that feminist bookstore for the first time—and all I wanted to do was to browse the shelves for information that might help me to understand who or what I was and what I was going through.

When I reached Womenkind Books, I pretended to be browsing and walked past the section on lesbianism several times. Why was this section so open, why wasn't it hidden in the back of the store, I wondered. Finally I stopped and grabbed the first book that caught my eye with the word lesbian on the cover, *Lesbian Passion*.

I put a twenty-dollar bill on the counter and fumbled in my purse to avoid meeting the eyes of the cashier. Had she given me my book first, I probably would have run from the store without my change. Anyway, I never counted the money, just stuffed it into my pocket and made a fast exit.

On the train home, I held my package tightly to me while different scenarios popped into my head; what if the train lurched and the book slid from its brown paper bag and everyone saw the word *Lesbian?* What if I left it on the train and someone picked it up and ran after me calling out, "You left your *Lesbian* book!"? Then I began to worry, where could I hide this book when I got it home? I almost tossed it into the trash can when I got off the subway.

Before accepting the new sexuality that married women who love women have discovered is truly theirs, women go through a kaleidoscope of emotions. Those lucky enough to have the support of the woman they have fallen in love with often report feelings of elation and rightness. Those forced to deal with this issue of unexplored sexuality alone frequently find themselves on a different path, filled with anxiety and terror.

Nearly all MWLW experience an initial anger toward their husbands, wondering "why didn't he do something about my unhappiness, about his inability to communicate with me?"

Those women who had acknowledged their tendency toward lesbianism, yet had concealed the information in favor of a traditional marriage, believed that if the communication with their spouses had been better, those feelings would not have surfaced again. They initially blamed their husbands for not meeting their needs and for letting them down.

Most women believed they had no choice but to marry. Still, for the women who knew about their sexuality early on, the decision had been a difficult one. Whether they went into marriage to try to "make themselves right" or to please their families, remaining in the marriage once they committed themselves became an all-consuming job.

MARION

Marion, one of those women who had known about her desire for women and gone into therapy before marriage to "make herself right," says, "I spent my energies and time pleasing him, moving from state to state as he changed jobs, being the dutiful housewife, supporting his efforts, caring for his children by a previous marriage."

When Marion joined a twelve-step program for overeaters, she realized that her problems with food were only a cover under which she had been hiding her deeper distress, her true sexual leaning. She was aware that she had been feeling a general unhappiness but had no idea why. Eventually, working through her food issues forced her to acknowledge for the first time that she had needs of her own. After this awakening came the truth—her needs were not being met. She realized that she had never been satisfied with the conversation or any sort of interaction within her marriage, and had turned to food for comfort.

Eventually she felt comfortable enough in the group to bring up the issue of her sexuality.

"Before I realized I had needs, I had no expectations of my husband to fill them. Sometimes, when I tried to talk to him, he would leave the house or he'd say, 'You don't know what you're talking about.' And I had accepted that. But now, as I was allowing my feelings to surface, I wanted him to acknowledge them too. It really didn't matter what they were.

"When I understood my reason for overeating was frustration because he wasn't satisfying me emotionally, my previous inclination started coming back."

Problems in Marion's marriage became apparent only after she discovered that she had feelings. This is not uncommon. Many marriages initially work because women, taught to be the caregivers, don't acknowledge their own needs.

Being unaware that we have needs is a problem that has been prevalent in our society. My parents survived the Depression and the war by hiding their feelings—being tough. They wanted my siblings and me to be strong too. And I found myself following their lead. When my young children fell or scraped their knees and came to me crying, I often caught myself saying, "You didn't get hurt. Stop crying. You're okay." I realize now the message they were receiving was: "I'm not important, what happens to me doesn't matter," or "It's not all right to have feelings."

Some women go through two or three marriages or numerous heterosexual affairs trying to find the "something missing" in their lives. Others, not understanding why, try to fill themselves with food or alcohol. Many sublimate their own needs by investing all their time and energies in their husbands and children, becoming the perfect wife and mother, or putting all their energy into their work and never making time for a husband or family.

BELLA

Bella, a free spirit of the 1960s, became a devout Christian woman. She says, "My husband and I were just kids in the sixties. We'd get high, get a little wine, play strip poker with friends, and just do it. We never called it anything other than 'having a good time.' A bell didn't go off that I shouldn't be able to be with women. It was so natural. No one told me that it was bad, wrong, or evil. My own inner self didn't tell me not to do it. I didn't know I had enjoyed being with other women. I just knew I could be with them. It was a kid thing we did before we grew up. It wasn't until 1989 that I found a label for it [making love with women].

"In a Christian home a wife is dutiful," Bella says, "so I did the Christian thing, I practiced being a good wife, and I am a very good wife. In those early years I just did what was scripturally correct. The Bible didn't say I was supposed to get anything out of this (making love). It never occurred to me that I should. But I felt an incompleteness, an inadequacy, compared with my picture of what a family was supposed to be like. In our intimate moments I felt I should be relating to my husband in a certain way. I should be more nurturing and caring toward him than I was. So I learned how to act. I didn't pretend orgasms, I really had those. But anything else.

"I went to church with my problem. The nuns said, 'Go home

and submit to your husband.' I went home and got pregnant. I still felt something was wrong. I went back to talk to the nuns again. Again the same advice. Again another baby. Eight babies later, it suddenly came to me. I was a lover of women."

While none of the MWLW interviewed said their relationships with their husbands had been perfect at the time they discovered their preference for women, they were divided as to whether or not a better marriage would have made a difference in the long run. Some believed that eventually, their true sexuality would have emerged regardless of their marital situation. Others felt it had come about only because of the conflict within their marriages. Still, the common feeling among many of the women interviewed was that if their spouses had been more sensitive, they would not have had a need to turn to their women friends for the verbal closeness and emotional intimacy lacking at home.

The belief that a lack of communication caused them to look elsewhere for validation and fulfillment, thus leading them to discover their preference for women, is a strongly debated topic among MWLW, and among therapists as well.

Girls and boys grow up differently because, while they are both mothered by women, for boys, that first love object is of the opposite sex, whereas for girls it is the same sex. "Because the child's first intense emotional/libidinal love object is a woman, it is the smell and feel of a woman to which both sexes are primally drawn, and according to Freud, feel the first sexual attraction." In his *Theory of Female Sexuality*, Freud and many other psychoanalysts since have struggled with this question. Heterosexual sons never make a transition. Their first love object remains female throughout their adult lives. Why would girls, then, "pull away from the same-sex attraction with their mother "to develop an 'inferior,' passive heterosexual attachment to men? Nancy Chodorow contends that indeed, women do *not* give up their primary attachment to their mothers, but add secondary heterosexual attachment to men later in life primarily because of the internal and external taboos against lesbianism and the deep ambivalence of this first love. Chodorow maintains that in heterosexual relationships women recreate the primary mother bond by intense attachment to their children, and particularly their daughters, rather than with their husband or lover. Because a man's masculinity is tied to being unemotional and therefore less connected than a woman often wants, a mother is inclined to see her child/daughter as a reflection of her own mother in order to bring the emotional connectedness to her life that she is missing with her husband."

A typical Oedipal configuration, even for heterosexual women, Chodorow suggests, is bisexual. . . . Thus, when a girl turns toward her father she is not necessarily turning away from her mother. "When a girl's father does become an important primary person, it is in the context of a bisexual relational triangle. A girl's relation to him is emotionally in reaction to, interwoven and competing for primacy with, her relation to her mother."

According to Chodorow, while a girl retains her pre-Oedipal tie to her mother, she builds Oedipal attachments to both her mother and father upon it.

"From this perspective it is much easier to understand that object choice for many women may be a more flexible matter, with much room for later developmental factors to have a significant role. Interactions with siblings, peers, and teachers may play their part. Social and cultural attitudes about sexuality from schools, churches, and the media also contribute. Finally, the circumstances of life can tip the balance. Sexual identity may shift accordingly over a lifetime."

"The traditional explanation of lesbianism is that it is founded on a psychic love affair with the mother, which the daughter never outgrows." Beverly Burch suggests that "because the psychic love affair with the father is either never experienced or is closed off for defensive purposes, the basis for romantic and sexual relationships with men has been foreclosed."

Though much has changed since the women's movement, in general women have been taught to be dependent and passive, to seek attention and approval from other people, and to attend to and respond to the needs of others. Where assertive behavior is rewarded in the male, an assertive female is viewed negatively as being pushy or aggressive. Women are taught that to be unassertive and caretaking of others is to be appropriately female. Since female behavior and characteristics are less valued than their male counterparts, to be gender appropriate, women must accept a status that makes the development of a positive self-image difficult. This often leads to low self-esteem or depression.

Communication is difficult for women whose self-esteem is low. They may have trouble carrying on a discussion if someone disagrees with them. They may become flustered or shut down, especially if it's a man doing the disagreeing. Having been brought up to feel inadequate and defenseless, believing that taking care of themselves or being assertive is unfeminine, women fear being criticized, saying no, and stating their needs clearly and directly. In the latest backlash against female advancement, some young women disdain the label of feminist altogether, fearing it labels them as either man-hating or lesbian.

Some accept being one down from men. Others attempt to redefine their position in society by glorifying traditionally female roles. The isolation in which MWLW exist, however, makes their growth even more difficult because they are different from other women. In order to build positive self-images, they must resolve the conflicts of gender difference.

For many women, those conflicts were exacerbated by hypocritical aspects of the churches in which they had been raised. Disheartened, many no longer attended services. Here, too, they found they were no longer welcome members. Several women did, however, enthusiastically report changing affiliation to the Unitarian Church, which they said was more accepting of their lifestyles.

GAIL

From an Irish-Catholic family, Gail, at thirty-five, is not certain if she considers herself bisexual or lesbian. She recalls being attracted to both boys and girls at a very early age. But she married and had babies—because she was supposed to.

As Gail began to come to terms with her own sexuality, however, she became more disenchanted by the Catholic church. "It disturbs me greatly," she says, "because basically I've realized it [the Church] is homophobic and patriarchal. It's sad because I've been raised in the religion, had twelve years of Catholic school, and have been educating my sixteen-year-old daughter through Catholic traditions. Now I face a dilemma. I have another child at that age where he should be enrolling in grammar school. I don't know if I want to perpetuate this [the Church's] negative way of thinking.

"I love my church and I was disappointed with the Church's stand on homosexuality. It's very hypocritical because there is so much homosexuality in the priesthood.

"But I don't think I would reject God because I don't think God rejects me. I don't think he rejects gay people. I think a bunch of men are making these silly rules and imposing their values on people."

Gail went on to say: "I read *Lesbian Nuns Breaking Silence.* It was so poignant, the way the women describe their relationships with the other women, very intense, very touching. I cried from cover to cover."

The women who were most strongly tied to their churches while growing up, the Catholic women, were the ones who most often cut the ties when they began to deal with their sexuality. As their consciousness rose, they could no longer be forced to follow the rigid rules of the Church. Some attributed their leaving to the lack of support and understanding offered by their religious institutions. Others believe it was the Church-imposed morality that caused them to turn toward women.

MARIA

A parochial school graduate, Maria says, "I am a Puerto Rican. I was a Catholic, raised to be a virgin and get married. They [the nuns] said getting pregnant out of wedlock was a sin. Nothing was discussed in school about birth control. Around me, all I saw were girls getting pregnant and nobody with them. I was afraid to get close to a guy because I didn't want to end up with a baby and alone. So it was safer to be with a girl.

"I lived with my female lover for three years and then we watched a friend's baby for the weekend. Being raised Catholic, you grow up, get married, and have kids. That's when I decided I wanted to marry a man so I could have a baby of my own. This was in the early sixties. I got involved and thought I fell in love with the first man I was with. I didn't take into consideration the kind of insensitive man he was. I married him to have my babies."

Maria's husband abused her, yet she remained in the marriage for the children . . . until he turned his abuse toward their eldest daughter. Then she took her children and left. Needing help to raise her young family, she married again.

"With my second husband I tried to recapture the intimacy I had shared with my lover. It was impossible. I became promiscuous, finding male lovers outside my marriage. They couldn't satisfy me either. I was so frustrated. Eventually I found another woman lover. I think if I was getting the emotional stuff I needed from my husband, I wouldn't have looked."

Arlene DiMarco, M.S.W., C.S.W., certified psychotherapist, feels that women turn to women for romantic love in lieu of support from their husbands. She believes that for married women who love women, "even if their husbands were more sensitive, eventually they [the women] would begin to feel that something was missing. Regardless of how good and how sensitive the man is, there is always that void. It needs to be filled by another woman."

She believes that "the need to be with women is something women are born with. By and large many women, afraid of the ramifications, will ignore this need. As uncomfortable as they are, they're not about to make any changes. It is only the women who are more in touch with their feelings who will search."

Religious persuasions, subtly instilled or more blatantly coerced, can strongly affect the lives of many women who have not yet come to separate themselves from their families and form their own identities.

MARYANN

Although most women, once enlightened, chose to leave their churches, Maryann, raised in a middle-class community in upstate New York, was an exception. She remained within the Catholic church which had always been important to her.

"While growing up, homosexuality was never discussed—in a positive or negative way," she says. "But when I found out about myself, it was painful, especially when people I cared about were telling me that it was awful and wrong [to feel the way I did]. What got me through was my faith. I knew deep inside me that it was right for me . . . and I found people around me who accepted me for who I was. My husband for one. I feel comfortable with myself and my church."

Maryann continues to be active in her church. She met another woman there and the two became friends, then lovers. Involved in the same activities, church allows them to spend time together. People don't question their relationship and her husband does not have to cover for her.

Those women who had strong religious upbringings had the most difficulty breaking with their childhood teachings. Some never did.

One sixty-six-year-old from an Orthodox Jewish background talked of having had her marriage arranged for her when she was a young girl. She lived with her husband for several months without being able to consummate the union. Eventually the marriage was annulled.

For years, believing that there was something wrong with her, the woman lived with the shame she had brought to her family— until she heard there was such a thing as women who loved women. She finally understood that that was the kind of woman she was born to be.

She was not alone. The more I talked with women, the more similar I found their stories and sentiments. I also received several notes such as this one: "I don't have a story to tell since it is impossible to act on my feelings, but your words literally jumped out of the page. For the first time, I realized I was not alone. Someone cared about me and women like me and the secret we are forced to live with."

LESLIE

Leslie, in her twenties, grew up in a small town in North Carolina. She describes her childhood home as being very homophobic.

"My Baptist upbringing made me nervous and uptight with sexual things. I thought that's why I hadn't really been interested in boys in high school. But as soon as I went to college, my life changed. I realized there was a whole world out there other than what I had been brought up to believe in. My friends talked about the wild things they had done with guys. That was all new to me.

So while in college I went out and fucked a lot of guys, thinking, 'Eventually, I'm going to like it.' But that never happened.

"Then I found a guy I actually thought I loved. I blame my parents for forcing me to marry him though. He and I were to-gether, but I still had this feeling that something was missing. My mother would call constantly and be in tears, accusing us of living together in a house of sin. She ranted on and on. As much as I didn't believe those things [about sin] from my religious upbring-ing anymore, it still made me crazy because it was part of my background and I didn't want to lose my parents. So we made plans for our wedding.

"Two weeks before the wedding, I had an affair with a woman. I guess I was curious, but afterward I knew who I was. I was honest with my fiancé and it made him a little nervous, but we had planned a big wedding and we didn't know what else to do. We got married."

In the sixties, the first wave of feminism brought about an internal revolution as well. The prevalence of support groups for women who had become isolated from family and friends in our mobile society increased dramatically. The word "share" replaced the word "tell." Terms such as "codependent" and "self-help" began to pepper our vocabularies.

Economics forced women back to the workplace. Others began to attend or return to college. Women were becoming part of the larger world outside the home. They were becoming aware that they had rights and privileges.

The feminist movement brought attention to women's prob-lems and new ways of seeing and addressing issues relating to them. Self-esteem grew. As women began to share their frustra-tions with one another, they became aware of their own needs— learning that it was all right to have them. Feelings and emotions, once denied, were now being acknowledged.

Consciousness-raising groups became popular. The groups provided safe environments where women could discuss personal roles, issues, attitudes, and needs. For the first time, women be-gan to talk about marital concerns they had kept repressed. Shar-ing their secrets helped them to realize that their problems and thoughts were not unique, and that they were not alone.

Open dialogue brought increasing awareness, helping women

to see that others shared the same frustrations as wives, mothers, and daughters. Taboo subjects such as sex and intercourse were no longer forbidden topics of conversation. Women discovered that not everyone had experienced an orgasm—although each had believed she was the only one who hadn't. For the first time, women began to feel good about their sexuality.

Nine percent of the women interviewed admitted to having been sexually abused as children. While they do not agree as to whether or not the violation made them turn to women, it is probably that while most women reject lesbianism because of cultural taboos, an incest survivor, who has been forced to live outside of society's rules since childhood, has the freedom to make that choice more easily than a traditionally raised woman. "I observe in my practice," says Karin Meiselman, "that virtually all of the lesbian father-daughter incest survivors reveal an intense longing for a nurturing, positive relationship with a woman, which I see as a distinctly separate issue from the survivor's anger at and difficulties with men."

Psychotherapist Eileen Starzecpyzel sees a correlation between the choice of women as a sexual object for both men and lesbians who have been victims of incest by their fathers. "A woman's relationship with her sons is different from that with her daughters and produces significant personality differences in her male child . . . her son, having a penis, will grow up to be more like his father than like her. Under the influence of powerful cultural and patriarchal pressure, the mother subconsciously relinquishes the boy to his father, who must teach him manhood. At the same time, her relationship to her son takes on strong Oedipal (sexual) overtones, because she begins to relate to him as a sexual 'other' or 'little man,' while her own husband remains distant and absent from her daily life, as is customary in this culture. This new, sexually charged interaction with the mother frightens the boy, who gives up the emotional link with his mother in favor of masculine identity and power. Until he gains a wife/mother substitute later in life, he loses the warmth with mother that girls retain."

Starzecpyzel hypothesizes that "the early loss of mothering, or severance of pre-Oedipal connectedness to mother, not only happens to boys in normal development, but also happens to girls who have been victimized by father-daughter incest. The loss of and longing for the early sexual pre-Oedipal bond with mother may be a significant factor in creating for the boy and the incested girl an unsatisfied longing for mother."

While Belinda, a Southern Baptist from Kentucky, feels that the abuse she suffered at the hands of men played a major role in determining her sexual preference, Joy, a Catholic from New Jersey, insists that her sexuality had already been determined before she was sexually violated by a woman when she was five years old. "It was a painful and confusing experience," Joy says. "Given that in my case it was a woman, it might have turned me away from women—and it didn't. If I really think back," she says, "I can recall instances even prior to that where the inclination was already there."

BELINDA

Belinda believes it was the sexual abuse she endured as a young girl, as well as her mother's desertion, that made her turn to women.

"My mother took off when I was four. My father slept with me, then he sold me and my brothers and sisters. The people who bought me took me to church every Sunday. Then the man slept with me every Monday. I was six when that started. How could I have trust in God? He represented men, and look what they had done to me.

"I married a man at sixteen to escape the abusive situation at home," Belinda says. "But I left a short time later. I kept being drawn to women. I'm forty now and I'm not certain what I am. I could make love to women and I love them to pieces. I would do anything to please the other woman, but I don't like anyone making love to me. I can't let anyone touch me. I only recently learned through intensive therapy that I have spent my life seeking the mother figure I never had."

For an incest survivor, be she a lesbian or a heterosexual woman, Psychotherapist Starzecpyzel says, "Sex is never just sex, and it is rare to experience pleasure, good feelings, and the vulnerability of orgasm." Sex brings with it difficulties with trust and a struggle to believe that letting someone be close will not result in humiliation, degradation, betrayal, and rejection as well as feelings of badness. While the paternal seduction is bad, "the primary wound of incest is the loss of the mother bond, which is damaged severely by the father's sexual appropriation and misuse of the child."

In father-daughter psychological/sexual incest, the father initiates incest consciously or subconsciously by appropriating his daughter as his "special" child, his possession. . . . The father may actively keep the mother from having a relationship with the child.

For the child, Starzecpyzel says, a sense of being unconnected to and stolen from her mother—the feeling of being a motherless child—is what results. Through his seduction, the father forces the girl into a tight father-daughter bond that replaces the normal mother-daughter bond needed for a girl's secure development. This replacement bond causes the child to develop an identity, not like the mother's, but similar to a boy's psychosexual development. Then like the traditionally raised heterosexual male, she may have a sexual response toward females.

If the father's intrusive disruption of the mother bond occurred early, the girl may be aware only of her rejection of mother as a worthy object to identify with, and she may be more conscious of having never wanted to be like her mother. While the core issues, as Starzecpyzel sees them, are identification with the father, protectiveness toward the mother, rejection of the mother, intense longing for the mother, and feelings of abandonment by the lost mother, the lesbian victim may initially enter therapy hating women and identifying primarily with men.

According to Starzecpyzel, despite the sexual abuse, it frequently occurs that the relationship with the father was the most available to the child. As a result, the child is inclined to value the power of masculinity as the healthier model of adaption. A turning away from identification with the mother and a preference for the identifying with the father is sometimes an important factor in the formation of lesbian sexual identity.

Many women who had accused their husbands of not fulfilling them emotionally came to the realization that the men had not changed. It was they who had changed. They realized that as their own self-regard and awareness grew, their expectations of their husbands had also grown—and so did their unhappiness at the men who were not fulfilling those expectations. This new under-standing led them to connect with other women who could fulfill their needs; and for some, that meant sexually.

According to psychotherapist Hedda Begelman, C.S.W.-R., board certified diplomate in clinical social work, and director of the Gay and Lesbian Counselling Center of Long Island, "Even after discovering their sexual preference and connecting with women who make them feel complete, some women come to therapy with their issue being 'How can I stay in this marriage and not explore this woman-woman relationship any further?'

"They have been disciplined by society's definitions of what is right and what is not," Begelman says. "Being a lesbian is one of the great prohibitions."

Many MWLW initially began therapy to suppress their feel-ings.

MARTHA

"I started therapy and told my therapist, 'I am thirty-two, married six years, and very unhappy. I can't communicate with my hus-band.' Not knowing I had other choices, I said to her, 'And I want to stay married.' My therapist took that as her marching orders. I didn't hold anything back. I told her how I'd felt about women all my life. She didn't say much.

"I spent twelve thousand dollars and eight years in therapy with a homophobic therapist, trying to make my marriage work. Still, none of this stuff [my preference for women] was obvious.

"Then a friend suggested I join a women's consciousness-rais-ing group to get more in touch with my sexual orientation. When I told this to my therapist, she said it was ridiculous."

Martha says, "When I look back now, it made lots of sense. If I had followed my friend's advice, I would have gotten in touch with who I was long before now. Finally I changed therapists and started to figure my life out."

LUCY

Not every MWLW will consider therapy to help her through her transition. Indoctrinated with society's attitude against same-sex feelings, some women perceive themselves as deserving of punishment for the crime of having fallen in love with another woman. They feel unworthy of help from a therapist.

Lucy, married, and the mother of a twelve-year-old son and fourteen-year-old daughter, was active in the PTA of her children's school when, suddenly, she realized she had fallen in love with her best friend of eighteen years. Needing an outlet for those new feelings, Lucy began to write poetry. When her husband accidentally found her writings, she was mortified. He said, "You're a foolish woman. Forget this nonsense. Forget your friend. Stay home and I'll buy you a new car."

She says, "I was so grateful to him for not throwing me out when he found out what a disgusting person I was. I sat home, buried my face in the refrigerator, and proceeded to gain almost one hundred pounds. It was easier and safer to eat than to think about the strange, unnatural feelings I had for my friend. I don't want to think about that time in my life anymore."

Almost too obese to leave the house now, Lucy will still not consider therapy. She continues to believe that she is detestable.

In the beginning of my discovery period, I thought maybe I was just in love with my best friend. Maybe the fact that she was a woman was insignificant. I could no longer talk to her, and I desperately needed to find someone who could answer my questions.

I went to a meeting for women who were dealing with the issue of loving women. It was at the Gay and Lesbian Center in New York City. As difficult as it had been for me to go to a woman's bookstore for the first time, my discomfort was nothing compared to what I felt walking into this redbrick building. My heart was beating so hard that I was afraid if I looked down I would see it straining against my shirt. I became slightly paranoid: Was anyone watching? Would they think I was like "those women" if they saw me go into this place? I walked around the block three times before I could get up my courage to climb the two steps.

In the assigned room I quickly took the nearest available chair. Afraid of any eye contact, I studied my shoes. Eventually, though, my curiosity got the best of me and I slowly raised my eyes. My first reaction was one of surprise. The other women looked so "normal." I could stand next to them in the supermarket or at a school meeting and I'd never know they were lesbians. I briefly shared my story with the woman sitting beside me and she invited me to join her for coffee the next day.

In my naiveté and ignorance, I assumed, as do many uninformed people I speak to, that the only thing lesbians do is have sex with other lesbians. Period. I remember feeling uncomfortable, but determined to do what I had to so that I would know the truth about myself. I felt absolutely no attraction toward this woman, but to put my curiosity to rest, I thought, if this is what lesbians do, I will do it. I must find out if I am one or not. I actually went out and bought new panties and a new bra.

We met at a diner. She ordered coffee and a Danish and I ordered tea and a large cookie. Like any two women would, we talked about our families and our jobs. We talked about ourselves and the newly discovered feelings we both had for our respective friends. Then we said good-bye and each of us went home to prepare dinner for our families. That was all that happened.

Months later, when we had become friends, I told her what had crossed my mind that afternoon and we laughed together.

When I began therapy soon after my trip to the bookstore and the open center, my mouth moved but the words wouldn't come out. I trembled as I tried to talk. At the time, I believed I was the only woman in the world to ever have fallen in love with another woman.

MWLW begin therapy for various reasons. Some, as I did, begin because they feel they are heading for a breakdown. Some start to deal with what their new sexuality means to them and continue to decide whether or not they can accept themselves as MWLW. Often, a client is in therapy for a long period of time before revealing her proclivity. Other women have already accepted what they have discovered—that they are lesbians—and now need to decide if they want to remain in their marriages or begin new lives altogether. They need to find out how to act on this new dimension of their lives.

Some of the women I interviewed were specific about what they wanted in a therapist—although some admitted that after being in therapy for a while, their requirements for a therapist had changed. Some preferred a male therapist, feeling a male perspective would be more detached. Some needed it to be a woman—their discomfort in sharing their secret with a man being too great to deal with. Others wanted only a heterosexual woman, fearing a lesbian might influence them when they were still unsure or confused about their sexuality. Yet once an internal frame of reference has been developed, many women are less fearful of being influenced and often seek a lesbian-identified therapist to gain further support or to use as a role model.

One homosexual therapist I spoke with is of the opinion that "the power of our heterocentric society is so strong that there are therapists today who believe no normal woman could want to be a lesbian. Viewing homosexuality as a disease, they are still trying to convert their patients to heterosexual lifestyles rather than dealing with the actual issues these women are facing with relation to their true sexuality. Unfortunately," she says, "even among those heterosexual therapists who are objective, many don't have enough experience with lesbians to help these women."

PAMELA

Pamela says, "After realizing I was attracted to women, I became depressed and went into therapy." Her male therapist refused to accept the truth in regard to her sexual preference. "He was convinced that I was not gay, that I was just unhappy and should work on my marriage, which I found difficult," she says. "My husband was into fads and toys, beautiful cars and women. He was into sex scenes, which made me uncomfortable."

Eventually Pamala's therapist acknowledged that maybe the problem was with her husband and suggested she try an affair with a man. "But the question of my preferring women kept coming back and I'd say to my therapist, 'We're not dealing with this issue.' And he'd say, 'It's not a problem. You're seeing a man. Continue seeing men.'

"I remained very depressed. I had rashes all over my body, hemorrhoids—any psychosomatic thing that could happen to my body was happening.

"Finally I left my marriage, my therapist, and my male lover, and I came out to myself. All of my physical problems went away."

Psychotherapist Hedda Begelman says, "A woman who begins to feel that she loves women has to accept that that's an okay way of life and there's nothing wrong with that. She's not perverted and not crazy and she doesn't have a disease, but for some reason, probably, she was born this way."

"A woman in transition should be going to a sympathetic therapist to help her deal with her situation," Begelman says. "Half of the women I see in my practice, which is primarily gay and lesbian, are married." She adds, however, that "whether a woman chooses a straight or a gay therapist, one of the same sex or the opposite, the most important issue to be dealt with is learning how to accept herself."

Not all MWLW have an immediate need to seek therapy or written information when they discover their differences. When love between two women is reciprocated, sometimes the close and intimate relationship they share is enough to give each of them the support she needs. The completeness each feels can also make her respective marriage work more smoothly.

JOANNA

Joanna says, "I loved my husband and I never wanted to hurt him. He was a very good man who always treated me fairly and with tremendous respect. I felt he didn't deserve this, yet he couldn't fulfill my needs. I needed to be able to communicate with somebody. I needed to have somebody know me one hundred percent. I needed to have somebody listen to and hear me. As wonderful as he was, he really couldn't do that for me. Because of this, I felt that it was okay to be with my best friend and lover.

"Actually, I believe he was relieved when I stopped nagging him to go out with me or to listen to me. Here I was, for the first time in my life, taking care of my needs and it was making the rest of my world better too."

Women who experience the deep emotional level they can reach with another woman can no longer settle for the contentedness they may have accepted as their lot in life before. Across the country, many of the same words were repeated as women described their newfound feelings. One said, "I never realized how two-dimensional my life had been until I discovered that third dimension within myself."

I would have to describe the new depth of feelings I experienced as "drawing back a curtain and having my dull gray world flow into a full spectrum of beautiful color." When I told others of this sense of leaving a black-and-white existence and entering one of brilliance, they said, "Yes. That's it. That's how I would describe it too."

Women talked about having lived with insatiable emptiness. Only in retrospect did they realize that they had been trying to fill that void by keeping occupied with work, in organizations, or in their communities. Others kept busy with adult education courses and workshops.

I was constantly busy and constantly eating, but I never felt satisfied. When I fell in love with Toby, even though the feelings were one-sided, it was as though my whole life and my whole system changed. Suddenly, I didn't have to be busy anymore. I could sit in a chair and daydream and that was all right. I had no desire for food. I found I was losing weight for the first time in my life without consciously dieting.

Most MWLW who become awakened to their new sexuality do not see divorce as the obvious solution. Frequently they say, "I wish my husband weren't such a nice guy." The overwhelming sense of guilt and duty, coupled with the fear of living a gay lifestyle, make staying in a marriage preferable for some women. Many of those I spoke with echoed each other with the following wish: "If only he drank or gambled away our money or hit me, then it would be easy to leave him." Yet even women in abusive relationships have a difficult time making the break. The idea of suddenly being alone, especially for those women who went directly from their parents' homes to their husband's, is difficult. The need of a man has been so ingrained in the education of most women that some even remain in marriages that are absolutely unbearable.

In *Codependent No More*, Melody Beattie describes a marriage where the man spends his days lying on the couch, drunk and abusing his family. The wife works, pays the bills, maintains the house, and cares for the children. When asked why she doesn't leave her husband, the woman says, "Do you think I can take care of myself?"

GERI

"I felt like sex was his payment for taking care of me. Sometimes I felt like I was prostituting myself. It was the woman I fell in love with who made me realize that I was, and had always been, an equal partner in my marriage. I had been the budgeter and manager and I had been responsible for raising three terrific kids. Yet all of these years my husband had made me feel as though I had been living off him."

Our society equates marriage with legal sex, and women used to be taught, even if they were not interested, that they did not have the right to say no when their husbands approached them. Sex came as part of the package. However, this notion, even among heterosexual couples, is changing.

Women taught to equate marriage with monogamy believe that if they do not choose to be monogamous, something is wrong with them, their partner, or their relationship. With education and growing self-esteem, women are beginning to realize that they can alter what society has mandated. Patsy, an MWLW and the mother of an eight-year-old daughter, has modified her life to meet her needs as well as the needs of her family.

PATSY

"What I've often seen in marriages are two people who are together forever and ever, bored stiff with each other, dull and uninteresting but together anyway because of the big pressure: 'If you don't stay, you're a failure.'

"I want my marriage to work because I am happy and therefore happy in it, not because society says if you leave it you are a failure.

"No one person can be expected to fulfill another person totally. Why can't I have my husband who I love and care about and also a woman who can give me what he cannot. To include Cheryl in my life is to make my life complete. For that, I have had to change my whole perspective of the world.

"Society has set up certain guidelines and the people who don't fit into its predisposed rules, like me, are made to feel different,"

Patsy says. "For a long time I thought there was something wrong with me. But the more I grew educationally and emotionally, the more I liked me and the more I saw other people liked me too. The way people responded to me became much more positive. So I thought, 'How could it be me? I must be all right.'

"That's when I started to question. I questioned the whole system, including all those definitions of a marriage, a husband, a wife. And I stopped wearing a wedding ring. I don't like all the connotations that come affixed with that."

Most people can live comfortably within society's established guidelines—but for women who have discovered that third dimension in themselves, the world must be redefined.

Patsy says, "Taking charge of my life and changing the rules was the critical turning point for me. I no longer bemoan the fact that I couldn't have the kind of marriage I was 'supposed' to have. Regardless of whether it's [proper] by society's definition or not, I have to feel good and happy about myself.

"When I come home feeling good, I can be open to my child and my husband. I can be open to the stranger I bump into on the bus. My guide is 'How do I feel about myself?' If I feel good about me and the interactions between the people that I care about in my life, then I'm happy—my life is working. I'm not hurting anyone and society can take its rules to someone else.

"I think society limits us and I think it's done intentionally. I want my life to be wide open enough that I can make any decisions based on what feels right for me and the people in my life. I don't want to be stuck into 'Well, I'm a mother so I can't do this,' or 'I'm a wife so I can't do that.' "

SHELLY

Married six years and the mother of a five-year-old daughter, she, unlike Patsy (who considers herself a lesbian), had been in relationships with men and women before she was married. "I never viewed monogamy as something I particularly wanted," she says. "It's not a style that really suits my nature and it's not a value I hold. But when I met my husband, he felt it was important for him, so I said I'd try. For two years it worked. My life felt all right, but in a certain way I felt like a part of me was dying. I was living a life that was not me."

□ □ □ □

Today it is common to find in alternative weekly newspapers personal ads that attest to the void many MWLW feel. "Female, caring, nonsmoker, married, seeks kindred woman for unending friendship," and "Married female with children seeks same for discreet correspondence, friendship." Another adds "Only therapied women need apply." In one center for gay men and lesbians, an MWLW started a support group for women like herself and within a few months the group had grown to more than sixty members and is still growing.

The process of an MWLW becoming comfortable with who she is and of defining new boundaries and understandings in her relationships is an ongoing one. There are highs and lows and periods of frustration and confusion. Hours are spent trying to understand the question "Why can't I just be happy?" Once I realized who I was, I was able to accept the fact that there was nothing wrong with me. A feeling of liberation and a tremendous sense of relief at being able finally to acknowledge my gender preference replaced my initial anger and frustration, and all the pieces seemed to fit into place.

I had been shocked when I realized I was a lesbian. I certainly didn't know when I married. I knew I wasn't very interested in sex, but I thought my low sex drive was the result of a thyroid condition. Over the last few years I found myself getting up earlier than my husband and going to bed after he was asleep. Only after I found out about myself did I realize I had gotten into this sleep pattern to avoid physical intimacy with him. I realized I would need more space for our marriage to endure. For this to happen, I would have to tell him about myself—but how?

PART TWO

A New Life

4

Do I Tell My Husband or Not?

ALTHOUGH she may think she knows her husband well, no woman can accurately predict his response should she choose to disclose her preference for women . . . and once the words are out, they can never be taken back. Therefore, to tell or not to tell is one of the most difficult decisions an MWLW must make, and one for which there is no easy answer.

When I learned about myself, I didn't believe I'd ever tell my husband. The whole thing came as such a shock to me. It was something I had never contemplated.

I agonized over my decision to come out to him, and then, when I decided to, over how I would tell him, and when. I chose a time when the kids were away for the weekend. But I couldn't find the right words. Friday passed, then Saturday was almost over. I couldn't say anything. I knew Sunday would be too late. It wasn't fair for him not to have time to digest this news.

We had gone to a street fair, but I was so uptight about wanting to tell him and not being able to get the words out that I can't remember what we saw that day. He led the way to an ice cream parlor and we sat down. He commented innocently on the amount of money I was spending in therapy, which I had finally told him about, and I just began to cry. Then all the words poured out. I told him I had been in therapy for months before I mustered the courage to tell him. I told him how I felt about Toby and how she had stopped talking to me when I told her how

I felt. I told him about the pain I had endured and the isolation I had lived with since the loss of my best friend.

It was a lot for him to take in, and we drove home in silence. Normally we'd go our separate ways once we got home. Today we sat together on the couch and cried. "Now each time you go out I'm going to wonder if you are looking for a woman," he said.

"Did you wonder if I was looking for a man each time I went out before?"

Darkness came and we remained in our places. Neither of us moved to turn on a light. After a while I asked if he'd like something to eat. "No," he said. "I need to take a walk."

That night was long and filled with sorrow. As I waited for my husband to return, I recalled the two innocent young teenagers we had been when we met, and my pain intensified. Still, the anguish I had lived with for the past two years began to lessen. My secret was finally out.

It seemed like hours before he returned. Exhausted, we went up to bed but neither of us slept. We lay side by side, talking and crying into the early morning.

I think my telling my husband everything helped him to have a little more understanding for me and what I was going through, but it didn't lessen his shock or the grief that soon replaced the first numbing blow. I tried to help him to see that there was nothing he could have done to change what had happened.

After a while I got used to being who I was and realized it was easier to live with the new me than with the detachment I originally felt from my family. They had been living with someone they didn't really know—and I had been feeling very incomplete.

My husband still went through periods of grief mixed with anger and for a while had days when the slightest upset could bring on uncalled-for fury. But those days grew farther apart and I kept remembering that it took me several years to come to terms with who and what I am, so it was only fair to give him the time he needed.

To his credit, he began therapy and is learning a lot about himself. When he talks now, it's with a deeper level of understanding. I'm finding him more interesting than I have in years. I don't know what will become of our marriage, but I think eventually we'll be better friends than would ever have been possible before.

□ □ □ □

While homosexual men have been the forerunners in leading the way out of the closet, women are only now beginning to feel the same freedom to be who they are. This may be due, in part, to society's begrudging acknowledgment of lesbianism, brought on by the shift in society's supposition that the cause of one's sexual persuasion was a personal choice and therefore could be changed.

Chandler Burr, author of *Homosexuality and Biology*, says, "Homosexuals have long maintained that sexual orientation, far from being a personal choice or lifestyle (as it is often called), is something neither chosen nor changeable; heterosexuals who have made their peace with homosexuals have often done so by accepting that premise. The very term 'sexual orientation,' which in the 1980s replaced 'sexual preference,' asserts the deeply rooted nature of sexual desire and love. It implies biology."

Prior to the sixties, it was not uncommon for a woman to grow up never having heard the word *lesbian*. Even when the word did begin to surface, it was generally in whispered conversations and in the most derogatory manner.

Now it is becoming common to see national magazines with articles on gay issues. Between June and October 1993, *Newsweek*, *Vanity Fair*, and *Cosmopolitan* featured lesbians on their covers and as their top stories. *New York* magazine's May 10, 1993, issue featured singer k. d. lang on its cover with the title "Lesbian Chic."

By 1996 top television series such as *ER* and *Roseanne* had announced shows with lesbian content. Then, on *Roseanne*, to boost ratings, the grandmother announced that she was a lesbian. The series *Friends* and *Mad About You* introduced lesbian characters as regulars, and in 1997 a landmark in American television was reached when Ellen DeGeneres, the lead character on the sitcom *Ellen*, came out in both her private life and on her television show.

Because lesbians are finding a voice and making themselves seen and heard, the isolation each MWLW has felt, living with her own "terrible secret," is slowly lifting.

Younger women, once they have identified their sexuality, seem to experience less difficulty coming out to their spouses, even when they have children. Perhaps this is because they have not yet been conditioned by our culture to see alternative lifestyles as taboo. Nor have they spent years being taken care of, and possibly losing their sense of self. They, therefore, have more confidence in their ability to survive without a mate than do older women.

The process of telling is one many "older" women do not know how to handle. They don't want to remain in their marriages on bad terms, nor do they want to leave on bad terms. They want everything to remain intact. The internal turmoil they feel leads to ambivalence or tremendous difficulty with decision making. The idea of deceiving someone else is so overwhelming that women often fail to recognize the way in which they are deceiving themselves.

Even when a woman has made the decision to tell her husband, her words are often met with disbelief or denial because a common misconception is that if a woman was a lesbian, she would be incapable of having a heterosexual sexual relationship. Yet, according to clinical psychologist and sex therapist Margaret Nichols, "The vast majority of lesbians have had some sexual involvement with men before coming out: More than ninety percent have had sex with men, and one third have been married."

Most of the MWLW interviewed believed that if they hadn't discovered their same-sex preference when they did, their preference would have eventually made itself known anyway. Initially, however, many of these MWLW who had recently learned of, or come to terms with, their new sexuality admitted to being extremely angry with their spouses, blaming the men for causing them to turn to women.

If the woman is in the accusation stage, it may be better to wait until she has gone through her own exploration and composed herself before sharing this information.

There are no specific guidelines for MWLW and no right or wrong solutions to this marital predicament. Each woman has her own agenda in choosing if, when, and how to come out to her husband. What works for one may not work for another. While disclosures often seem to come about gradually, the timing of the "official disclosure" in relation to business or financial pressures, family illness, or problems with a child, has a lot to do with how the husband will react.

One woman says, "We were married eleven years before I finally felt I was in a place in our marital relationship where it felt safe enough for me to share who I was with my husband."

Another says, "I waited two days. Then I couldn't keep it to myself anymore. It made so many other things so clear."

Whether or not the couple decide to continue in their marriage, if there is to be peace, the way an MWLW tells her spouse about herself and the way he is able to listen to her are very important. Often, sharing what she is going through serves to create a greater understanding and a closer bond between husband and wife.

When she tells her husband, the MWLW should keep in mind that it is she who has changed. He has not. Every man's reaction is going to differ depending on his own security. Even a man certain of his own sexuality will experience a variety of reactions. Shock, anger, rage, and denial are common feelings. Some men go through depression. Even men who are compassionate and sympathetic to their wives' plights will experience hostile feelings at some time. This confirmation of suspicions, or explanation or excuse for sexual incompatibility, may bring relief to others. Being as honest as possible without being hurtful will help.

The ease with which an MWLW has been able to communicate with her husband is one important aspect in determining whether or not she will share this information with him. The negative or positive feelings she has about her own sexuality—often related to her upbringing, education, and level of self-confidence—is another. The agony brought on by the deception of not telling causes other women to come out. Women who have never acted on their impulses to be with another woman, but who know they are more attracted to women than they are to men, face the same turmoil. They would like to share the truth about themselves, but can't.

PAT

"I had gotten to the point where my feelings just weren't going anywhere," says forty-five-year-old Pat. "They weren't changing, they weren't disappearing, and my husband and I knew something was wrong. In a fit of honesty and openness I told him that while I'd never had an experience with another woman, I always knew there was something 'different' about myself.

"He never believed me," she says. "In his mind, if I were gay I would be incapable of having a heterosexual relationship."

Frustrated after various unsuccessful attempts to broach the topic, Pat simply decided to let it drop.

"It's a subject that's now avoided," she says. "We don't talk about it, but anytime we have a fight or a disagreement, I feel it simmering in the background. I regret having said anything and I can't take it back."

Pat, brought up to put the feelings and needs of her family first, has been living unhappily in this "stuck" state for the past eighteen years.

NORMA

Norma fell in love with a woman who was going to die. She says, "I had never felt this way about another woman before and I didn't think I could feel this way again. I was very happy with my husband. I wasn't looking to get out of my marriage. I wasn't looking for 'it' but 'it' found me. Marcia would have liked me to come out of the closet, leave my husband and family, and join her in her life, but I was afraid.

"My husband knew her. He knew that she was my best friend. He also knew that she was a lesbian. I had even told him that I loved her. He asked me how I meant that and I said, 'Like I love a lot of people.' I never told him that we had a physical relationship, so he was tolerant.

"I told my husband that she was sick and I wanted to be all the friend I could be to her while she was alive. He seemed to understand and allowed me the time I wanted with her. Whether he knew or not I don't know. I think when she died, it was a relief to him. I know that he had been very jealous."

JANETTE

Janette never had any sexual experience with another woman, but always knew she was different. Her friends in high school had posters of male actors covering their walls. She remembers thinking, "Why would they want to look at these?" She married a man who was her friend because, like so many others, she thought marriage was something she was supposed to do.

"My husband knew but didn't know," she says. "We joked about my feeling anxious and scared. I thought I was going crazy. I loved him but I wasn't in love with him. I had two children and another coming, a house, and a dog. All that and it wasn't me.

"Three years ago I thought I could be married forever. Then a feeling of 'it's not fair' started growing. I know now I can't spend the rest of my life faking something I don't feel. I needed to share my feelings with my husband.

"Recently I went to a store and picked up a few books," Janette says. "One was *Call Me Lesbian*. I showed it to him. He took it as a joke and wouldn't talk to me about it. I asked if he wanted to know what page I was up to and what the book was about. He wanted no part of it. He said he was going to call Howard Stern, a New York talk show host known for insulting his listeners.

"Then a program, 'In Bed with a Secret,' aired about straight spouses. I asked him to watch it with me. I said to him, 'I don't know what to do. Am I supposed to act on my feelings? Am I supposed to suppress them? What should I do?' He got very mad. He said I could do what I wanted, but his kids would never be in a house with women like on that program. Then he wouldn't talk about it anymore.

"That night, afraid he'd call me an unfit mother, I got rid of the books. Now he seems to have forgotten the whole thing like it is no longer an issue."

Janet thought open communication might have saved her marriage, but her husband's refusal to deal with the truth has stopped any chance of that possibility.

Janette has started therapy alone. "My husband knows I'm in therapy and says to me, 'Did you tell her [the therapist] how good you have it? What a good husband you have?' I say, yes, of course, and I save my money and plan for my future without him."

Within a marriage it might come to light that sexual preferences differ, but lesbianism alone is rarely the only problem a couple faces. Each partner enters the relationship with his or her emotional baggage. The sexual issue, however, is often the catalyst through which other problems are identified.

LIZ

Liz, thirty-seven, was brought up in an independent, female-headed household where the women did everything. She never imagined herself in a subordinate position to a man. She and her husband both had careers in the theater; they spent much time traveling and living in hotels on the road, which they both loved. But then Liz's career began to outdistance her husband's. He grew negative and withdrew. She, not able to break through his shell, began to feel isolated.

Unconsciously, although she had always believed herself to be heterosexual, she was drawn to a woman employee who traveled with them and she initiated an affair with her. Liz describes the woman as "vivacious, energetic, and, most important, incredibly supportive."

"When my husband asked me what was going on, I fessed up. It was a loud, horrible dialogue. But I felt what I had done to him was pretty horrible, so that whatever he wanted to dish out to me, I should just take. He became really angry more at my friend than at me. Now he basically thinks all lesbians should die.

"He's throwing 'you don't need anyone' at me, but that's not the point. I didn't need him when I married him. I married him because I wanted him. If I had had to be a spineless female just to prove to him that I loved him, I wouldn't have grown in my profession as I've done. He feels women should be weak and that he, as the man, must always be in control and take care of the woman.

"All he can see is that my friend ruined everything for him. He'll take no responsibility for his actions and the behavior that pushed me away from him. He chooses instead to pass the blame and responsibility rather than look at the underlying causes that turned me from him. He's got so much misplaced anger now, I don't know if he would ever be able to bury the hatchet."

At times, the decision to tell is taken out of the MWLW's hands. Some husbands suspect that their wives are no longer interested in them sexually and sense that their feelings for women are powerful, and perhaps even sexual. Several women were "outed" accidentally when their husbands overheard phone conversations.

One husband found a letter inadvertently left out, and another came home to find his wife embracing her woman friend.

DAVID

"Ellen got pregnant and we married, so you can't say we started off our relationship in love with each other, but it's something that has grown. As far as our sex life is concerned, I've never questioned any of that. I believe the man ought to satisfy the woman in a sexual relationship, so she's always been satisfied on that part."

Now the father of two and an educator at a midwestern college, David said, "I had been to a meeting and walked into the house. Our children were away at camp. I saw my wife, Ellen, with a young woman from the neighborhood. They had lost track of time and were actually making love.

"I'm not the kind of person who gets real angry and screams and yells. I'm the kind who wants to talk situations out, and I guess I wanted an explanation more than anything else. The other woman left and Ellen explained that it isn't an uncomplicated thing. She didn't think it was something women went out looking for. It was just something that happened. She said she had these feelings.

"I could understand when she said she didn't know what they were all about. I could accept that. Now I'm not only trying to learn about Ellen's life, but I'm trying to understand my fascination with her life.

"We're not doing anything [sexually] more frequently, but . . . there is definitely more emotional intimacy because we've both been so open with each other. She has begun to confide in me in terms of her relationships and the way she feels about other women and who she's attracted to."

David hesitantly admitted that after recovering from the initial blow of seeing his wife in the arms of another woman, "I was more intrigued watching the women than shocked by the idea of them together. I'm turned on by the fact that Ellen is with another woman. What intrigues me is not that it's two women but that it's *Ellen* and someone else. I don't think I would enjoy literally being in a threesome, but I did enjoy the watching part. If she were with another man, I can pretty well predict that my response would not be positive."

David is not unique. Human beings, by nature, are sexual beings. While society would try to repress this notion, it was not uncommon for men to relate an increase of their own sexual appetites after learning that their wives were attracted to women. The idea of two women together excites a great many men. We need only to look at billboards or glance through magazine ads to see beautiful women in intimate poses with other women. Popular rental choices for men at video stores are movies of two women making love. As one man explained, "Because there is no man performing on the tape, no comparisons need to be made, and I can visualize myself in whatever capacity I choose."

It can take some women years to discover and then accept their own sexuality before even beginning to consider sharing who they are with their husbands. While that is not unusual, it is also not unusual for a perceptive husband to discern what is happening between his wife and a woman friend before the women are aware of the sexual component of their friendship.

SHARI

"My husband saw things before I did—noting that my friend and I were getting very close, he asked me if we were in love with each other—so the groundwork had been laid by him to have this discussion. Our relationship and my own style is such that I would be open with him on any matter—as he is with me—so this was no exception. Knowing I had the understanding and support of my husband was an incredible load off my shoulders.

"When I finally admitted to myself what was happening, I first ran it by my therapist for some guidance. Then I sat down with my husband one night and told him pretty straightforwardly that I'm gay. He said, 'We'll work it out.' His response set the course for all the work we've done since."

While the majority of men take their wives' preference for women as a personal affront to their own manhood, men with a strong sense of self understand that the preference doesn't necessarily reflect on them. Because of her husband's self-confidence, Shari felt comfortable sharing her discovery with him. She was able to go through the agonizing questions, trauma, decisions, and changes brought about by her breakthrough, with him at her side.

Still, a husband's emotional support does not guarantee that the marriage will endure, because it isn't always the man who chooses to end the marriage when he learns about his wife.

LYNN

"I was married to my first husband for seven years. When he accused me of being a lesbian, I thought he was crazy. My second marriage lasted twelve years. I was very much in love with my husbands, especially my second husband, and when I was walking in the street with him, I'd look at women and say, 'Doesn't she have nice hair or breasts or legs.' I thought all women looked at other women. I still had no idea about my sexuality. Sometimes before we had sex we'd look at porno films. I was always watching the women. The first seven years were wonderful, but then we started having some trouble, not getting along.

"I began spending more time with my girlfriend. In the beginning I thought, 'I'm just flirting with her. This is fun.' Even after we had been going to bed for six months I believed I was doing it because I was really pissed at my husband.

"When I realized eventually that I was a lesbian, I told him. He said, 'I always thought it was so innocent the way you used to look at women and comment on them. I never really thought you found them attractive, but I guess I'm not surprised.'"

Once she came to the realization that she was a lesbian, it was Lynn who chose to end her marriage.

Women who know about and discuss their sexual predilection with their husbands in advance of their marriages, and truly believe that they will be able to honor the contracts they have created—having families, working together, caring about each other—also find that open communication and understanding are not always enough to make their marriages work.

FLORENCE

Florence, thirty-three, says, "I knew I was a lesbian and was scared that even if I married, my life would be difficult. But I thought I had to get married. When I married my first husband and kept my secret, the marriage fell apart. I believed it was because I had not been honest with him. When I met my second husband, I told him that I was gay the day we met. I still thought getting married would take my gayness away from me.

"My husband didn't take this information as a threat to our marriage. He just thought it was one of my attributes, like having brown hair. So I was gay. I was able to be with women when I was married to him. As long as I didn't flaunt what I did, it was all right with him. I'd tell him I was going away for a weekend and he was comfortable with that as long as I came home again.

"We were married for three years when I ended our union. He would have liked me to remain, but I couldn't. As time went by, I became more strongly attracted to women and less comfortable living with a man. Although he accepted who I was, and I cared about him, I still felt that I was living a lie. Finally I couldn't do that anymore."

Some men hadn't fully comprehended the ramifications of their wives' lesbianism or bisexuality when they said they could stick it out. Some confessed that at the time they had chosen not to believe it, while others made it clear that they didn't want to talk about it or even to hear their wives' stories. Others, who continued to have a physical relationship with their wives, related an increase in their sexual appetites after hearing about their wives' true sexuality.

The bottom line is that having your wife tell you she is a lesbian is a lot of information for anyone to process. While there is no way to predict how any husband will react, it became clear that those women who hadn't become alienated from their husbands in the process of discovering their sexual preference were more likely to maintain an intimate partnership if not a sexual one. In the rare instance, a husband might even help his wife explore her new identity.

PAULA

"We were married fifteen years," Paula, the mother of three, explains. "My husband is one of my best friends and has always known about my struggles with sexuality and my strong feelings for particular women in my life. He supported me lovingly when my journey finally brought me to recognize myself as a lesbian. Believe it or not, he helped me to write this ad to place in a local women's newspaper:

> Married lesbian wants to join or form a lesbian support group for friendship, conversation, and understanding.

"I don't think either he or I ever expected that this realization could have much of a practical impact on our lives. After all, I had no intention of leaving my marriage or breaking up the family. Instead, I simply embraced the newfound internal peace that had come to me with this ultimate self-acceptance, and I began to explore ways to feel comfortable in the lesbian community without turning my back on my world as it was."

Paula's husband was sensitive to her needs and knowingly helped her to learn of her sexual identity. But lesbianism can also be extraordinarily threatening to some men. There are husbands who are simply incapable of understanding their spouses' needs and pleasures. Others can imagine women together only as a sexual turn-on for their own fantasies. In Melinda's case, it was not until her husband expressed a desire to see his wife with another woman that she finally acted on feelings she had secretly harbored.

MELINDA

"When my husband told me he wanted to see me with a woman, I thought I would do it as a gift to him for his birthday. And at the same time, I could explore my own sexuality. A friend put me in touch with a woman who helped me to make his fantasy come true. It was a very positive, wonderful experience," she says. "What I really want to do now is to be with another woman without my husband present."

After her experience, Melinda told her husband of her feelings for women. "He said it would be fine with him if I was involved with a woman as long as it was not a relationship that took up the amount of time and energy that my relationship with him does. He doesn't want to be pushed aside. He wants to be the main focus of my life. Maybe because he is turned on by the idea of two women together, he is not opposed to my being with a woman."

Melinda's husband is fairly accepting and he doesn't want to lose her. Other men, however, cannot stand having their wives involved in relationships with women. They cannot cope with any aspect of their wives' new sexuality.

MARTHA

When Martha told her husband about herself after having been in therapy for eight years, his response was "I thought so."

She says, "He had figured that because I didn't respond to him sexually, there must be something wrong with *me*. So now it was 'Okay, so you are. That explains things.'

"He was thinking that what I told him solved the mystery of my not being physical. He still figured that I was going to stay with him forever and was very upset when I told him I was thinking of leaving him. He hadn't considered that fact.

"We went through months of crying together and he would hate me then he would try to get me to feel sorry for him and not change *his* life. I realized that the bottom line was he didn't care that I was in pain. He only wanted me to continue keeping things the way they were for him."

Martha's husband's reaction is not uncommon. No one wants to be embarrassed, to have his life changed, to have his job affected. Human beings become comfortable in their worlds; it is human nature that people try to maintain the status quo. For some, the threat of change can be devastating.

Realistically, women must be aware that their revelation may provoke outrage. Some men have become physically violent. Others started withholding money, or using it for revenge. One husband told his child, "Mommy doesn't love us anymore." MWLW who divulge this information must understand that they may be faced with consequences not of their choosing. Even for those who have shared open channels of communication with their spouses, or believed their husbands to have surmised their true sexuality, the actual admission can come as a shock.

Likewise, the MWLW who believes she has her husband's support and understanding when she gives this information to him must understand that although his reactions may be delayed, at some point he will likely experience a sense of bewilderment and loss. This time of transition differs for each individual. Even those men secure in their own identity must recognize that their world is going to change. And that change may mean the dissolution of their marriage.

5

The Reality of Marriage

I AM GRATEFUL every day that my husband and I can communicate, that he is understanding and supportive, that we have a sense of caring for and about each other, and that there is peace and respect in our household, because this was not always so. Recently I picked up my old journal and was reminded of those bitter struggles that almost led to divorce at the beginning.

Those first few months after coming out to him had been hell. While I felt relief that I no longer had to be deceitful, he went through total mental chaos.

It was during a sailing trip with my brother and his friends that I made the decision to leave my marriage, not because of my sexuality, but because of the growing bitterness and hostility between us. Even attempts to be civil failed. I'd say, "Here's the sunscreen," and he'd grab it from me snapping, "I am perfectly able to take care of myself." My stomach was in a constant knot. He spent his time swimming and snorkeling with the others. I spent my time thinking about what would be.

The way we were going on was not healthy for either of us. Until then, I had been considering everyone else: how the kids and my mom would feel or what others would say or how his family would react. Now, for the first time, I thought of myself and my frustration. I would tell him I wanted a separation.

Rather than speak up, however, I chose to avoid my husband instead. When we docked for the night, everyone scattered and he and I wound up walking together. Eventually we sat down on a bench in a town square. Almost immediately he said, "I've been giving it a lot of thought and I can't see any other way. I want a separation."

I breathed a sigh of relief. I didn't have to be the one to say it. We talked quietly about how and when things had started going bad in our marriage. There was no blame or fault. We both realized it was over. I did feel a sadness, though, thinking that neither of us had ever really shared the kind of passion that I had learned was possible within a relationship. I wondered how I would feel if he were to discover it with another person. We talked of him moving out. It made sense, since he could be happy with a comfortable chair and a television, while I was a collector and needed my things around me. Our daughter, Laurie, was in the process of finding a job and her own apartment, and so we decided to wait until she had before we told the kids. I didn't want her thinking she had to change her plans or look for a larger apartment so that she could take care of her father. My husband agreed.

That night I lay awake. Surprisingly my thoughts were not of finances, logistics, or losses, but of how I would redo my bedroom with the large downy quilt, fluffy pillows, and the ruffled edges I'd always wanted.

It is only in today's modern marriages that we have come to expect the perfect state of being, derived purely through the love of a man and a woman for each other. In some cultures, until recently, young people were generally paired in arranged marriages. "You'll learn to love each other" was as common a mandate as terms such as "marriage broker," "matchmaker," and "arranged marriage."

In the 1960s, Dr. John F. Cuber, a former marriage counselor turned sociologist, along with his wife, delivered a paper known as the Cuber Report. "Cuber and Harroff interviewed 437 highly successful Americans in depth, to discern the real quality of their marriages. Fewer than one in four had unions that could be described as intimate and loving and that in any way resembled the ideal which most people hope to attain.

"This is not to say that all of the others were actively unhappy. In many of these enduring marriages a *modus vivendi* [manner of living]—sometimes comfortable and sometimes not—had been achieved. Husbands and wives made their own lives and went their own ways, often avoiding each other, devoting their real attention to work, to children, and (sometimes) to other sex partners. These marriages were described as 'utilitarian.' "

While the ultimate state of marriage would be the perfect union, in reality, marriage is a working arrangement which serves, or should serve, the mutual benefit of both parties involved. The reality is that most people do what they are "supposed" to do. They search for security, stability, and respectability within society's social constraints.

Before the idea of feminism and equal rights for women in the workplace took hold, women commonly married with economic reasons foremost in their minds.

"For many women, marriage [was] one of the few forms of employment that [was] readily available. Not marrying could easily mean becoming a domestic or factory worker or going on welfare."

In the early 1970s, University of Pennsylvania's Dr. William Kephart asked one thousand college students, "Would you marry a person you did not love if he or she had all the other qualities you desired?" Most of the men said no. Most of the women said maybe. One woman explained. "If a boy had all the other qualities I desired and I was not in love with him—well, I think I could talk myself into falling in love."

The Kephart study showed that American girls were trained to approach marriage with practical considerations. College women could not afford the luxury of genuinely free choice because, according to the studies, they knew that their station in life would depend almost entirely on their husband's status.

While today's women are generally becoming more educated, more independent in respect to their earning powers, and more focused on what they want in a life partner, many, like Sally, still feel the need to be taken care of, as women did twenty-five years ago. Some, however, do change their minds and leave their marriages.

SALLY

Sally knew of her attraction for women at sixteen, when she fell in love with her best (male) friend's girlfriend. When she met a much older, well-to-do man, she was totally open about her earlier experience with the other woman, and her feelings for women in general. She was also honest about her economic needs. He married her.

"When I sent for your questionnaire, I was intending to remain with my husband," Sally wrote. "Prior to our marriage he was kind, generous, and seemingly open-minded. Upon moving in, I discovered a variety of restrictions—those of money and freedom. He limited the friends I could have. He became very controlling, and I felt as though I were being smothered.

"There was a significant age difference between me and my husband, and he often used that to treat me like a child and override the validity of my knowledge, learning, and experience. I was coming to hate him."

Still, Sally says she would have kept her part of the bargain, except that he changed. "Within three or four months, the conditions became intolerable.

"To not leave would have assured me of life-long income, land, and a comfortable large house. It would have meant enduring unpleasant sex, the degradation of myself, and my beliefs, dreams, and desires, and infliction of pain on myself, selling myself for material goods.

"I left because I was hurting inside. I was being controlled, manipulated, and used. And I had sold myself."

DIANNA

"My husband and I met when we were sixteen years old in high school and got married when we were twenty-one. Church wedding, High Mass. Our first two children were born two years apart and then, three years later, our third. We hadn't discovered who we were sexually or otherwise. When did we have time to do that? We just evolved. My evolution was into being a gay woman and owning it, confronting whatever had to be confronted.

"I think I knew I was gay when I married him. I told him, 'I really care very much about you, but I'm in love with Nina.' And he said, 'No. That's not possible.'

"I told him about how soft she was and how her smile made me feel alive and he said he understood what I was feeling for her. We shared the same love object, you might say.

" 'But you want to have a normal life, don't you? You want to have children and I love you. I want to marry you,' he said.

"I was weak. I had an unhappy family situation and wanted to get away from home and I didn't see many alternatives in terms of how else I could do it. So I focused myself on getting married and setting up a household and there really wasn't another woman in my life for the first nine years. Then I did meet someone and I couldn't repress it. What actually happened was that my husband started having an affair. Our relationship had grown very cold and bitter and withholding sexually on both our parts, and I think I was depressed and repressed at that time. Sexually I was very unhappy and feeling probably guilty and a whole bunch of negative things and I used his affair as my excuse, my ammunition to say its over. I was twenty-nine at the time."

SYLVI

I met Sylvi on the subway going to New York City's Gay and Lesbian Pride Parade. She was easily identified, not only by her rainbow-colored suspenders over her white T-shirt, but by the exuberance and excitement she gave off on that day.

"Going to the parade?" I asked. She smiled and we began to talk.

Sylvi, it turned out, had known she loved women when she was fifteen but married anyway. "It was my only choice. I was so concerned with society's rules. I had the desire to maintain something relatively stable."

In order to do this, Sylvi became an avid churchgoer. She laughed. "It was at church, over the years, that I met my lovers. Some of the women I became involved with were straight when we met. Others, like me, knew they needed to be with women.

"Eventually, I realized that it was possible to be true to myself, and I left my marriage," Sylvi says. "It took some time for my husband to understand and accept who I was, but now we are friends and truly care about each other's well-being."

That marriage serves as a camouflage for the "unacceptable" lifestyles of gay men and lesbians is evidenced by the number of men and women who stay in their marriages as well as by those who seek its protection. It is not uncommon to read personal ads that say: "Gay male seeks gay female for marriage of convenience." One woman said, "I sought safety in a heterosexual marriage because I was terrified of how I had been treated when my family found out I was gay." Being able to fit into "traditional" society brings acceptance and simplifies the lives of lesbians by providing an acceptable partner to take home to Mother, a readily available escort for office functions and parties, or a date for Cousin Sal's wedding.

Not every lesbian who marries a gay or straight man does so as a smoke screen, however. Marriages of convenience are often warm and companionable. They can alleviate loneliness, offer unconditional friendship, and be a source of security for both partners as well.

Honey, an out lesbian who married a gay man, was encouraged to do so by her mother. While her mother accepted Honey's sexual preference, she was concerned that her daughter was alone. Suggesting that Honey consider her childhood friend as a possible mate, she told her daughter, "You'll have someone to take care of you, someone you truly care about in your life. You both understand each other and you'll both be free to be who you are."

After actually analyzing their respective financial situations, Honey and Carl decided marriage made a lot of sense. They don't intend to raise a family, but they do intend to take advantage of all the tax benefits offered to married couples.

The economic and sexual union of man and woman, the very nature of the institution of marriage through the ages, has been to serve the interest of society, not to assure a couple's personal happiness. Marriage has often been used as a political device or to better the family's holdings with little regard for the woman's needs or desires. And so, throughout history, MWLW, especially those born to influential families, have been forced to create separate lives of their own. Two examples of such married women in the public eye were Eleanor Roosevelt and Vita Sackville-West.

While we know now that Eleanor Roosevelt was an MWLW, any private correspondence that even hinted of the sexual being within her has been suppressed or destroyed. Most of what we have learned has come from oral interviews, says Blanche Wiesen Cook, author of *Eleanor Roosevelt*. Until the 1970s, when the papers of Lorena Hickok, Roosevelt's long-time friend and intimate companion, were opened, her life was obscured by closed archives and court biography.

"Over the years, in Greenwich Village and at Valkill, Eleanor Roosevelt created homes of her own, with members of her chosen family, private, distinct, separate from her husband and children. Even as First Lady, ER established a hiding house in a brownstone walk-up that she rented. . . . Away from the glare of reporters and photographers, she stepped outside and moved beyond the exclusive circle of her heritage to find comfort, privacy, and satisfaction. . . .

"She never considered her friends or her friendships secret or shameful. Her family and her friends lived in one extended community. For decades, there was Eleanor's court and Franklin's court, which included Missy Lehand, his live-in secretary and companion. After ER's death, her friends might deny one another, in private or in print. But during her lifetime they had to deal with one another. They sat across from one another at Christmas and Thanksgiving. They were invited to the same parties, and the same picnics.

"Until recently, historians and literary analysts have preferred to see our great women writers and activists as asexual spinsters, odd gentlewomen who sublimated their lust in their various good works," says Cook. "But as we consider their true natures, we see that it was frequently their ability to express love and passion— and to surround themselves with like-minded women and men who offered support, strength, and emotional armor—that enabled them to achieve all that they did achieve. The fact is that our culture has sought to deny the truths and complexities about women's passion because it is one of the great keys to women's power."

Vita Sackville-West was another highly visible woman. She was a prolific writer, wife, mother, and lover of women, Virginia Woolf among them. In 1920 she wrote: "I believe it will be recognized that many more people of my type do exist than under the present-day system of hypocrisy." *Portrait of a Marriage*, written by her son, Nigel Nicolson, is the story of West's marriage, which not only survived infidelity, sexual incompatibility, and long absences, but grew better and stronger as a result.

▢ ▢ ▢ ▢

Reasons for leaving a marriage are rarely as simple as "I realized I was a lesbian," although that knowledge helps to magnify other deficiencies in the marriage. MWLW, upon deciding to leave their marriages, either act upon their decisions quickly, or remain on a temporary basis while they prepare for the economic responsibilities they will face as single women and mothers. Usually, because children are involved, there is much to work out, often lengthening the amount of time it takes to make the transition.

Some of the women I interviewed who opted to remain temporarily in their marriages were in the process of completing their educations, reentering the job market, finding positions in which they could advance, or working on upgrading their present job skills while planning for future needs such as housing, finances, and medical benefits.

The consensus of opinion was that there was no one perfect time to leave a marriage. Each woman decided according to what felt right for her. Some chose to wait until the last child had finished high school or began college, or until they felt that the youngest child could better handle the change.

Other MWLW who had every intention of temporarily remaining in their marriages until they could leave without jeopardizing their own financial security as well as their children's found that continuing stress caused by hostile and bitter husbands took a physical and emotional toll, forcing them to leave their intolerable relationships before they were ready to.

For many women who came of age in the decade before the sexual revolution, living in their parents' homes and then going directly to the ones they would share with their husbands made the idea of moving out, and being totally alone for the first time, frightening. More often than not, these women left their marriages only when they knew another woman was waiting for them. Shelly, however, felt the need to give up her lover to be able to eventually make that move.

SHELLY

"When I met my husband and he satisfied me sexually, I thought I was in love with him. We were married for nineteen years. Over that period of time he became more and more abusive. He wanted me to participate in bondage and other sex games, which made me uncomfortable. He cheated on me openly and I remained silent. It was quite a few years before I could even admit to myself that I wasn't happy . . . sexually or emotionally.

"Eventually I became friendly with the mother of a child in my class. We became best friends, then lovers. I wound up in therapy. My therapist convinced me that I wasn't gay . . . just unhappy. Even when I told him about the kinds of things my husband wanted me to do, he said I should leave my lover and work on my marriage.

"As a result of my mixed-up feelings and depression, I was willing to do anything. I left her and tried to go straight because that's what the shrink told me to do. That didn't work."

Shelly began an affair with another man. "That didn't work either," she says. "I knew my therapist was wrong and I reconnected with my woman lover.

"Eventually I decided to leave my marriage, but the only way I could leave mentally and physically was to leave because it wasn't working. I couldn't leave for her. I didn't want to put that responsibility on anyone. I didn't want to ever say, 'Look what I did for you.' So, actually, in order to leave my husband, I also left my lover."

The same economics that might liberate one woman might keep another in her marriage. In some cases, women who had enjoyed a higher standard of living found it less frightening to leave their marriages, while others remained because of their financial security.

Aware that leaving her marriage would cause a tremendous decline in her economic status, and would also mean losing old friends, a large home, an affluent lifestyle, and an unlimited bank account, Elaine, nevertheless, opted to leave.

ELAINE

The wife of an influential and prominent man, Elaine says, "For twenty-three years my husband took care of the bills, handled the money, and gave me everything I wanted. In return, I spent my entire married life decorating homes and finding friends and then leaving them behind as my husband's growing success necessitated one move after another." She says, "With each promotion, I went into therapy to fix me so we could move again.

"My husband had an inability to see what was going on and I had an inability to talk about what was going on, so we politely ignored it.

"I had been unhappy for a long time, and so lonely at this point. I took a part-time job for something to do. And I met Hilary. She was a friend of my boss's and she'd visit with me while I worked in the store and we'd talk. There was a strong emotional, mental, and then physical attraction.

"When her vacation was over and Hilary left the city, I told her I'd go to visit her. And I bought a plane ticket and went. It was something I absolutely needed to do."

After the visit, staying in her marriage was no longer an option Elaine could live with. "I felt tremendous guilt and nothing at all. I was so cut off from my own feelings."

With barely more than her clothes and personal things, she moved in with Hilary while she temporarily sought public assistance. Eventually she found a job and a small place of her own.

Elaine believes that she was able to leave not because she was confident and worldly, but because she was so naive in money matters. Her husband had always taken care of things such as health insurance and she had given no thought to life's necessities.

Elaine explains that the failure of her marriage was due to a lack of communication, not sexual incompatibility. She believes that it was the ease with which she was able to communicate with Hilary that led to their love and union. "I went into marriage with a whole package of expectations colored by my childhood experience," she says. "A wife stays at home and is cared for physically. The house is provided, money is provided. Material things are provided by the male. The female partner makes the home, raises the children, makes the social arrangements, provides the artistic touch, plays the piano, cooks.

"When I met Hilary I didn't have expectations. I could meet her on a one-to-one level. We explored ideas and attitudes and feelings. From that grew love and caring."

Unlike Elaine, who would have been financially secure but still chose to leave her marriage, Helene talked about the high standard of living she enjoyed and the status she held within her community. She admitted that as much as she would like to leave her husband, she could not give up her material comfort or the large circle of friends and activities she enjoyed by virtue of her financial circumstances.

HELENE

As a young bride, eager to do her part, Helene spent her time and energy being the perfect helpmate, wife, and hostess. Her activities revolved solely around her husband. She acclimated herself to his needs and desires, until he grew to assume that her only purpose in life was to serve as an adornment to him.

Never able to communicate her growing frustrations, she grew apart from him, and, over the thirty-five years of their marriage, her feelings for him gradually diminished. In search of the missing element in her life, she became involved in several heterosexual affairs. They proved to be unsatisfactory. Eventually, she acknowledged her attraction to women. Still, having learned so well to hide her own needs and feelings, she has found it difficult to become emotionally intimate with anyone.

While she prefers to spend as little time alone with her husband now as possible, she is not willing to change her marital status because of the lucrative lifestyle it affords her. Helene is aware that she uses her unlimited financial resources as a buffer. She describes her life: "I go from one activity to another and one friend to another: tennis, golf, theater, luncheons, dinners, movies. I travel constantly. I have two homes. I immerse myself totally in each activity, so as not to have the time to think of anything else."

Living on a treadmill serves a twofold purpose for Helene. It keeps her from being alone with her husband and it also makes it impossible to establish more than a superficial level of friendship with any of her numerous acquaintances or her female lover.

Although there is a widely held misconception that all women, once they identify their lesbianism, leave their marriages, MWLW often choose to stay. Seventy percent of the women who responded to my self-selecting survey have remained in their marriages, some for more than thirty years and one for more than forty. One therapist I interviewed asked not to be identified because "half the women I see in my practice, which is primarily gay and lesbian, are married women."

The reasons women marry in the first place play a large part in why they remain in their marriages. The need to be loved, wanted, approved of, and taken care of is of primary importance. The conflict between wanting to be free and wanting to be protected paralyzes them. Most MWLW remain in marriages, even unsatisfying ones, for the same reasons that discontented heterosexual women do. They are tightly woven in their established lifestyles and families and cannot bring themselves to change everything. Protecting children and keeping the family together are priorities. Another reason, according to Dalma Heyn, author of *The Erotic Silence of the American Wife*, is that "the average income of women of all social classes who are divorced in this country decreases by roughly 30 percent.

"Data from a study of 5,000 families by the University of Michigan panel Survey of Income Dynamics found that married women averaged 744 work hours a year. In the year before a separation, however, the hours of work jumped to 1,024 because women sought to protect themselves economically from the effects of divorce."

Especially in states with new "no-fault" divorce laws, divorce had a catastrophic economic affect on women. While the standard of living for divorced men went up an average of 42 percent in the year following the divorce, divorced women's standard of living plummeted 73 percent—even counting alimony and child support.

Some MWLW cite love for their spouses as their primary reason for remaining. However, these same women frustratingly describe that love as platonic. Also operative, of course, is the fear of change that keeps most people from taking risk—especially where their security is concerned.

GAIL

For Gail, being in an unemotionally involved relationship felt safe. Gail, thirty-five, has one child from her previous common-law marriage and one with Ralph, her current husband. She always had a sense that she liked women. After her separation from her first husband, which came about because of his violent outbursts, she dated women for several years.

"In the four years I was single again I dated a lot of unstable people and I didn't want to deal with that anymore. Then I met my second husband."

Gail chose to marry a second time because she craved a stability that she didn't see in her lesbian community. Her choice of a lifestyle was influenced more by our culture and her personal priorities than it was by her sexual identity.

"I wanted the whole nine yards," she says. "I wanted another baby. I wanted to correct all the wrongs. I wanted to have my cake and eat it too."

In describing the relationship between herself and her husband, Gail says, "We used to get stoned together and really have fun. Our relationship was loving, kind, communicative, we were on a roll. We were the same age, we had a lot in common, we both came from a working-class background. And he knew about me.

"We had been very heavy drinkers when we met, frequenting the same bar, smoking a lot, partying. We thought, 'This is going to be a fun, modern marriage.' Then, after we were married less than a year, all of the responsibilities of home buying brought a tremendous financial burden. He didn't have a clue as to how to write a check. He was very inept in financial matters. I had to take on that burden. Then I got pregnant and we had a mortgage and a baby. I thought it was time we settled down and made an attempt at a mature lifestyle. He continued to smoke and drink and do all of those wonderful things, and I was at the point where I was hardly getting high at all because I had to keep my head about me. He maintained a working-class mentality while I strove to become professional." Ralph has a G.E.D. Gail now has a B.A. and hopes one day to have her M.A.

"It's complicated, why I have chosen to remain in my marriage," she says. "Part of it is financial, but there is also a lot of love there. It's a crazy relationship. I tend to take on the male role, he tends to take on the female role, which is very much to my liking, because I am somewhat androgynous. I have a lot of male hormones and he has a lot of female hormones, and it seems to be a very natural thing."

□ □ □   □

Being a lesbian does not necessarily mean that one wants to live in a gay community. Choices are influenced as much by cultural and personal priorities as they are by sexual identity. Several of the women who had had every intention of eventually leaving their marriages but had opted to remain temporarily found different ways to "reinvent" their marriages, and make them work instead of leaving.

This "holding period" created an opportunity to begin open communication for both spouses. For the first time in their marriages, they were able to achieve a clear understanding of what was going on for each partner. Some MWLW reported mutual growth. This led to a new or awakened respect. And in a few cases, a decision to remain within a redefined marriage became a possibility. They said they related better as friends in their newly redefined marriages than they had as sexual intimates. In several instances, after disclosure, it was the husbands who suggested that their wives remain.

MAGGIE

Not wanting to be considered an old maid, Maggie had married at twenty-one and had a baby at twenty-two. Then she divorced at twenty-four. "When I met my second husband, several years later, I was past looking for love," Maggie says. Now forty-three years old, she has one grown child and three small ones.

Before she knew about her own sexuality, Maggie knew that sex with men repulsed her. She told her husband this and he accepted that fact. "He was a good provider and a good person, and still is . . . and I had no idea I liked women.

"I decided to come out to my husband before my ex-lover's husband, who knew because he had put a tap on her phone, told him. Now he knows I'm a lesbian."

Maggie admits things didn't go smoothly in her marriage when she first told her husband. "He told me he loved me and he'd never stop loving me. I told him I was really sorry for that. I said I'd like him to get into a relationship with someone who could love him back.

"At first he wanted to kill himself. For two months my life was in total upheaval. He had an outing party. He called all of my friends and told them I was a lesbian. He didn't do it to be nasty. He was crying. He didn't know what else to do.

"I said I wanted a divorce. He's a corporate vice president and he convinced me that divorce would not be beneficial for me or the children. I'd end up losing part of my house, health insurance, everything. I realized I'd be living at poverty level if I left, because although I could get a job that paid more money, that would keep me away from my children and I wouldn't do that. So I said okay.

"He's past the point of telling everyone. Now he wants to keep it a secret.

"I would leave him with the kids and go spend the weekend with my lover and he would do the scrubbing and cleaning. We don't have sex, but we share the responsibility of raising the children together."

When Maggie's lover wanted a full-time relationship with her, Maggie felt forced to break off their relationship. Now she feels frustrated and trapped, although the decision was hers. "I still get weak knees when I see her, but I can't give her what she wants. I can't pack my bags and show up on her doorstep with three little children."

MELINDA

Melinda also chose to remain in her marriage. "There's a shared history, which, as I'm getting older, seems to feel really warm to me. Like putting on an old slipper. Financially, things are better than they've ever been, which offers us the freedom to do the thing I really enjoy: travel."

Then, she confesses, "There isn't a day that goes by that I don't imagine myself being with a woman, whether going on vacation or lying next to one another or talking or cooking dinner. There is nothing I could see in my life where I wouldn't include a woman and don't sometimes think of that happening. *It's definitely an 'and' situation to me, not an 'or.'*

"The only thing that scares me is: What does it mean in the long term in my lifestyle? I know what I have now and it's comfortable, yet I don't want to give up the other part, which is clearly part of who I am. That part doesn't scare me. What scares me is the potential disruption of my life as I know it."

□ □ □ □

For many people, family serves as an insulation against the world. The idea of it "collapsing" is frightening. "Who is going to take care of me when I get old?" "Who is going to be there when I'm needy?" are constant worries.

According to Catherine Whitney in her book *Uncommon Lives*, "The family has not collapsed so much as it has expanded in context to reflect who we are at the end of the twentieth century: A population whose average life expectancy stretches to seventy and eighty years, a society where nearly seventy percent of women work outside the home, a people whose technological advances expand our options for movement and communication. . . . But many couples are afraid to risk change and instead they watch their twenty-five and thirty-five-year marriages cease to hold any meaning or give any joy. In this context, divorce might be the only way some people know how to move from one stage of life to another."

Not all of the MWLW remaining in their marriages have been able to make their lives work for them. Some have resigned themselves to living a lonely existence, forgoing their own needs, bemoaning the fact that their lives are so flat.

PEARL

Pearl, a young woman with one small child, remembers being sent to a Catholic boarding school. "I thought I really liked this one person a lot, in a different way, but I never told her. She was one of the sisters. We were really good friends and we could talk about a lot of things, so I thought of becoming a nun. Then I went back to a regular high school, pretty much a normal teenager."

Pearl had her first experience with a woman as a teenager at a party. "I really got stoned out and there was this woman . . . I thought I was rebelling, then I put it to an emotional thing because I had attended an all-girls' Catholic boarding school. I put it on the back burner.

"I married about three years ago. After a while it seemed like my husband wasn't connecting with me emotionally, then physically. Eventually I realized that I really was attracted to women."

While she acknowledges her feelings to herself, Pearl believes that she has no choice but to suppress them.

"I am very lonely in my marriage, but I will remain because I still care for my husband and because of my child. There is a lot of pressure. A woman is automatically expected to do so much. I work and have a child and keep house and organize and cook, while all he has to do is work. No strain. He feels everything is perfect the way it is."

When asked what she was doing about her unhappiness, Pearl said, "Nothing. I think of what could happen if I met another woman and we became close. . . . I'm not putting myself in that situation.

"I have to be the strong person. I've always had to prove that I could be strong and handle. Now it really doesn't matter. I'm used to that place. My needs are not being met, but I don't know what I can do about that. My husband's needs come first. That's just how it is. I'm not as important as him. That's why there is a problem in my relationship. But I know it's not his fault."

BARBARA

Barbara, like many MWLW, vacillates between wanting to remain in and wanting to leave her marriage. "I wonder how things would have been if I had had the courage to leave when I was so angry and frustrated with my husband initially. I also wonder if that was what led me to fall in love with Jill in the first place.

"Had Jill been in love with me, might I have given up thirty-two years of marriage for her? I don't know. I often think about what might have been. But the reality was that Jill chose instead to exit my life.

"I made myself believe I could not leave my marriage because I wouldn't be able to support myself. Then I got a job and I still used finances as a reason for remaining. Then Michael lost his job and I became the sole supporter and that was why I couldn't leave. I don't know why I am staying. At times, when we're alone, I shudder to think of our empty future together, yet when the family is around, everything feels right.

"After four years of becoming acquainted with the real me, I came out to my husband. He went through a lot of emotional stuff. Finally we decided to separate. What relief I felt, like a heavy weight had been lifted from my chest. We decided to go to therapy to ease the separation, and we began to talk. Sometimes he is so sweet now, I think, why should either of us leave? Then I can say something as innocent as I'm meeting a friend for dinner and he'll blow up and scream, 'You have time for everything you want to do but you never have time for me or the house.' And I think to myself, let it be over. I can't live with his yo-yo reactions. I feel like I'm on a roller coaster. . . .

"But I still don't have the courage to make the final decision, nor am I certain that I want to."

Barbara believes, "I have been able to remain in my marriage primarily because I never felt the passion for Michael that I did later on for the women in my life and I never felt the highs and lows that come with that passion. So actually little had changed in our marriage except that we slowly ended the sexual part."

It is possible to have a strong desire to keep a marriage together and make it work and also to protect children from divorce, yet still have an equally strong desire to grow fully as a person and a sexual being. For some women, this requires going beyond their marriages.

BETTY

Betty had been in a relationship with Joan, also an MWLW, for two years without her family knowing. She says, "All the while I was with Joan, I was so happy that my relationship with my husband was better. Although we had stopped having sex several years before, we were more comfortable with each other. I had Joan to talk to, so I wasn't at him all the time to listen to me and to talk to me. I stopped accusing him of not understanding me. I enjoyed spending time with my family because I knew I'd have special time with Joan too. My children were happier sensing my peacefulness."

The relationship between Betty and Joan might have continued indefinitely if Joan's husband had not been transferred. Joan and her family moved across the country.

"Neither of us had ever considered leaving our families. Suddenly I was desperate for the kind of closeness and companionship we had shared," Betty says.

"At women's bars I was shunned because I was married. I realized how fortunate I had been to have Joan in my life. More than a year has passed without my being able to find another special woman to take her place, a woman who is also married and understands family obligations and, therefore, limitations. At home, surrounded by my family, I feel totally alone."

As some MWLW grow more aware of their own feelings and needs, they also become more aware of their rights to make their own choices. Sex within marriage often becomes less frequent or stops completely for both the lesbian-identified women who have come out and those who haven't. For those who consider themselves bisexual, coming out often improves the sexual aspect of their marriage.

Within the group of women I interviewed and who have chosen to remain in their marriages, 39 percent have come out to their husbands. For them, the term "marriage" began to take on different meanings. Often, although celibacy replaced sex, the relationships became more solid as lines of communication opened and understanding deepened.

ANDREA

"I had an affair with a woman in college and I wanted to marry her, but she turned totally against me, so I married the first man who didn't try to jump into bed with me on the first date. I was convinced I was in love with him and was married for five years. When we separated, I was convinced I was in love again and married again.

"I looked at lesbian books but I didn't pursue anything. I guess there was a fear of the unknown. After memories of incest surfaced and I read *Wild Fire Igniting* and *Ship That Sailed into the Living Room*, I realized that I did not want to be physically married.

"I told my husband I wanted separate bedrooms. He wasn't particularly happy about it, but I had been telling him I didn't want to be sexual with him and he was denying it. So I moved into another bedroom and he went into a period of anger.

"I came out to him several months later," Andrea says. "I had started seeing someone and she was not willing to spend time with me until he knew. I was really nervous about telling him because of all I had read about the man taking the children away, etc., but it finally got too painful not to tell him.

"By that point he wasn't really shocked. He had to go through a lot of grief and denial but we co-parent. Now we consider ourselves friends. We support each other emotionally and we share everything. We did peer counseling, taking turns listening to each other to give emotional release, which has helped us.

"I would like to go back to school to be able to get a job. Marriage right now is being a full-time mother to three children. I don't have a job history and I'm not making enough money to support myself and he's fully willing to have me stay here indefinitely.

"I didn't have a lover when I came out to my husband but I do now. I bring her here. She likes my kids and my husband and he wants to be friends with her.

"He's not in a relationship, but I think he would like to be. He's seeing someone who he's becoming a little more intimate with. He's taking control of his life. I've seen him grow tremendously."

Andrea concedes that "my husband would like more family time with me. I don't choose to, although I know, when we sit down and compare notes and recommit ourselves to the family and communications, we definitely get along better.

"We are more equally sharing the family and household chores than we ever did. He's doing things around here that he never would have done two years ago, not to please me, but because he's shifting his values. He never thought of me leaving and taking the kids, but he values their presence in his life more than before. He wakes them in the morning and helps them get dressed and cooks for them and sees that they have clean clothes."

While bringing up the issue of sexuality initially causes resentment and anger, it is often the starting place from which other old baggage is dragged out, aired, and then discarded. While spouses may no longer be sexual partners, with sexual issues and accompanying tensions out of the way, friendships may eventually develop.

Andrea and her husband have chosen to remain in their marriage because they have gotten it to work for them. "We share everything. Neither of us wants to be a single parent. He loves the kids.

"Actually, I have it pretty good, because I know a lot of single parents don't get the freedom that I do because he's there. I was a single mother after my first marriage and I remember what it's like. The emotional support isn't there when you're shuffling children back and forth. I'm very committed to my kids. I've got responsibility. I think if money were no object, I'd like to turn the garage into a room of my own. It would be easier to let the kids live here and have another apartment, where we could take turns going to.

"Our kids know how our family functions. There is no side taking or having to defend one parent or the other. We don't fight. There is no hostility. We get along better now."

ROSALIE

Rosalie responded to my ad with this note: "I live in a rural setting in a midwestern state and have been married for twenty-five years. For the last five years my husband and I have shared our lives with my friend. We consider ourselves a family. My husband helps her with many things. She spends time at our house.

"My family accepts her as part of the family and she attends most functions, although no questions about the nature of the relationship have ever been asked."

Rosalie has since sent me holiday greetings, information on concerts, and photographs of her country home, herself, her husband, Jack, and Brenda, the woman in her life.

I felt privileged to have been afforded insight into the life of this family who, against odds, has expanded its household and created an atmosphere of love and acceptance that works for them.

In a child-free marriage for twenty-five years, Rosalie and Jack, who had sensed something different about his wife when he married her, are totally open and honest with each other. And Jack and Brenda, Rosalie's special friend, are friends now. "Brenda is a very enlightened person," Jack says. "She has a brain. She's an independent woman. There is a lot of similarity between this woman and myself. . . . It's a very comfortable thing."

When the truth came to Rosalie that she was a lesbian, Rosalie says, "I was concerned that I would remain lonely in that particular aspect of my life since I knew I had the life I wanted and was not interested in a divorce.

"There has always been a personal freedom in my marriage and I have been able to pursue my interests without guilt. With that comes responsibility, and I had no desire to ruin what we had built. I would never be willing to hurt my husband or others to satisfy my own need."

While traveling for business, Rosalie met the friend of a business acquaintance. She was attending a dance and invited the other woman along, thinking she might meet someone. "The someone turned out to be me," Rosalie says. "The next day she came to my house, met my husband, and began coming down every weekend.

"Jack had been aware that this friendship was different, and when he discovered Brenda and me in the kitchen, hugging, he asked us not to be afraid to talk to him. The three of us talked a lot about this situation. I actually believe that Jack was the one who began to talk about a life that included all three of us. He did not want to lose me, or have the life we had together ruined, and knew that Brenda had become important to me.

"Jack chose to accept Brenda because he realized that she truly loved me. . . . He also saw that I loved her and needed her. And it became evident during her early visits that Brenda sought a similar sort of life to the one we had built.

"When Brenda got a job nearby, it was Jack who made the offer to rent to her until she bought property down the road and built her house. We have rarely been separated since.

"That we have been able to achieve this family of ours is due to Jack's willingness to confront and accept the situation. In return, we have been given an extended family. Brenda and I can attend lesbian events and be open in that community, which gives us a needed outlet. Occasionally Jack comes along, but generally these times are ours alone."

Rosalie says that her marriage to Jack works well. "We talk more about things than we did before, and I am able to be open about things I never would have talked about before.

"Brenda sometimes has more trouble with our arrangement than Jack. While she and he are friends, she does regret that she will never have me to herself; at times she feels we aren't alone together enough, but we have always been able to work through that by taking a weekend regularly to attend a concert or function somewhere else."

While Rosalie continues to be sexually active with Jack, she says, "I don't consider myself bi . . . but I didn't want to change what I had that was working for me. I also know my primary attraction is to women. If something happened to Jack, I would never look for another man.

"Changes in our sex life have more to do with Jack's being older than with my coming out to him. He has said that it has taken the pressure off him to try to perform more than he is able. Brenda is his gift to me since he is sensitive to the fact that I am younger [more than ten years] and might like sex more often than he can provide it.

"We have a 'three-cornered hug' that we engage in with each other in the morning and before retiring at night. That has become a family practice. There is no other physical intimacy between Jack and Brenda or the three of us together.

"I am sure there are times when Jack feels left out. He says, however, that he is genuinely happy that I have found someone with whom I can express my feelings for women, and I believe him. He seems glad when we are together, and when he has to be gone for several days to care for his mother, he says he is glad I do not have to be alone. Being alone has never been a particular concern of mine, but Jack has always worried that I would be left behind.

"Jack is more of a feminist than I am in many ways. His support has enabled me to accomplish things [create a business] I would never otherwise have had the freedom to do. When all four of our parents became ill, he was the one with the skill and willingness to give up his career to take care of them. That resulted in a role reversal we had not planned. I became the sole financial supporter of our household, and since my traveling job gave me no time, he assumed household duties.

"For many years I had so little vacation time that Jack and I did not do much. We might travel for a few days, but mostly we would be at home. When Brenda entered our lives, he and I did not change that practice. Brenda has a greater need to get away and to be alone with me. Jack claims not to mind. He traveled the world while he was in the navy and he is glad that I can do some of those things without his having to go himself.

"I try to be especially considerate of Jack and to try to express appreciation for the many things he does for me and for all of us. Now that I am home more, I try to do more of the work that he has normally done for some time. When Brenda and I are going to be gone for a weekend, I try to buy a special card or gift and leave it under his pillow so that he'll know that I'm thinking of him.

"There are times that I feel I am shortchanging Jack. I express it to him and do have guilt feelings and feelings of low self-worth. He does not feel that way and does not like it when I beat myself up. I feel the same about Brenda. While she cares for Jack, I know that her dream would be for there to be just the two of us. However, Brenda knew from the beginning that I was married and that it would not change. She chose to come; I never felt I had the right to ask either of them to accept this. She wanted to stay, and while it bothers her more to have to share, she also knows that we truly are her family. . . .

"I feel caught in the middle sometimes and sometimes I feel like the one shortchanged. My own friendships and activities have suffered to some degree because I always feel like any time I have belongs to either Jack or Brenda. I rarely plan anything alone or with another friend since I must accommodate their needs for time with me."

Initially, after my husband and I had talked on our trip, I thought a lot about our separating. But of late, the bickering and arguing that had been the constant source of irritation since my announcement had been replaced by a calmness and now, with the Jewish holidays approaching, my thoughts were on the dinner we were preparing for the following evening. So I wasn't expecting it when, while peeling potatoes beside me, he said, "I've been looking for an apartment."

My eyes, already tearing from the onions I was dicing, felt an additional sting. I had expected to feel relief, but I wasn't feeling that. A jumble of emotions ran round my brain. Suddenly I felt overwhelmed by everything. Saddened. Here we were, side by side, preparing for our traditional Passover Seder for people we both loved, and talking about changing our lives. Then he continued. "But I've been going over our finances and I can't move. We can't afford to pay a mortgage and a rent."

I didn't say anything. We continued working side by side.

I had come to terms with my female-oriented sexuality, and now was also coming to terms with my marriage, which I decided I'd rather redefine than leave. For many years my marriage had been a traditional one. I saw myself as the hub from which my husband and children ventured forth into the world and returned again to its safety and comfort. Now I, too, wanted to be free to venture forth and return again.

But what kind of man would agree to this. What kind of man would want to stay with an MWLW?

6

The Husbands

ONE PARTICULAR QUESTION that never fails to arise when the subject of MWLW comes up is "What kind of men are these women married to?"

Just as there is no common denominator among MWLW, their husbands also come from a wide variety of backgrounds. Their occupations range from factory workers to professors and from civil service employees to CEOs; their hobbies range from motorcycles to botany. Like any diverse group of men, some were described as virile, others not. While some were intuitive and knew their wives' preference before their wives realized it themselves, others preferred to live with their heads in the sand, even after full disclosure. Depending on their own level of self-awareness, the men saw their wives' same-gender choices as threatening or stimulating.

One man said he saw his wife's relationships with women as a prelude for more stimulating sex. "I was the one who brought it up," he said. "I started asking her questions, purely sexual and descriptive, not emotional. I thought, 'If we could be honest, it could be a good relationship.' And I found she was excited by it. It improved the sexual part of our life together."

Another man has looked the other way while his wife has been in a relationship with her best friend for more than thirty years, nearly as long as she has been in her marriage. She vacations with and spends weekends and every spare minute with her friend.

"My husband is glad I have Cynthia and I don't bother him," Susan says, "since he chooses to live with blinders."

Not all men wear blinders, nor do they all see their wives' announcements in terms of their own sexual fantasies. For some men it was their wives' coming out that caused them to look at themselves analytically for the first time. Not every husband felt the need, but several went to therapy as a means of working out marital issues. Admittedly, the decision to see a therapist was a difficult one for most to make. One husband, who went only twice, talked about probably going back "some other time." Another spoke of developing a greater awareness of his own problems, unrelated to his wife's sexuality. He said part of the reason he was going was to gather the courage to make changes for himself.

MICHAEL

Michael had always resisted the idea of therapy. It wasn't until after his wife had started seeing another woman that he finally decided to go. However, he remained adamant that therapy could not help his marriage. "There is nothing in it for me anymore," he said bitterly. He agreed to go only because he was in a bad way and was desperate to find some help. What came to light during his therapy sessions was his own baggage. He had refused to acknowledge or deal with any of the problems that had accumulated since childhood. He began to focus on himself, working on long-buried childhood issues instead of his floundering marriage.

Michael began to understand how his problems were related to his slow withdrawal from his wife. He stopped blaming her for his anger and hurt and began to accept responsibility for his share in the way things had gone between them. He came to realize that the marriage, although altered according to society's general definition in regard to the sexual component, still held much for him. Barbara and Michael have been working at renegotiating and stabilizing their new relationship.

TOM

Tom, like Michael, was finally able to see and understand that problems with his marriage began long before his wife made her discovery, and may even have affected her discovery.

"My wife, Frances, knew there was something bothering me and wanted to talk to me about our situation, about how I was feeling, what I was thinking, and what was happening with us long before she turned to her friend for the comfort she wasn't getting from me. But I was in my own world. She kept pleading with me to talk," he says, "but, like always, trying to talk to me must have been frustrating as hell for her. I was brought up to keep my emotions in check, and I am a pro at that.

"I told her that I was ambivalent to the situation and it didn't matter to me what she did, but that's not true. It does matter. What's really bothering me is me. I'm down on myself. She's doing what she wants to and I feel like I'm stuck. I'm jealous. I know it's my fault for not being able to communicate. She says she probably would have discovered her identity sooner or later anyway, but I wonder about that. Our marriage was going bad before she found out about herself. Maybe if it wasn't . . . I know it was my fault. I think it started when I lost my job and I took the one in the city. I was miserable with the commute. No. I think it started before that. I was withdrawing: from her, from life. I was submerging myself in my work, in the television, in books.

"I feel real unhappy about myself. Frustrated, like I missed something my whole life and I don't know why. Basically I've given up on everything. Now I'm very lonely. I have no friends. She goes out with her women friends and I have no one to do anything with. I have a hard time making friends on my own. I always expected her to take care of the entire social part of my life.

"Since I couldn't talk about my feelings or show my feelings in any other way, sex was my only way to get really close to her, and now that's gone too. How should I feel?"

It is not surprising that most of the men who agreed to be interviewed seemed secure in their sexual identification. Their wives' same-sex orientations didn't threaten their sexual identity, nor did the idea of homosexuality in general seem frightening to them. They were open and able to talk about it. Perhaps more noteworthy, these men were also able to step back to see and appreciate their wives as separate individuals.

HOWARD

"I love my wife and want what's best for her. The fact that she loves women, I think, is something important to her and I want to respect that. If this is a part of who my wife is, I have no right to tell her to be different. That would be like denying her a part of what makes her her."

Asked if her revelation made him question his own sexuality, Howard said, "I guess I'm not particularly attracted to gay men. I had an offer to play around with an older male cousin of mine when I was younger. It just didn't interest me. If the same situation was to come along today, I don't think I'd be interested.

"Actually, I think I'm more attracted to women than I have been. I realize now they have another dimension that they're struggling with and working with and trying to be accepted for.

"I think, had my wife said, 'I want a divorce,' when I found out, it would have been painful, but I think after the initial shock and adjustment was over with, I would still have walked away with a deeper appreciation for women."

NATHAN

Nathan, like Howard, explains his unusual marital situation philosophically. "Whatever makes a person happy is what that person has to do. My wife has certain needs. She's not a happy person, but she strives to be happy."

Eighteen years ago, while his children were small, his wife told him of her need for women in her life. He nevertheless chose to remain in his marriage. "I'm a creature of habit and convenience. I didn't want to have to go out and start a new life all over again, so I made the necessary adjustments so as not to rock my existing boat.

"When I first realized I was never going to be able to fill her emotional need, that was a tough time. I was also a little bit angry because she never told me that she had had sexual feelings for women earlier," Nathan says about the timing of his wife's coming out. "I resent that I didn't know in the beginning. I should have been told right off the bat. I think it would have made a difference.

"I can't deny that's what I'm mad about, but the fact that this is what she is, I can't take that away from her. Once I knew about her, I chose not to change my life.

"After I realized I had to make my own settlement, everything was fine. We went on normally for a long while; then we sort of arrived at our own lives."

JACK

Jack was attracted to his wife, Rosalie, because he sensed something different in her than in other women.

"At thirty-five I got to the point that I was ready for marriage," Jack says. "There was something in Rosalie that wasn't the female touch I felt in other women. There was nothing girlish or whiny about her. There was something different that I couldn't identify. We complimented each other's personalities and I needed what was in her.

"Rosalie had no great desire to be a mother. We would have had children if it had been important to her, but it wasn't. Besides, I had been the diaperer for my younger siblings and I didn't mind being relieved of that burden.

"When Rosalie identified her feelings and came out to me, it made me feel lost for a while, until I realized that that part of her had always been there. I wasn't angry, but I felt lonely at times.

"I'd rather have this woman be able to sit down and talk to me and relate to me than cater to me and cook for me. There was an honesty about her. This was one of the things I always admired about her."

Jack believes that lesbianism is more about the emotional support derived from another woman than strictly sexual issues. "For some, sex may be more important. But I think most important is that you've got to be able to talk and sense and feel for each other.

"I couldn't fulfill all of her needs. I had sensed that for quite a while but I didn't know what they were. She had to take the necessary steps before I could understand. I feel more secure now knowing that there is another person, Brenda, who also cares about the person I care about."

Rosalie's friend, Brenda, lives nearby. Jack and Brenda each have a separate physical relationship with Rosalie but not with each other. Jack and Brenda have, however, become good friends. Brenda was even invited to stay at Rosalie and Jack's house while her house was under construction.

Admittedly, this new arrangement was not always easy. A lot of dialogue went into creating the open and honest rapport they now share. Jack admits, "At times there was resentment in the beginning that Rosalie had someone else to talk to, but knowing how important Brenda was to her, I wanted to make it work.

"There were times I'd sleep alone at night and curl up with a pillow because she wasn't there. That was hard. At times I resented Rosalie for this. But it wasn't important as far as affecting the way I felt about my wife. It was just time to say, 'Damn it, what's this all about?'

"I was able to tell Rosalie how I felt. Sometimes she cried a little. I'm sure she felt she was letting me down and I'm sure she still struggles with it, but I'll help her in any way I can."

Jack's acceptance was not arrived at overnight. Much time was spent in thought, and then discussing and evaluating the situation, before coming to the realization of their individual needs. "I know that as a man I can't give Rosalie everything she needs, and as a woman she can't give me everything I need either."

Society would have us believe that marriage makes for completion. This places a tremendous burden on both partners: the one who believes that there is something wrong with him or her as an individual if his mate occasionally turns to another whether for physical, emotional, or spiritual connection, and the one who does not feel complete but agonizes over the possibility of hurting a mate if he or she finds someone else who can help to fill the void. If one mate feels content but the other doesn't, the stress can be even greater. Yet, it is almost impossible for one person to be able to fill all of another person's needs.

FRANK

"There was always a sexual problem between us," Frank, married for eleven years, says. "And why we stayed together this long I don't even know. Maybe there's a bond, or sense of security. Anyway, I had a feeling, so when she told me, I didn't really think anything of it. It wasn't like she said, 'I have a girlfriend and I'm in love and I'm leaving you.' She just said, 'I like girls.' I sort of knew already. I wouldn't call her a feminist but she had always been sort of antimale.

"So even when she presented it to me it wasn't like it was a big thing. But as time went on, she progressively got more and more obsessed with the idea of lesbianism. It was like she was searching for something that's never been. Every minute, every chance, everything revolved around that. She was on America Online eighteen hours a day, like till four in the morning with these women.

"We work together, we're partners in a small manufacturing business, and we also have a son. So very quickly, things started to fall apart. From the America Online she started talking on the phone. There were all kinds of calls and then she started meeting people.

"I was livid. Really mad. The lesbian part didn't make me as angry as what she was doing to my life, to my son's life, and to the business. Probably that's where I had the most anger. I was getting up at five in the morning, getting the kid and doing everything for him, working all day till seven o'clock, and at nine I was like beat. She totally neglected my son, totally neglected the business, and everything was just in a complete upheaval. We had lots of fights or I would go for a week and not say a word to her."

While Frank admits to constant conflict, he also acknowledges that during the early months of his wife's coming out, their sex life was good. "That was the strange thing," he says. "As far as sexuality goes, there had always been something lacking, and now, sexually, she was charged. So sex was better than it ever was. And more often, and more frequent. But at the same time she was also flipping out.

"After about three months the sex was cut off. There was a lot of lying going on, things behind my back. She was meeting people and telling me she was going someplace else.

"I got really, really mad and at that point said, 'Why don't you move out,' but I felt really bad kicking her out like that. She suffers from depression, which was compounded by her feelings of guilt. She wouldn't get out of bed and was constantly crying. It took more than a year. Anyway, once she got off the antidepressant she got much better. She got an apartment and she is moving out, but now we talk. We made a joint decision for her to leave my son with me. At first she wanted him and I finally talked her out of it. Our workshop is at the back of our place. I wouldn't have felt comfortable coming to her house to work if she stayed and I left. I'd be subjected to her lifestyle with her phone calls, etc. Now I see us being friends and jointly raising our son.

"I still care for her a lot. I'm not in love with her anymore, but I still love her. We have a bond, married for eleven years, a kid. That just doesn't go away."

EDDIE

Married for sixteen years and the father of one, Eddie says, "I look at our relationship like a giant organic thing. It's part of both of us. We've been together sixteen years. We have a son. We have a history and our lives are built around this history. Anyway, Shari was always very open communication-wise, and she came out to me within a day of her realizing it herself. She had been working through issues of abuse as a child, reliving them. So my reaction was 'We'll work it through.' I wasn't really shocked until I realized it was fairly serious stuff. I guess I thought it was just something else to put on the pile."

Shari describes Eddie as "a man with high energy, and sometimes high tension. He is enthusiastic and has strongly expressed opinions that can also be tossed to the wind. He is distant emotionally in some ways and very loving and supportive in others. He throws himself full tilt into a successive series of hobbies, but always finds one more to move on to. Always being involved in one project or another is one of the things that attracted me to him at the beginning. I was in love with him when we married and I love him now."

Still, Eddie and Shari led very different lives. Eddie says, "We hadn't always done everything together. We have very distinct tastes, our interests aren't parallel, and our hobbies don't coincide. We both have our own releases. She's into horses. I like motorcycles. We allow each other to grow in many different directions."

Although their sex life had diminished over the years to "a rare event," Eddie initially believed they should remain monogamous when Shari told him about herself. "At first it bothered me." Eddie explained, "I didn't want her to be with another person, male or female. I was jealous that she might take her sexuality elsewhere and that became an issue.

"In the back of my mind I was hoping I could change this," Eddie says. "Then I realized that was very unrealistic and I had to somehow cope with it and kind of weave that into our marriage, hoping that our marriage could survive. Still, just because I'm understanding, it isn't easy to deal with. I wish it wasn't this way."

"I've thought of divorce," Eddie said, "but I didn't want that. I saw the pain my sister went through with a divorce . . . get a machete and chop it in two.

"We had to work it through," he says. "Eventually, I realized that this was something society had put upon me: 'You make your wife loyal to you.' But it wasn't something I really felt inside. So I kind of let that go and it really changed things. It lifted this burden off Shari's shoulders too."

It is not uncommon when a wife brings her new sexuality out into the open for her husband to wonder whether or not he is to blame, to question his manliness. In Woody Allen's film *Manhattan*, the wife, played by Meryl Streep, leaves him for another woman. To prove his manhood, he enters into a physical relationship with a seventeen-year-old girl.

One woman said, "In reexamining my relationship with my husband, I realized that it was not that he loved me, but his ego and his manliness were at stake. Here he is, a CEO, making over six figures a year. He handled all of our money, controlled my whole life, even decided what we would and wouldn't eat. He had me cleaning the house, shopping, cooking, and taking care of the children. But he couldn't change my feelings.

"If it was another man I was in love with, he could beat the hell out of him, but it was a woman. He couldn't touch a woman. He felt deflated. He didn't feel anger or rejection. He felt resentment."

□ □ □ □

It is also not uncommon, when a wife comes out to her husband, for him to question his own sexuality.

"Sometimes I wondered if I could be gay," admits one man after his wife's disclosure. "When I saw men who were attractive, I'd think, 'Maybe I could have an affair,' but then I really thought about it. I never questioned my sexuality before, but I did recently. And it's cut and dry. I am a heterosexual. I am not attracted to men and I don't consider myself bisexual, although I see men as potentially attractive. I can't see myself wanting a man as I do a woman. But then, I don't want to be married to a lesbian, but I am. It's a difficult thing."

Another woman wondered if her husband might be gay years before she had any clue that she was a lesbian. "When we were young marrieds," she says, "we were at a picnic with friends. The guys were tossing a ball around and running to catch it. For a fleeting instance I thought my husband looked effeminate as he ran, but I didn't give it much thought. After all, we had three children.

"The more I thought about it, though, the more I wondered. Although he was generally a kind and considerate man, he made ridiculing comments about 'fags' and 'queers' whenever the opportunity arose. He sort of talked about them too much, like he was trying to show how different he was from them.

"When our sex life dwindled, and came to an end, he never said anything about it. Neither did I. I think we both felt relieved. Looking back, I realize it had never been anything to boast about. Never any experimentation, a little foreplay, him always on top. It was sort of like, okay, we did it. I made you come and I came. Good night.

"After twenty-seven years of marriage, I realized that I was a lesbian and told him. Even though I had no intention of leaving, it was real hard for him. He was not in the habit of making phone calls, so he couldn't talk to anyone about it. He saw his male friends only when we went out as couples. So he was really alone. I felt so sorry that I had told him, but I needed to talk about *me*.

"We don't talk about my sexuality now, but we do talk more about general things. Other than where the topic of gays and lesbians is concerned, he's a very good and gentle man and a wonderful and involved father, and I care about him a lot.

"I really believe that one of the reasons he's so homophobic is because he's afraid to deal with his own sexual issues. Recently, in conversation, I said to him, 'If you find people you truly care about, gender shouldn't matter.' He jumped down my throat, shouting, 'I'm not queer.'"

Not every husband struggles with the question of his manhood or his sexual identity when he learns of his wife's predilection. One husband talked of feeling relief. "I had felt constant pressure to be 'sexual.' There is this thing in our culture which equates masculinity with being aggressive and with wanting frequent sex, and that's not what I'm about. I would describe myself as being passive sexually. I was willing to do whatever it took to please my wife in the bedroom department," he said. "But that was really never my thing. I was always more interested in the companionship part of our marriage. I think I must be basically asexual. I know I'm not gay. I'm not attracted to men at all.

"Now that my wife came out, I don't know if my marriage is going to last. I'd like it to, but it's not up to me alone. I would feel very bad if it broke up, because I care about her and I'm comfortable with her. And while I would describe myself as being sensitive to women's needs and most of my friends are female, the thought of having to prove my sexual prowess with women in the dating scene all over again is very uncomfortable."

According to Robert T. Michael's book *Sex in America: A Definitive Survey*, "American society is structured to reward those who play by the marriage rules. You are likely to gain the approval of your friends and family and colleagues at work by being happily married by an appropriate age."

Still, Michael and his associates, relying on a survey of 3,432 randomly selected people, found that "Americans fall into three groups. About a third have sex with a partner at least once a week, a third have sex with a partner a few times a month and the rest have sex with a partner a few times a year or have no sexual partners at all."

This finding concurs with findings of Masters and Johnson in their book *Masters and Johnson on Sex and Human Loving*. They say that "In the last few years, celibacy has become more talked about as a sexual alternative."

The general public assumes that something may be wrong with a man who chooses to remain in a marriage that becomes celibate or in one that offers reduced sexual activity, but "for people who get no pleasure out of sex, celibacy may be a welcome relief, like being released from imprisonment."

According to the *Almanac of American People*, while 86 percent of the people surveyed listed having a "traditional marriage" as a "most important life goal," when asked what they looked for in a relationship, the majority said love or companionship. Only 1 percent said sex.

CHARLIE

"The sexuality part of it is really secondary. It's not even secondary, it's probably like ten on the list," Charlie says in speaking about his marriage of fourteen years. "It's the whole social aspect of it, like a complete change of lifestyle. Over the years single friends kind of drifted off. All our friends were basically married and she doesn't want to hang out with straight people all of the time anymore, so I've been doing tons of lying. If she didn't go to an event or birthday party, everyone would say, 'Where's the Mrs.?' I would say, 'Oh, she's working' or 'Oh, she had to do this or she had to do that.' My biggest problem with my wife's disclosure was how it would reflect on me if others found out.

"I was in pain for two years. My stomach was killing me. It was the lying to, being lied to, having to lie. I had no one to talk to. Then my wife joined this support group for women like herself. She met a woman there and we went out with her and her husband a few times. It's funny. Men don't talk much. They're closed. The guy never said a word to me about any of this when we got together.

"Then my wife told me about a support group for spouses of gay men and lesbians, and I went. It was mostly women and four men. These people were really really angry. At this point I had been starting to get over my anger a little bit and I didn't want to surround myself with such angry people, so I never went back.

"The hardest part of my wife's announcement was knowing that people might find out. I tried to hide it from my family especially. The whole thing made me very uncomfortable. I was always conscious of who she would tell. When I was with people,

I'd think, 'Do they know?' I felt that people would ostracize me, or they would think it was my fault or I did something wrong.

"My stomach was getting so bad that I knew I just *had* to tell someone what was going on. Finally I told my brother. He was very understanding. Then, one at a time, I told a few other people. They were compassionate and understanding about it too. They basically said, 'Look, it's not your fault. You didn't do anything.' "

ANTHONY

Anthony, in his mid fifties, has been married to Claire, his second wife, for twelve years. He believes the reason she turned to other women was that he shut down and stopped listening and talking, and was unable to sustain the intimacy they had shared in their early marriage.

"I think Claire was trying to let me know that she needed someone and I was unavailable. She had asked me to go with her a few times on business trips, but I didn't have the time. So that's when she met this woman. That's over now, but she wants to live on her own for a while. She told me she wants to go to every lesbian workshop, meeting, and movie she can find to see who she really is, but I'm hopeful that we may get back together again.

"We talk all the time and see each other every other week or so. She's trying to find herself, and I'm willing to wait.

"Claire had said I was physical but not intimate. It was hard for me. I started thinking about myself and what I was doing wrong. I've been celibate since she left. I'm a very flirtatious guy. I bullshit a lot, I talk a lot, but that's about it. Sex isn't number one on my hit parade priority anymore. At this point in my life I'm looking for someone to mellow with. I just want compatibility. It doesn't have to be sexually great and it doesn't have to be active sex. I want to have a comfortable relationship, a walk in the park.

"Claire came over to help me put the Christmas tree up and then to take it down. She comes and stays overnight sometimes and we're building up a new comfortability. While we have been sleeping together again and there has been no sex, there has been more pleasurable holding and cuddling. I'm not pushing anything. Tender kisses. I'm giving her space. Not getting angry. She appreciates me showering in the morning and shaving and then coming back to bed to cuddle."

While none of the men who remained in their marriages liked the idea of their wives needing women to make their lives complete, and would not have chosen the situation given a choice, most came to understand and accept that another woman might be able to fill a specific need that they, as men, could not. The husbands who left, once their anger had subsided, also came to understand this. And eventually all the men came to realize that their wives' female-oriented sexuality was not an affront to their own manhood.

BARRY

"My wife left me for her childhood friend, another woman. We went to a therapist to make the separation easier, and I broke down and cried. For me, the saddest part was not that I was losing my wife, but that I was losing my best friend. I told her how I felt, and she cried too. She said, 'No, you're not. We'll still be friends. We have two children we have to raise together.'

"I was very angry for a while. Until I started getting my life back on track. Now we see each other on the holidays. We raise the kids together. I even send her Mother's Day cards telling her that she's a wonderful mother, because she is. We've remained part of each other's lives."

I found that the husbands and ex-husbands of the MWLW who consented to be interviewed all became more actively involved in their children's worlds following their wives' disclosure, taking on their share of child care, feeding, and chauffeuring, some for the first time. Those who had a strong desire to keep their families intact, now aware of the kinds of problems they faced within their redefined marriages, were working with their wives to resolve them.

"It's funny," one man said, "a lot of people tell me I've grown since this experience. I guess you're just forced to. Sort of an enlightenment. Just living it. Now I have more understanding of the communication problem between men and women and what makes a woman happy. I don't think the sexual part was our main problem. It was an emotional connection that I never filled with her and that she just had to search for in other places. I think the next relationship I have will be better because of that."

7

What Do the Kids Think?

A WOMAN who discovers that she is an MWLW has a tremendous number of issues to work through. Whether she chooses to share her new identity with her family or not, changes in the household will be inevitable. She will often find that children are intuitive. Even children too young to have the words to describe what they feel nevertheless have insight.

"It was kind of confusing," one young woman said, remembering back to the time when she was nine and began to sense that her household was different from those of her friends. "From what I would see on television, the mothers didn't have women friends really, and when they did, they played cards or they exchanged recipes. They didn't have big fights, they didn't have big emotional anythings. I knew my mother's friendships were different."

Should we try to hide our true identities from our children? Are we protecting them if we practice duplicity rather than honesty? Can being open hurt them? Each woman must come to her own decision.

The decision to tell my children, Ian and Laurie, twenty-six and twenty-four at the time, was not one hastily reached. I deliberated at length with myself, my husband, and friends who shared my secret.

At first my husband was uncomfortable with them knowing, but I felt strongly that it was really about me and who and what I was and I needed them to know. He finally agreed. I decided to tell them separately and, one evening, when my son and I were alone, I reminded him of an article I'd written on this topic and told him that my interest was actually a personal one. I told him how I had made my discovery and then handed him the introduction that I had just finished for this book. He read it as I sat quietly and waited. When he finished he looked up at me. "What about Dad?" he asked.

"Dad knows. We've talked about it and we're dealing with it. Neither he nor I is walking out the door."

"Okay," he said, accepting what I had to tell him at face value, neither evaluating it in the context of pain or pleasure nor seeing it as an emotional thing. To him it was a piece of information.

A while later I asked him if he felt any anger or resentment toward me or his father.

"No," he said. "You haven't done anything to make me angry. You haven't done anything to make me resentful either. The first three things that went through my mind when you told me were: Are you breaking up? Are you moving out? Do I have to find another place to live? But my life continues pretty much as it has before. The way you and Dad dealt with this has enabled me to think about it less. Neither of you has changed much. You've both become a bit more of a pain in the ass about needing separate space, but I can accept that. I need my space too."

When I asked him how he would feel if his friends knew about me, Ian responded with questions of his own: "Does it make me a different person? Do you respect me any less? Do you like me any less because you know? Does it change your opinion of me? If knowing a fact about my life, or your life, since it affects my life, will change someone's opinion about me for the worse, then I don't consider that opinion to be worth anything. With a few notable exceptions, I don't care what other people think."

Ian is a writer, and as such has done research on a variety of different topics, so he hadn't connected a previous article I had written on MWLW with my personal story, but Laurie had, so my disclosure to her didn't come as a surprise.

"I kind of figured something since your friendship with Toby began."

"But that was a year and a half before I realized I had fallen in love with her," I said.

"I could tell from the way you talked about her. It was kind of like the way I would talk about my boyfriends, just casually slipping her name into conversation and stuff like that. You acted different with her, in a way that you never acted with any of your other friends. And then you wrote that piece about married women, so when you told me, it was just kind of confirming what I thought."

Still, Laurie's first concern was very much like Ian's. "What about Dad?"

I assured her, as I had Ian, that her dad knew and he and I were dealing with it.

"How did knowing about me make you feel about your own sexuality?" I asked after she had gotten used to the "other me."

"I know how I feel toward men and women, so it didn't scare me like 'Am I going to be that way now?' You are you and I am me and your sexuality isn't going to change my life."

While I'm certain Laurie would have preferred me to remain my old self, she was glad that I had shared with her. "I don't like to be kept in the dark," she said. "And I want you to be able to tell me anything, just like I tell you anything about my life."

Still, she made it graphically clear what she didn't want to know. "I'm not ashamed of who or what you are, Mom, and I don't resent it or anything like that, but if you were to have an affair, I wouldn't want to know about it. I don't know of many kids who want to hear that their parents are screwing around on each other. What you do with your sex life and what Daddy does with his is your business. Just like I wouldn't want to hear the details of the sex life you and Daddy had before and just like I wouldn't tell you the details of my sex life.

"I want you to be happy, and if this will do it, great. Just remember, I'm your friend, but I'm your daughter first, and there are some things left better unsaid."

Ian had no need to share this information, saying, "It's your life, Mom, you can tell who you want." Laurie, on the other hand, has talked about it with her friends. She confided that she told a new boyfriend too. "I guess I was sort of testing him," she said. "If he's close-minded about you, he'll be close-minded about other things, and I don't want those kinds of people in my life."

While I had spoken to my children of tolerance and understanding, by hiding the real me I had denied them the chance to put these thoughts into practice in their immediate world. Being honest and straightforward has led to more open communication and a stronger family bond. They have learned to think independently and to stand up for what they believe in and we have all developed a stronger awareness and sensitivity for others.

One of Laurie's friends had been going through much distress in regard to his own hidden homosexuality. His relief after hearing about me enabled him to talk about himself for the first time.

This announcement to one's children will not always be met with acceptance, however. Various factors affect the way children of any age respond to the disclosure: the comfort level with which the mother deals with her situation, the emotional maturity and sexual security of the child, the relationship between the parents, the relationship between child and parents, and the level of tension the child feels in the home. Initially, every child's biggest concern, regardless of age or independence, is not the parent's sexuality, but what will happen to *our* family? How will *my* world change? How will *I* be affected?

"If children feel loved and secure, they adjust," says psychotherapist Lois Wadas. "They are much more resilient than we give them credit for being. What hurts them is not telling them the truth when they have ears to hear and eyes to see. Children are intuitive, and when you discount the reality, you do more damage than talking about it.

"Naturally, telling is a whole different scenario for each age group," Wadas cautions. "All ages require a special approach, but with an adolescent, you definitely should have outside help. Adolescents are volatile. They are moving into their own sexuality, and to be confronted with their parents' is very unsettling. Because they are in the process of forming who they are, they need things to be steady and predictable."

JUNE

June had four children who were married and on their own. Facing a terminal illness, she made the difficult and painful decision to, at last, acknowledge her true sexuality, a part of herself she had rejected for more than forty years. Although she could not predict the response her loved ones would have, or how her disclosure might alter her own life or theirs, June believed she had to come out. She did this, not for her family, but for herself, because she needed to be who she was. She could not die peacefully knowing she had lived a lie.

First she told her husband. Aware that being on her own would be difficult because of her disease, yet wanting to be fair, she offered him his freedom. He opted to remain nearby. While they chose to reside in separate units in the multifamily dwelling they owned together, they remained caring and supportive of each other throughout the remainder of her life.

Admission to herself and then to her family brought her closer to her daughters. One daughter said, "Mom had always seemed so strong, so unapproachable. Even after her disease was diagnosed, she was like a rock. Then she told us about herself and we were able to see her as a woman with human frailties."

But June's married son, ignoring the fact that his parents' separation had been a mutually acceptable agreement, and that they still cared for each other, could only see his mother as having abandoned his father. He developed a growing fear that if she could leave his father, his wife could do the same to him. He became an angry, suspicious, and abusive husband and eventually his wife did leave him.

ARLENE

Arlene relates the difficulty one particular son had with her disclosure, of taking it as a personal affront.

"He's a yuppie: makes excellent money, lives downtown. He's up and coming . . . and I stigmatized him. I've associated negativity with his perfect self. It's like I came up with a bruise on *his* ego.

"I am the person he loved the most, who gave him his life, his mom, and now he could not live with me. We are a very God-oriented, loving family," Arlene says. "He needed that bond back. He could not continue to get prosperous unless he came back to his family. That's exactly what he learned. Eventually he came back to me and said, 'Mom, I was wrong to turn away.' "

□ □ □ □

While not all children are straight, children raised by gay or lesbian parents or couples are *no* more likely to grow up to be homosexual than are children raised by heterosexual parents. According to *The Kinsey Institute New Report on Sex*, "There is evidence, in fact, that parents have very little influence on the outcome of their children's sexual partner orientation." *Reinventing the Family*'s author, Laura Benkov, concurs. Study after study revealed no essential differences between children raised by heterosexual parents and those raised by gay or lesbian parents. These children were "no more prone to confusion about their gender identities or to emotional disturbance of any kind."

When gay parents face custody or visitation battles in court, legal precedent usually deems gay parents unfit. The irony of this is that "children of gays are most often born to parents in heterosexual marriages who subsequently come out." Because today's gay father or mother is much more apt than those of a generation ago to be honest, however, a larger percentage of today's children who have gay parents will grow up aware that they do.

Still, children of MWLW have generally grown up with little exposure to lesbians or gay men and have absorbed some of mainstream culture's homophobia. "The Bank Street study tapped into the fact that many teachers, and educational administrators, like everyone else in our culture, harbor subtle or blatant homophobic views—views which are reflected in the classroom in a variety of ways, ranging from a lack of sensitivity to specific children's families, to exclusionary curricula, to rigid ideas about the role of gender in children's lives . . . often even the least homophobic teachers and administrators are ill-prepared to address issues lesbian and gay families raise.

"For these children," says Benkov, "the revelation of a parent's homosexuality requires a total shift in perspective. Coming to terms can be complicated if there is an acrimonious divorce, an atmosphere of threat, or homophobic family members. Traversing this territory can take years, and is sometimes never accomplished. But many children—even those steeped in homophobia—are readily moved by love for a parent to reconceptualize their world."

Although living with a mother who is an MWLW does not necessarily cause a child to feel that his or her sexuality may also be out of the norm, having a parent, sibling, or child who is gay may trigger the question "Could I be gay too?"

ROBERTA

Years before Roberta identified her own sexuality, she knew that her teenage son was gay. Confiding this to her daughter, who had known about her brother for some time, made the young girl comfortable enough with her mother to say, "I once experimented with another girl to see if I was a lesbian. I'm not."

Living with a sibling who is gay or with a mother who is an MWLW does not inevitably necessitate wanting to explore alternative sexual choices. The close exposure, however, to a person who lives outside of the conventional norm makes these children more aware that options other than the traditional male-female relationships do exist and they are often more able to put same-sex relationships in proper perspective. As a result, lesbianism eventually loses its taboo status; it becomes not bad or good, just different.

CARLA

Carla, the twenty-one-year-old daughter of an MWLW, experienced her mother's disclosure differently. She says, "I had all kinds of questions about my own sexuality because that's how I am. . . . I read a book in one of my women's studies classes about coping when you're a lesbian. Some essays were sexual and some totally emotional, so I've had exposure to diversity as far as their philosophy of it is.

"I have one really good friend who is a lesbian. While I don't consider myself a lesbian and I don't have my primary relationships with women, this friendship has allowed me to be even more open and questioning about how I feel."

Carla remembers that she was seventeen when she first began to talk about her mother's gender choice. "I wasn't comfortable with my body. I was in relationships with men but I wasn't comfortable with them sexually. I wasn't comfortable with any sexuality at that point. So when I started to think specifically about the sexual part, I thought it was disgusting. I started to picture it in my mind and I started to think that it was really gross."

"You mean with women?" I asked her.

"Women with women, but for some reason women with men also seemed pretty gross at that age. It also had to do with the fact that it was my mother. You know, it's a parent thing. Picturing my mother having sex with anyone was weird."

Now comfortable with her own sexuality, Carla realizes that what had made her ill at ease about her mother's was that she had no prior knowledge that two women might be both emotionally and physically attracted to each other. "You didn't usually see two women being together on TV. I don't mean seeing two women together in a porno movie, to turn on a man, but seeing them in a respectful way. I think if I had been more used to seeing women with women, I would not have been so uncomfortable."

From the time she was nine, Carla had surmised that her mother's relationships with women were unconventional. She remembers sensing emotional changes in her household. "I don't know if I had the words then, but I definitely knew something. My mom and dad weren't fighting so much. There wasn't anything there really. The fighting was going on between my mom and different women friends, which, to me, showed more of an investment. The emotional intensity she had with women affected her more."

She was able to remember the specific friendship her mother had that had given her a sense that something was going on. It was with another married woman with whom her mother worked. "From a business relationship, all of a sudden it became very personal and our families did everything together. Then my mom and the other woman had a fight or something and my mom was totally depressed."

Carla felt that in her household, the roles of mother and daughter had been reversed. "My mom was in bed all day long for like a couple of years. I was around ten and I had to do a lot of things for her. She was very sensitive and it was important for me to be a good girl and make Mom happy."

Although she had had suspicions, since she couldn't formulate her thoughts Carla believed that there was nothing to talk about, and so did her mother, until Carla was getting ready to leave for college.

"I started to get a sense that my mother wanted to tell me something. I couldn't even say, 'I think my mother's a lesbian.' I could have notions about it, and feelings, but to put the word on it, that was something different. I started to feel that if my mom talked to me without me being ready, I would freak out and be really unsupportive. I didn't want that to happen. I knew it would destroy her."

When Carla felt she was ready, she and her mother talked. Carla says, "I think my mother has a lot of internalized hatred from society, like this is dirty, this is disgusting. She's so closeted, and this keeps her trapped in a circle. I don't really know what she should do, it's her choice. But I feel that while there are, on a practical level, a lot of intelligent reasons for being secretive, this perpetuates the 'well, there is something wrong with what I am and so I can't tell anybody' idea. It leaves her closed off to other women who might find her and connect with her and help her as well as them."

Carla's concern for her mother and her desire to help her has fostered her own interest in women's issues. She attributes her strong feminist tendencies to the women's studies classes she attended while in college as well as to her voracious reading which began as a way to understand better what her mother was going through. "If it wasn't for the pain I saw my mother living with, I think I might have had internalized hatred or oppression toward people who are different. I've learned a lot of things through this. I've become more aware about being who I am rather than being who I'm supposed to be."

The ability to reason can be temporarily affected by the stress and anxiety MWLW frequently feel during their transitional period. According to Carla, it was her mother's own internalized hatred about what she was that affected her physical health, and, without realizing it, put extra pressure on her children.

ALLISON

"My mother specifically said, 'Don't tell your roommate, your best friend, your father.' I felt a tremendous conflict of loyalties. Because I was not supposed to know, I could not show support for my father, and therefore, the only person I could be supportive of was Mom.

"I was very torn. I was very angry at her for making me choose.

Probably more so than because of the actual information about herself. She was putting me in an impossible position. I was getting angrier and angrier. When I get angry, I have to talk. I felt like I was betraying her, but as soon as I got off the phone I told my friend. I had to tell someone.

"In some ways, my mother was like a brand-new baby discovering things for the first time. For a couple of years I really felt like I was raising her. No kidding. I was living it and I've got the labor pains and stretch marks to show it. She lost her inhibitions and it was difficult for me to deal with. In one way she was a woman and having these great, wonderful, mysterious feelings . . . and, at the same time, she's my mother."

Initially upon hearing that the mother is an MWLW, children often see their father as the wronged parent. After a while they may become angry with him for choosing to remain in a compromising situation in the marriage.

STACY

"I felt like my father was a martyr. I felt like he was the best person in the world. He was giving everything to everyone else, doing everything for me and my brother. . . . We were his life because he didn't have any outside friends. Here Mom is, changing her whole lifestyle, investing time and energy elsewhere, and he's totally flexible. My mom is bringing home women she's involved with and my dad continues to be not only flexible, like 'I won't see what's going on,' although that is part of it, but engaged with these people and helping do things for them and really bending over backward.

"I got to a point where I felt I had to do everything to make my father happy because he's doing everything to make everyone else happy. Now I have this immense pressure on me."

Stacy's compulsion to assure her father's happiness caused her to assume a parenting role, taking on responsibility for him, until therapy changed her way of thinking. "I started getting the point, like, 'Wait a minute. This is my father's choice to remain in this relationship and it's his choice to be flexible about things. For some reason it's worth it to him to be bending over backward. Not because he's a martyr but because it's his choice.'"

She has suggested to him that he not necessarily seek a divorce, but "get a life." He said, "I have a life. This is what I choose."

Although Stacy thinks she now understands her parents' relationship more fully, she still gets angry with both her parents. "I get angry at my mom for putting my dad in this position and I get angry with him for staying in this position, or putting up with it.

"Sometimes I feel that he has contributed by not being emotionally supportive. There are so many different levels. I feel like they shouldn't be together and my mom should be out, but it's their lives."

Stacy knows she doesn't want what her parents have for herself and has struggled to find the relationship that will meet her own needs. She says of her old boyfriends, "I went out with someone like my mother, meaning he was really emotional and then I went out with someone like my father, really distant and unemotional. Now I'm working on a place in between."

LISA

Lisa also acknowledged anger at her father's inability to be there for her mother emotionally. She describes him as being "emotionally dormant," and while she believes that the issue of her mother's sexuality still would have come about had her father been more in tune emotionally, "it wouldn't have felt so desperate."

Having examined the possibility of a separation for her parents, she says, "I would feel great for my mom because she would be free and happy, or happier or more capable of being happy. I'd want to be supportive of her as a person, but apart from her being a person, she is my father's wife. Her happiness would be to some extent at the expense of someone else I care about, so it would be very difficult.

"I love my father dearly, but I think the important thing is they both have to acknowledge that they deserve to have a life, and this doesn't have to be with the person they've been with. They also have to realize that they can stand on their own and be whole people. I think my mom can do it. She's capable and ready. My dad's the one I'm concerned about."

Her dad was not the only one Lisa expressed concern for. "I have concerns for myself," she said. "Because my dad doesn't have much of a life, I can see him on my doorstep, so as great as it could be for my mom, I'd like my dad to have a playmate or a distraction or something so I don't have to be his entertainment center, his hand holder."

Lisa sighs. "My parents love so differently. They care so differently. They're both good people but they need different things so they have to be allowed to be different and they can't do that together.

"I certainly want my mom to feel fulfilled and know what being in love is like and I don't think she knows with my dad."

All the adult children of MWLW I interviewed said they were glad they knew the truth about their mothers' lives even though it had been difficult information to take in and deal with. The only studies that corroborate this information, however, involve single lesbian mothers, not MWLW. While one study done by Hanscombe and Forster in 1982 did not describe how the children were told, it did report that where lesbian mothers were open with their children, the children felt closer to their mothers emotionally.

Another study on mental health in single lesbian mothers done by Rand, Graham, and Rawlings in 1982 did not record the family's reaction to disclosure, but reported that admission to ex-husbands, children, and employers positively correlates with the psychological well-being of the lesbian mother.

While some women who wanted to tell their children about their gender preference talked about waiting until the children were certain ages to begin their dialogue, others found age to be of no concern.

LOUISA

Louisa had been married to a man for over six years and had a five-year-old daughter when she came across the woman who had been her lover fifteen years earlier. "I fell in love with Pattie, but for many reasons we ended up not staying together." Upon meeting again, they reconnected.

"I wasn't looking for this to happen when it happened," Louisa says. "I was not expecting the intensity that I did feel. Pattie and I have been struggling to sort out what's been going on for the last year and a half, and we're both very committed to being in this relationship."

Louisa, who considers herself bisexual, is out to her husband, and endeavoring to make her marriage, as well as her same-gender relationship, work. She and her husband have chosen to raise their child in an open environment.

"My daughter is seven now and she's grown up around all kinds of people. Her godmother is a lesbian. She knows women can be married to men, women can be married to women, and men can be married to men. That's normal for her because this is her world. I'm not particularly physical with Pattie in front of my daughter, but we are demonstrative. She isn't at a point where she realizes it isn't common for everyone."

Louisa, encouraging her child to form ideas with openness, says, "I don't say gay, straight, bisexual and define those terms, because I think, in some way, giving her this language would limit her to thinking in categories.

"So right now she just assumes that people love each other in different ways. When she asks me more, like she asked me if my two very good [women] friends were married [to each other], I said yes. And that was it. That was her question and I answered it. When she wants to know more, she will ask me and I will give her truthful answers."

The desire to bring together all the people they love is not uncommon among MWLW regardless of whether they are out to their families or not. If that special other woman is single, the MWLW may try to incorporate her into her family by including her, as a good friend, in family functions and activities. If both women are MWLW and have children of similar ages, their families may become close and they may share their lives while keeping their relationship secret.

CYNTHIA AND SUSAN

Cynthia and Susan have been intimately involved with each other for more than thirty years. Between them they have six children. While they have chosen not to tell their respective families about their committed relationship, because they have been best friends since their children were infants, their families have grown up sharing birthday parties, holidays, and special occasions. Recently, one of their daughters was married in an orthodox Jewish wedding in which men and women dance separately. "Something I had dreamed of happened," Cynthia said. "Susan and I were able to dance together at a family wedding."

On occasion, if the other woman is unmarried and occupies much of a mother's time, rivalry between the lover and the MWLW's children might result.

PENNY

During Penny's high school years, her mother formed an attachment with a single woman. Penny remembers feeling resentful when this particular friend entered her mother's life. "I was away at camp and I got a letter from my mom. She told me that she had met a new friend, and I could tell from her letter that she was happy, so I was happy for her. But then, as I saw their friendship progress, I didn't like her anymore. This woman wasn't married. She came over alone and she wanted all of my mother's time. My mom was buying her things, doing things for her. My younger brother thought she was pretty and he loved her. He had a very simple relationship with her. They played ball together. But I definitely felt some kind of competition and jealousy. She had all of my mother's attention.

"And then, at some point, this woman got engaged and that was the last time I saw her and my mom never saw her again."

Penny's mother did not consciously try to ingratiate her lover, but other women work very hard at making the special woman in their lives become special to their children too.

GERRY

Unlike many spouses of MWLW who went through their discovery period alone, Gerry's husband, aware of her inner turmoil, was supportive and understanding of her needs from the beginning. He was even glad for her when she found Cathy.

"When I became involved in a relationship that finally brought me to the new awareness of my sexual orientation, my husband and I made integrating Cathy into our family a priority. We agreed that our fourteen-year-old daughter should be informed of my relationship with Cathy, although we felt our sons were too young to understand.

"My news elicited a loving but questioning response from my daughter. Her major concern was about the future of our marriage. She expressed satisfaction and relief when I explained that her father and I were very committed to each other and intended to keep the family intact. Still, she was obviously struggling with the very idea of homosexuality, and I can't say she was pleased for me in any way.

"Cathy, also married, but childless, has participated in important family events with us and has scheduled outings with each of the children, and they have been to her home. While my daughter knows what my relationship with her is all about, the boys simply understand that she is an important person in my life, and I hope they are beginning to recognize that she is truly an honorary family member.

"As for my daughter, my relationship with her is excellent and the subject of my sexuality is one of many serious issues that we work on together. She seems to have gotten used to the idea to the extent that it is not one of the major issues in her life, and by all evidence she is a lovely, well-adjusted young lady."

Gerry had no intention of discussing her sexuality with her eight-year-old son, until one day when they had been in a bookstore near a display for Gay Pride Month.

Jarret said, "Oh, this is a lesbian book."

Later in the car, Gerry asked, "Do you know what a lesbian is?"

"No. But you are one!"

"How do you know?"

"Because you listen to that lesbian music."

"Oh, yeah! Well, what do you think the word *lesbian* might mean?" Gerry asked him.

"Maybe women who like to march in Washington?"

"A good guess, but you're still not right," Gerry said.

"Well, what is it?"

"A lesbian is a woman who is in love with another woman instead of in love with a man. Or she might be in love with a man too, but the point is, she can be in love with a woman."

"Oh, weird."

"You think so? Some people do think it's a little weird. But I think it's pretty great," Gerry said.

After a long pause, Jarret asked, "Well, what woman do you love?"

"I love Cathy."

"I'm not surprised."

Later Gerry said, "There's one more thing I have to tell you about my being a lesbian. It's kind of private. It's nobody's business but my own, so it's not the kind of thing to talk to your friends about or anything, okay?"

"Hmm, I don't really think much about it, to tell you the truth."

"That's fine, great, but I still want you to understand about privacy."

"Okay. Well, I really do hate that music you listen to!" Jarret said.

"Well, I hate that music you listen to too!"

Gerry says, "We laughed together then, and that was that. I'm pleased that my second child can now understand more fully just how important my woman is to me. I'm proud of this interaction with my son and the special relationships I enjoy with each of my children."

A tiny minority of MWLW said that because of the difficulties gay people face, they might have reconsidered having children had they known about their true sexuality before becoming parents. Most, however, were happy they had families. Yet some women voiced feelings of guilt in regard to difficulties their children might encounter owing to society's intolerant attitudes.

One MWLW said, "My daughters were watching a talk show on television. Two women declared their marriage and kissed. My seven-year-old said, 'Yuk,' but my ten-year-old said, 'Wow, cool.' She thought it was wonderful that two women could love each other. I'm glad that my girls are learning that they have other options, that their choices aren't as limited as mine were. Still, I hope that neither one chooses this lifestyle. I would not have chosen it for myself, not in the conditions gay women are forced to live in now. It's hard, bigoted. I'm living the lie of heterosexuality. It's driving me crazy."

Some women believe this information is too challenging for

their children. Others believe in being honest because, while it is easy to monitor a young child's environment, the increasingly social nature of children's lives as they grow will present them with constant threat of exposure: overhearing adult conversations, or hearing from other children. In Bea's case, it was her lover, in an angry moment, who let the secret out.

BEA

Bea, the mother of two, had been married for seven years, then divorced. Not yet aware of her true sexual identity, she had three unfulfilling relationships with men before she connected with another woman at a Little League baseball game. "Marcy was married and I was engaged. We hit it off, becoming friends. We were friends for a year and a half before we became lovers, the first for each of us. It just happened very suddenly."

While the women were together for fifteen years, they maintained separate households. "I knew I wanted to be with her and she with me, but with five kids between us, we had the need for separate households. I never told my children. I thought Marcy and I had this tremendous secret," Bea says. "They saw my lover constantly, at holidays, etc. We were a family, she and her three kids and me and my two. Although we didn't live together, we practically raised our five kids together. Then we had a tremendous argument and she told her children about us and they told mine. My oldest son knew I was in pain so it made it easier to discuss things with him. I admitted that Marcy and I had been more than friends for fifteen years. He said, 'I know.' I asked how he felt about it and he said he didn't want to discuss it right then. After a time, though, he said, 'I know you would accept anyone who would make me happy and I will accept anyone who will make you happy.'

"But my younger son and I had always had trouble communicating, and when the other kids told him about me and Marcy, he got so angry that my relationship with him became totally estranged."

Most MWLW discover that there is no perfect time to come out to their children. The process of discovering and outing oneself is an ongoing one.

Once told, children of MWLW face the dilemma of whether or not to keep their mothers' inclinations secret or seek friends to confide in. Teenagers, especially, worry about telling their friends, not only because of what their reactions might be, but because those reactions might reflect and reinforce the hidden anxieties and fear in themselves. According to Laura Benkov in *Reinventing the Family*, adolescence is the period in a child's life that generally poses the most significant challenges. Children are struggling to separate themselves from their families and at the same time to establish themselves in friendships. It is a time when they are intensely focused on their own personal identity, especially sexuality. It is also a time when homophobia in the environment can be the most intense.

When an MWLW remains in her marriage, regardless of the renegotiated contract she and her husband may have agreed to live with, her children have the option of keeping their mother's lifestyle a private matter. When the parents are separated, however, and the mother has a female lover in her life, keeping the circumstances from friends becomes more difficult for a child.

ANGELA

Angela had left her husband and was living with her seventeen-year-old daughter. Her daughter knew Angela was gay and accepted it. Still, it was uncomfortable at first for the teenager to tell her friends about her mother.

Angela says, "My daughter tried to keep it secret, and that was very difficult because her friends were always here and I had a lover who was out and had lived her whole life out and resented being asked to be closeted in the house she was now living in.

"So it was necessary for my daughter to come out about me to her friends and she did, one by one in whatever way. First she came out to the people she felt safest with, her camp friends who don't live nearby. They were wonderful. She didn't have any negative feedback. Then she came out to her other friends. The kids were just wonderful too. They liked me before, so they like me now.

"The difficulty was my daughter hated my lover, who had tattoos, very dyky. I guess she would have been more comfortable with my lover looking like a schoolteacher."

The mother's true sexuality was not a major issue in most children's lives, and most MWLW reported building stronger, more open relationships with their children in the long run. Three women who had left their marriages, however, reported having children who no longer spoke to them. They believed that the children's anger and resentment came because of the breakup and not because of their own gender preference.

EVELYN

Evelyn and her husband had appeared to have the perfect marriage: affluent home, three nice children, respect of the community and of the corporate world the husband inhabited. But neither could communicate with the other. His ambition drove him farther and farther from the family, leaving Evelyn with emotional problems.

"I knew my marriage was dead before I met Katie. Visiting her only confirmed it. It was one of the few times I got in touch with myself, and I realized I had to leave my husband."

Having no money of her own, and seeing no way to support her teenage children, she made a painful choice, one she says was the only one she had. She left them behind in their large and familiar home.

Although our laws have some equity of marital property, Evelyn felt that demanding what was rightfully hers might have meant long-drawn-out court battles and she refused to put herself or her children through this.

Over the last twelve years, while two of her children have come to understand and forgive their mother for what she had done, the third child never did. "I haven't seen or spoken to my middle daughter for about ten years, and she lives blocks from me. It makes me feel terrible. She is living with a cult group and blames me for all her pain and unhappiness."

All the women who had decided on separation or divorce said it was more difficult to tell the children about the dissolution of their marriage than about their sexual inclination. Dr. Lee Salk says that "Although there is little stigma to divorce these days, studies have shown that next to the death of a loved one, divorce is the most stressful situation an individual can face."

Judith Wallerstein and Berlin Kelly, in their study *Surviving the Breakup*, found that "more than half the women were better off by psychological indicators and by their own judgement. . . . Somewhat fewer of the men seem to have used divorce as a device for changing the course of their lives for the better. Their most important finding in regard to children is that the children's development and the way they view the divorce depends directly on what happens to the adults after the divorce—on how successful the divorce is for the parents . . . when one or both parents cannot achieve a successful divorce, the children pay a high price. In particular, if the parents continue to fight and blame each other, the children have a hard time."

JACKIE

Upon returning to college in her early forties, Jackie fell in love with her female professor. She says that once she realized her true sexual inclinations, she wanted a divorce. Fond of her husband, and concerned about his well-being and that of their children, she suggested couples therapy. She felt this would be a good way for him to slowly get used to the idea that things were going to change.

After several months they decided together that it was time to tell their children. Piece by piece, they prepared their sons, who were home from college, for the announcement of their coming separation. "We formed a united front and told them we had pulled apart," says Jackie. "We didn't tell them about my feelings for women at the time because I wanted to tell each of them about that separately.

"Because we had seemed so happy on the outside, when we told our children that we were going to separate, one son broke out in tears in the middle of the restaurant, saying, 'I thought we were perfect.'

"I wanted to say, 'But we're still perfect. This doesn't mean we're any less perfect.'

"When we separated, our children were devastated." As a result, Jackie was very concerned about how they would deal with her other announcement a short time later. She needn't have worried.

Her oldest son said, "You know, Mom, maybe it's for the wrong reasons, but I'm glad." I think what he meant was "I'm glad you're leaving Dad because you're a lesbian and not because he did anything wrong."

Jackie's sons have adjusted well. While they are protective of both parents and try hard to steer a middle course, her oldest son talks about his family situation openly and even kids about it.

"While he was in college, my son wrote a play," Jackie says. "He said to one of his friends, 'This is a heavy weekend. My play is going to be produced and both of my parents are coming up— with their girlfriends.' "

While shaken, Jackie's children were able to adjust to their parents' divorce and then to Jackie's announcement because of the relationship they had with their parents prior to the change in family structure. I believe that was why my kids were able to deal with my announcement. When I came out to them, I wasn't thinking: Are they going to reject me, be angry, resentful? We had always had open communication and my kids had always been involved in family matters. I felt this is just another hurdle and we'll make it through. While I was a little anxious about how they would receive my news, my thoughts were, "I need to tell them and we'll deal with it."

8

Coming Out to Friends and Family

REALISTICALLY I knew that it was my feelings for Toby that had made her uncomfortable and caused her to pull away, but I also knew that it was being truthful with her that had ruined our friendship. And so, sharing sensitive issues had become more and more difficult for me. It was only after I found the courage to confide in other women that I was able to break through my newly established patterns of isolation.

Occasional evening walks with a neighbor, Lorraine, had become an enjoyable daily routine, and we'd recently begun to become friends as well as neighbors. Our conversations covered a wide range of topics. Once, I tentatively mentioned that I was working on a book about MWLW.

"Why?" she had asked.

About to tell her, I lost my nerve. "Because I'm a writer," I answered. Several times I came close to telling her about myself, but I was afraid. So she remained another person to keep my secret from.

One evening Lorraine stopped by for some help with an embroidery piece she had begun. I was so pleased with the pages I had just completed, that in my excitement, without considering possible consequences, I asked if she'd like to hear a few. She listened as I read to her from across the room. We were alone in the house, but she said, "I don't want to ask you this question out loud. Come sit next to me on the couch."

She said, "Once you told me there had briefly been someone very special in your life." I nodded.

"Was that someone a woman?"

Normally one to blurt things out, I was suddenly silent. Was it right to tell Lorraine? Would I be burdening her with this information? Frightening her away?

"Yes," I said quietly.

There was a pause, then she said, "I don't think you're really a lesbian."

I had to keep from smiling. I knew she was trying to make me feel better, but I actually felt fine. By this time I had realized that having same-gender feelings was not the horrible thing society portrayed it to be.

"I work with some of *those women* and you're nothing like them. You don't dress like them or look like them," Lorraine said with the authority of one who knows.

Then awkwardly, she said, "I have to ask you something. Do you like me . . . like that?"

"No," I reassured her. "I like you as a friend."

"But if you're a les—" she began.

"Lorraine, are you attracted to every man you see in a sexual way?"

"No," she said.

"Well, it's the same with me."

She breathed a sigh of relief, but things between us had changed. In the past she would stop by for a brief chat when she'd see me coming home from work. Now she began to wave from her doorway instead. She stopped calling. When I called, she rejected my invitations to walk as we used to. I felt saddened. I missed Lorraine's company.

A couple of months passed before she called me again. She said she had missed our chats and asked me if I'd like to join her that evening. Still, through our entire walk she kept a noticeable distance from me. I could sense her nervousness. Each time we passed a man, she would comment. "Nice buns" or "great ass." And while she never had before, now she talked incessantly about how good sex was between her and her husband, until finally I found it difficult to constrain my laughter. "Lorraine, it's all right. You're safe with me," I told her.

"Was I so obvious?"

"Yes," I said, and we both laughed like we used to before the *L* word interfered with our growing friendship.

Lorraine asked numerous questions and I shared some of my findings with her. One letter I received from an MWLW about her own discovery was so poignant that I read a part of it to Lorraine.

After I'd finished, she said, "Wow, this is very scary."

"What?" I asked.

"This whole thing. How do I know I won't wake up one day and realize I love women? If you don't look like one but turned out to be one, could that happen to me too?"

For Lorraine, the jolt of my announcement was compounded by the similarities she saw in us. Besides both of us being married, we shared similar child-raising philosophies, had comparable homes, and before this surfaced, shared similar frustrations about our husbands.

No woman is automatically exempt from the frightening possibility that she, too, might sometime realize she is a lesbian. Suddenly Lorraine had to face the same realization that countless others have struggled with. Being married was no guarantee that she or her husband couldn't realize a new sexual preference.

Most people simply need time to process the surprising information when a friend comes out, unless they suspected all along. For others, the disclosure may bring hitherto unresolved sexual or social issues to the surface. People who have difficulty dealing with their own sexual uncertainties are less likely to be able to accept this type of disclosure.

One woman realized that her inability to come to terms with her daughter's same-gender preference stemmed not from her daughter's revelation, but from her own inability to deal with the sexuality she had repressed since childhood.

Only after years of therapy, while going through her menopause, could this woman finally acknowledge her own preference for women. And only then was she able to make peace with her daughter.

Several women told me of friends who deserted them upon learning of their sexual orientation. They also told me that years later, some of these same women, once horrified, sought them out to tell them of their own enlightenment when they, too, discovered or acknowledged their attraction to women.

LOIS

Lois was tormented by the belief that she had done a horrible thing to her husband by discovering her true self. She was unsure of what her future with him would be. While the people she worked with knew of her relationship with her woman friend, she had not told her good friend, Gina, in whom she confided almost everything via phone calls or letters. Lois was afraid that sharing her same-sex preference might affect their friendship, and kept her problem to herself.

Even when Gina came for a visit and asked how her marriage was, Lois lied and said fine. Then Gina said, "Mine broke up. I went away and met a woman."

Lois laughed. "I had known Gina since high school, more than twenty years. For the last ten years she had been too afraid to say anything to me that might affect our friendship, and here I was doing the same thing.

"The only reason Gina told me now was that in our business the rumor mill is very active and a mutual friend I worked with let my secret out."

Finally Lois confided in Gina. "It was great and it made me feel like I wasn't such a two-headed monster because Gina was like me, yet she was the nice, sweet person I always knew."

While telling does get easier with time, initially it feels like an earth-shattering event. We choose the recipients of this information carefully.

Early in my discovery process, I had received a Christmas card from an old friend. We had each moved, and our correspondence had dwindled, then ceased. Still, her card brought back fond memories of long, chatty visits. I decided to confide in her. Although at the time it was still difficult for me to tell anyone, I sent her a four-page letter telling her what had happened to me.

Why did I choose her? Something in me wanted her to know who I was. Maybe because she was living halfway around the world. Maybe because I'd always admired her, I wanted her validation.

Time passed without acknowledgment to what I then believed was a huge confession. Had I been wrong to tell? Did she think I was awful? Was she rejecting me? More than a year later, I received a letter from her. There was no judgment, only curiosity as to how I was getting on with my life. She filled me in on hers, the busy life of a mother with young children and a husband often traveling for business. I could feel the warmth of our old friendship.

I realized that while I was working my way through a major trauma in my life, it was not a major priority in her life, which was moving along its own track.

Even though we got together only two or three times a year, I also felt the need to share my concerns and feelings with my two oldest friends, Beth and Sherry. But we had all double-dated since junior high school and then married at about the same time, and our husbands were friends too. This weighed heavily on my decision as to whether or not to tell the women about myself. Even if I asked them not to, they might tell their spouses. This could affect my husband. Would it be fair to him? Would he be comfortable with the other men knowing? Would he feel ridiculed? Blamed?

I thought about consulting him, then decided that my sexuality was not about him, of his being the cause or the catalyst: It was about me and who I am. And I needed the support of my friends.

Over the years, due to distance, family priorities, and busy schedules, our visits had dwindled to two or three times a year. Our deep, endless girlhood talks had evolved into quick phone calls for updates on the kids or occasional evenings spent as couples. And then, except for the few minutes we would find ourselves together in one of our kitchens, cleaning up after having shared a meal, all conversations, as they had for years, took place in the presence of the men.

On one such visit I had driven to the store with Sherry while the men prepared the barbecue. This was at the time when my husband and I were talking separation. "What's wrong?" she asked. "You seem so unhappy." I was uncomfortable talking about my revelation and what had been going on at home, but at the same time, it felt like such a relief to be able to talk. Sherry listened, nodding from time to time. "You weren't having your needs met," she said, "and the person who gave you what you needed just happened to be a woman. I never thought of being with a woman—but that doesn't make it wrong, it just makes it different. I guess you can't help your life circumstances."

Before we got out of the car, Sherry assured me that she still loved me and that this didn't change her old feelings of friendship toward me. During a phone conversation afterward she said, "I was surprised about your gayness. I thought, where did that come from? In all of the years we've been friends I didn't see that in your life at all. I don't think it was something you thought about. I think it just happened."

A few weeks later I told Beth what was going on. Beth was my very oldest friend. She, like Sherry, assured me that this didn't change her feelings of friendship toward me.

While I feel the same old warmth and caring each time we speak, our lives are presently taking different paths. I don't know for certain if they ever told their husbands. No one has ever brought up the subject in front of my husband or me, but invitations to their homes have become fewer. I understand their discomfort with our situation, and their fear of dividing their loyalties.

JAN

"My best friend Emily and I met through our husbands at a company dinner and, because neither of us lived near our families, we became surrogate families for each other. We celebrated holidays and birthdays together and we had gone with our husbands on some business trips too. Now her husband had changed jobs and they had moved to a different state. We spent hours on the phone. Still, it took a long time for me to build up the courage to tell Emily my secret. I thought I was past the emotional part, but as soon as I started talking, I started crying. Through tears I told her what I was and how I knew and everything that had happened to me since she moved and how I felt, etc. Emily didn't know what to say after 'oh.' There was a pause, then she said, 'I have to go now,' and hung up. I was devastated.

"Normally we took turns calling each other. But when she missed her turn, I called her. 'I'm sorry if I said something to offend you. I thought you would understand.'

" 'No,' " she said, " 'you didn't offend me. You just hit too close to home. I've been going through hell for the past few years wondering about myself, but I never had the guts to find out for sure. And I was afraid to say anything to anyone, even to you.' "

"It was my turn to say, 'Oh.' "

CAROL

When friends are intuitive, coming out to them is not always necessary. Carol, married and the mother of two small children, works in the film industry. Between her private life and her work life, she balances a very busy schedule but has always made time for her friends. Until, while working closely on a special project with another woman, she felt an odd sort of pull. She had never consciously thought about her sexuality, and kept telling herself the feeling was only because they worked so well together. Still, she says, "When our project was completed, I was afraid she would go out of my life, and I couldn't bear that. I asked her to join me for dinner, and that was the beginning of us together."

Carol laughed. "One old friend said, 'What's been going on with you?' I said, 'I've been working incredibly hard.' She said, 'You've worked long hours before, but you've returned my phone calls. You're having an affair with a woman, aren't you?' She said she knew because, if it had been a man, I would have confided in her. She was right.

"All of my friends know now and every one of them has been very supportive."

Carol's mother also intuitively knew. Carol says, "Before I told my mother about us, I told her there was stuff going on in my marriage and I didn't know how long I could stay in it. She got really upset about the kids and what would happen to them.

"I realized she was bringing up her own fears and eventually I began to retreat from her. But she was so concerned that finally I said, 'Mom, I'm really happy, but I'm going through a difficult period.'

"Although we don't fit the traditional stereotypes of lesbians, once she met my friend, my mother had a feeling. She told me she felt a tremendous energy between the two of us. She's been really terrific about it. She hasn't told my father, nor have I. I never had a terrific relationship or communication with him, so if my mother is comfortable with him not knowing, that's okay."

□ □ □ □

While I had a need to be known and accepted by my mother, I once told a friend, "I tried to tell my mother about myself, but she just doesn't get it."

"Your mother doesn't get it because you didn't give it," she said. I knew she was right. I had been sidestepping the topic. I had told my mother about the book I was working on, about going to Washington to join the march for gay rights, and even about two of my friends who had played a part in bringing about domestic rights for same-sex partners, but I had never said, "Mom, I recently found out that I am a lesbian."

Telling my mother was not easy, especially over a long-distance phone line, but I was tired of the shallow chitchat that had begun to pass for conversation between us. I needed to know that she loved me unconditionally, not based on an image she had created of me.

There were pauses and I could hear her quiet sobs as I told her about my feelings for Toby and how they had caused me to lose her friendship, of the pain I had endured and the isolation I had lived with since making my discovery.

"I knew you were unhappy," my mother said. "But I had no idea why. I'm glad you told me. I wish I could have been there to help you." She said she was sorry that I was a lesbian because she knew how hard being different could be. She would have preferred my life to be less difficult. And while she was saddened by how my being a lesbian would affect my husband and the security of the life I had created with him, by the end of our phone call I felt closer to my mother than I ever had in my entire life, and I believe she felt the same toward me.

For many MWLW, the decision to come out to their mothers is one of the most difficult. Still, Sherry Zitter, M.S.W., L.I.C.S.W., says that a daughter's coming out to her mother can be a positive step. "For a mother, a daughter's coming out may revive her own early same-sex attraction; it may feel like abandonment, rejection, sexual intrusion, or affirmation and validation; it may precipitate a mourning process for the wished-for heterosexual daughter; and it may induce altruistic satisfaction that her daughter has the opportunity for sexual and emotional reciprocity.

"From a family systems perspective, coming out often creates a clearer boundary between mother and daughter. . . . The coming-out process rejects cultural norms, proclaims a woman's sexuality, and challenges the heterosexual assumption. . . . Coming out to one's mother, as an appropriate and well-informed decision, can be a vital and life-affirming developmental task."

The reluctance to tell a mother, for most MWLW, stems from their societal upbringing in which different often equates with unacceptable. Fear of losing the "good girl" status women hold within their family is often enough to warrant their silence. These fears are not unfounded.

" 'A son is yours 'til he finds a wife, but a daughter is yours for the rest of your life.' This proverb succinctly describes what many mothers expect of their children. When a mother raises a son, she generally expects to lose him to another woman someday. When she raises a daughter, however, she usually anticipates that even if that daughter marries a man, Mother will always be the most important *woman* in her daughter's life. This myth, which runs deep in our culture and our psyche, may be primary in a mother's reaction to her daughter's coming out."

One reason some women initially keep their sexual preference from their mothers is the fear that they will be consumed with guilt, and assume responsibility for their daughter's homosexuality.

ROBIN

"My mother did so much for us kids that I didn't want her to think this is something she fucked up about. She would blame herself. When we were growing up, although my father had left us, she never trashed him. She had every opportunity and every reason. She let us grow up to be rational adults and to make up our own minds about our father and to establish our own relationships with him.

"I thought, if I tell her, she'll go through her own mind, thinking, 'Did I do something to make it seem like men were horrible? Was I too strong?' She would blame herself."

Eventually Robin realized that her reasons for not telling her mother were not as selfless as they first appeared to be.

When Robin told her mother she was having marital problems,

her mother said, "I hope you're not being influenced by your homosexual friends. Are you?"

" 'Oh, no, Mother. God forbid,' I said. I was nervous as hell. Later in the conversation I took that back. I'm thirty-seven years old. Why should I be nervous in front of my mother?"

While some families open their arms with acceptance and love upon receiving the information that their daughter or sister is an MWLW, others totally reject their own children. One woman said, "I thought I was disapproving of my daughter because she had left her husband and gone to live with another woman. Then I realized I was harboring a tinge of envy too. She had had the courage to do something she really wanted to do. I had spent my entire life being held back by what I was 'supposed to' or 'not supposed to' do."

Some parents fail to see their children, even their adult children, as individuals. They view their offspring only as extensions of themselves and are interested in the persons their children are supposed to be, while their true identities are discounted.

Parents are not the only ones to discount their daughters' true sexual inclinations in their need to keep their own world unaltered. MWLW often have a strong need to conform to what they believe are their parents' perceptions of how things are supposed to be. Trying to be the daughters they are supposed to be causes them to stifle themselves, or to develop two different personas, one for the family and one for themselves.

JUANITA

Juanita had never considered her sexuality, although she remembers being frustrated with her friendships as a teenager. Though they were intense, they never seemed intense enough. She felt like she wanted more but she didn't know what. She knew she was supposed to get married and have a baby and that's what she did.

"I was connected to the me that other people wanted me to be," Juanita says, "and that was connected to my sexuality. Because to be the daughter my mother wanted, my father wanted, my sister wanted, I needed to play certain roles, and in order to fulfill these roles it was critical that I suppress my sexuality. Looking back, I think that was a big part of it."

While Juanita has now learned who she is, and is able to feel powerful and positive about herself, she still has problems dealing with her family. "I still turn to my family, and it scares the shit out of me to ever say to my mother, 'Mom, I'm a lesbian' or 'Mom, this is the person I love and she makes me happier than anyone in the world ever did.' She would have a heart attack and drop dead and I would feel like shit, so, even though I feel great about myself, I'm Latina and in my family it would be such a major shock. Forget it."

Because Juanita's strength and confidence have grown and she is now able to accept herself, she is able to accept her family with their limited ability to understand. While she may or may not ever tell her family about the secret she lives with, she does say they have noticed a positive change and commented on the "new Juanita."

MIRIAM

Miriam speaks for many women when she voices this common complaint. "I have felt for years that my parents don't know me, and that was long before my sexuality. They see what they want to see, and they are very limited, so I decided long ago not to waste my breath. It's a shame though. I am out to almost all of my friends. Although I would like who I really am not to be so jarring to them, I don't think I could ever sit with my mother and swap confidences.

"I feel, under the circumstances, that I am a mythical being. I hate the myth my parents have constructed about what my life is and who I am. They have the constant assumption of heterosexuality. They don't love me but some construct."

Still, for this need of family approval, Miriam, a grown woman with a child of her own, leads a pretend life, always being "the good little daughter." Presently, Miriam's bedroom remains as it always has, with one large bed the focal point. While she or her husband sleeps on the couch, Miriam ponders, "How could I explain separate bedrooms to my mother?" Although they have the space for another bedroom, the other room remains the den. She says, "I find it painful and annoying that I have to accommodate for that all of the time. It makes me wish I lived nowhere near my parents."

□   □   □   □

While coming out created discord for some, the majority of MWLW felt that revealing themselves almost invariably strengthened whatever bonds already existed between themselves and close friends or family members.

JOSIE

Josie remembers the day she told her mother. She had only recently discovered her feelings and found herself crying throughout the long drive from her home to her parents' in a neighboring state. "When I got there, I took my mother out for lunch. My dad didn't want to join us. After lunch I just cried, telling her that I was in love with two people. She listened. I wasn't going to tell her that the second person was a woman. She brought it out.

"It was very relieving. She said something beautiful. 'Look how lucky you are that two people love you. Most people go through life never knowing that even one person loves them.' "

At some time Josie's mother told her father. "He knows but he doesn't talk about it much," Josie says.

AMBER

The majority of women who were out to their parents said that they communicated primarily with their mothers, and that their fathers didn't talk much. Amber, on the other hand, says, "I was raised in Texas by a very racist Catholic family. My mother was awful. She and my husband felt it was their duty to notify all my relatives when they found out about me. She sees my relationship as dirty and has referred to it as 'rolling around on the floor having sex in front of your children.' You can see how uneducated and homophobic she is. But my father's and brother's reactions were wonderful. 'Amber needs someone to love,' they said."

ANTOINETTE

Antoinette came from a very privileged home in the South. While in college, she spent a lot of time photographing women, clothed and unclothed. She had overnights with friends. "I remember I touched one of my friend's breasts and she stiffened up. I apologized and felt ashamed and guilty."

Antoinette was in denial and never realized that she might be attracted to women. "These are things I sort of put away," she says. "Still, I always had a sense of being different. Maybe that's why I dated the people I dated." Antoinette entered into an interracial marriage, even though both her parents and her in-laws were opposed. She looks at that decision, in retrospect, as a stepping-stone to coming out.

Eventually, she connected with a woman and privately acknowledged her sexuality. Before she was ready to make the news public, however, her mother guessed. They were driving together, when her mother said, "Are you attracted more to men or to women?"

"I thought I'd drive off the road," Antoinette says. "I wasn't ready to tell her, but I had to." She gave her mother *Loving Someone Gay* and *The Other Side of the Closet*, which she had also given to her husband.

"My mother had picked up on a comment I had made during a visit. She had told me of a young man they knew who was gay. 'So?' I had asked.

" 'His parents don't know and he doesn't acknowledge it.'

"I said, 'That's really too bad that he can't share that important part of his life.'

"My mother said, 'That was something overly sensitive for you to say and it started me wondering.' "

Antoinette's mother told her father. He said he wasn't surprised. "I knew things were not going well with your marriage, and when you had come to visit us and got a call from your girlfriend late at night, I thought, 'Why would a friend be calling so late. It must be more than friendship.' "

Still, Antoinette says, "My father was very upset when he found out . . . not because his daughter liked women, but because he didn't want the neighbors to know."

Antoinette had the rector at her church send her parents a book called *Now That You Know*. She says that since then, her mother has bought and passed out five copies to family and friends. Now her father is reading the book and they are working it through.

□ □ □ □

Not all parents are concerned with what the neighbors will think, or how same-sex relationships reflect on the family. For most parents, the primary concern is "If you leave your marriage, who will take care of you?" They want their children to be safe and cared for.

CHARLENE

Charlene is another woman who has confided in her father. He is one of her most staunch supporters, although that was not always the case.

When she came out to her parents, everything came out, including the incidences of abuse she had lived with: having been molested by a cousin when she was three and having been raped at seventeen. While she does not feel that these events made her a lesbian, it was only after her father learned of them that he was able to accept her for who she was. Charlene says, "I got total restitution. My father then wanted to protect his daughter, he wanted to champion my cause. He said, 'So that's why you turned to women. It all makes sense now.' That's the way he thought, so I said, 'Okay, Daddy, that's fine.' I was just glad to have my parents back."

Once family and friends learn to ignore labels and see people for who they are, most women report fondness on the part of their families for their special women friends, even to welcoming them into the family with open arms.

LETTY

Letty had been attracted to women before she married, but because she also liked men she felt marriage would work. Yet when her first lover reappeared in her life, she couldn't bear to lose her again, nor could she give up her husband or children. "I had to step away from the prevailing culture and really claim my right to define what's right and wrong in my own value system. That is what I have tried to do." While Letty still lives with her husband and child, Rebecca has become another family member.

"It's taken a while for my family to take to all of this. It was funny, because it was like coming out all over again. I came out years ago, before I got married. It was no longer an issue, and then I thought, oh, God, I have to go through this all over again. Still, everyone in my life is incredibly supportive of what I am doing. I am fortunate. My mother knows Rebecca and she thinks she's bright and really likes her. She also loves my husband. My brother also really loves Rebecca and gets along with my husband. We all have mutual friends and basically everyone knows and is supportive."

ROSA

Rosa never came out to her family, but simply went about the business of incorporating her lover into her life. She believes that her family sensed the special importance of her friend.

"Since my father has been in a nursing home, my mother has been preoccupied with the whole subject of homosexuality. She read Rock Hudson's story as soon as it was published and seems to expound on the subject a lot of the time. I don't know if it's because my father's absence creates a less oppressive atmosphere or if it is a natural interest of hers or she senses the relationship that Lillie and I have and wants to project her understanding.

"When Lillie arrived, she began attending most family gatherings with us. My family accepted her as if she had always belonged, never asking how we'd gotten to know her or why she moved in with us. My parents had never included 'outsiders,' and I found this immediate acceptance interesting."

While Rosa has never explained explicitly to her mother the part that Lillie plays in her life, she believes that her mother knows how important Lillie is to her.

Often, hearing that a daughter is considering divorce is more distressing for her parents than hearing that she is a lesbian. The fact that the secure world they have envisioned for their daughter might be toppling can take precedence over discovering her new sexuality, especially when children are involved.

MARTHA

"I'm a better mother since finding out about myself. Therapy has helped me to experience all of the pain that I'd held back. I'm much more compassionate toward my son and toward my friends. It's helped me to be able to relate to people better.

"For my family, though, I have no desire to be more understanding. My mother doesn't want me to be divorced. She is upset that I have changed everything and it's not even the issue of my sexual orientation. It's the fact that I've changed everybody's lives by saying I don't want to be married anymore. She condemns me, so there is no support from my family. My brother, who was on my side, has taken my mother's side. He's not judging me, he's not against me for coming out or for wanting to get divorced. But he thinks I should be treating my mother differently. That I should be making peace with her."

LESLIE

Leslie, although not out to her family, is facing the same kinds of accusations and rejection from them as Martha because of her announcement of divorce.

Throughout college Leslie had been able to deny her suspicions about her same-sex attraction. Her suspicions were confirmed, however, when she was intimate with another woman two weeks before her wedding. She thought her feelings for the woman, and women in general, would go away at that point, but she wasn't certain, so she discussed them with her husband-to-be. He believed he could deal with her inclinations and they proceeded with the wedding as planned.

Nevertheless, after the wedding Leslie realized she had made a mistake. She really cared about her husband, and didn't want to hurt him any more than she already had, so she decided to leave him.

Leslie then realized where she fit within her family's priorities. Their need to maintain status quo, as well as their need for acceptance within their small community, took precedence over her happiness.

"My family is very nonsupportive," Leslie says. "They're so upset that I'm leaving my husband that they can't deal with anything else. My brother thinks I'm crazy and callous and that I traumatized my husband. I really am not these things. I've been honest with my husband the whole time, but how honest could I be with my family? They say they're so humiliated about my wanting to leave my marriage that they're talking about moving out of town.

"Divorce is *not* something that happens in our family. I don't want to be cut off from my family, but I'd almost rather be cut off than be treated like I'm being treated now: all of their phone calls telling me what an awful person I am, my mother crying all the time, my dad screaming at me that I didn't go to church.

"Can you imagine how they would behave if they knew the real reason for my divorce?"

An MWLW, when she tells her parents about herself, must understand that there is no guarantee of acceptance. How parents process the information or to reject it is based on their own resolved or unresolved issues. While some parents become estranged from their daughters, others choose a path of understanding, acceptance, and unconditional love, and still others choose denial as a way of dealing with, or not dealing with, the information they have been given.

DARCIE

"I am a WASP," Darcie says. "My family is very straitlaced. I remember calling my mother and telling her that I was moving in with Melissa after my divorce.

"My mom said, 'Are you taking a two-bedroom apartment?'

" 'No,' I said, 'One.' "

Her mother said, "Twin beds?"

"No," Darcie said.

"Is there any hanky-panky going on?" her mother asked.

Darcie said, "Mom, do you really want to know?"

She said, "Yes. That's why I'm asking."

Darcie said, "Okay. There is hanky-panky going on."

Her mother said, "Oh. I have to turn the vacuum cleaner off," and she hung up.

Although her mother had been in the habit of calling several times a week, she didn't call for three weeks. When Darcie resumed the phone calls, her mother's conversation began as though nothing out of the ordinary had happened. Darcie took her cue from her mother and since then has not discussed her sexuality. "This 'if we don't talk about it, it doesn't exist' attitude works for us."

Initially, the two major concerns parents seem to have upon discovering that their married daughters are gay are morality and the survival of their family. However, the reasons that cause people to accept or reject a situation are far more complex.

Family dynamics are likely to change as a result of the information an MWLW gives to her parents, and deep psychological issues may come to a head.

For instance, "In a family where a father has had an overclose relationship with his daughter, a mother may view her daughter as a rival," says Sherry Zitter in her article, "Coming Out to Mom." "Coming out as a lesbian in such a family may actually engender a sense of relief in the lesbian's mother, who might see her daughter as less threatening to her own marital relationship. Father, however, may feel quite rejected by his daughter's choice of women as sex partners. Possibly his own repressed incest fantasies must be given up, as well as feeling a fantasized sexual rejection. This may be a factor in a family where a mother has accepted the lesbianism much more easily than a father. (In view of high incest statistics, we must confront the reality that in many families, a father has had an actual incestuous relationship with his daughter. His reaction to her coming out could then involve anger at her rejection of sexual involvement with him, as well as some guilt at 'causing her lesbianism.')"

In-laws don't have as much of a personal investment in the MWLW as her own parents do. Their primary concern is with their son, who is being affected by his wife's sexuality, and with their grandchildren, who they may see as being harmed by their mother's lesbianism and a split within the family. Some women spoke of support and understanding from their mothers-in-law, while others had stories such as Phyllis's.

PHYLLIS

Before they were married, Phyllis had confided in her husband that she thought she was bisexual. He said he didn't think it was a problem. Still, aware of the prejudices of others, she was always careful not to reveal her secret further. She especially had no intention of telling her in-laws about herself, and he agreed.

Seven years later, what had at first appeared to be of little consequence in their marriage grew into a major problem as her husband's angry moods and drinking escalated. "While I was at the Gay Pride Parade, my husband, drunk, told my in-laws I was out trying to find myself. So my mother-in-law called me to ask if I was a lesbian. She was asking questions and answering them for me: 'You can't be a lesbian because you have two children,' 'I know you're not,' and on and on. So I let her rant and rave and when she was finally done, I said, 'I choose not to discuss my sexuality with you.'

"It's never been a great relationship. I felt, in spite of that, I had done everything I could to make it better. But this news rocked their world and for a while they didn't want to kiss me when they saw me. It was a bombshell."

Just as an MWLW may choose to come out to one parent and may not necessarily feel the need to come out to the other, like-wise, anticipated negative consequences may prevent her from sharing her identity with all of her siblings. The bond she shares with each individually will usually determine who she decides to confide in.

SHARI

Although they don't see each other often, or talk much on the phone, Shari describes her relationship with her brother as open and intimate. Still, she was amazed at how easily he accepted her disclosure.

She says, "When I came out to him, about a month after I came out to myself, his reaction was really surprising—even more so considering that he belongs to a fairly strict Christian denomi-nation. He actually laughed and said, 'I was wondering when you were going to tell me!' That felt great—that he had for some time been aware of my sexual orientation and accepted it as part of the whole me."

When I decided to tell my siblings, I wasn't actually involved with anyone. There is a big difference between confiding your sexuality to someone and introducing them to a lover. It was easier for me to tell them in the abstract, and it was probably easier for them to get used to the idea.

The very close relationship I share with my sister, four years my junior, emanated from my disclosure to her. While we had always been devoted, and I would have done anything for her, other than a biological connection I felt as though we had little in common. We saw the world from different perspectives. Once, before coming out to her, we had been walking in the city and I led the way into a gay bookstore. "Let's check this out," I said, wanting to get some sense of how she felt. She said she'd wait for me outside. She was so uncomfortable that not only did she wait outside, she waited down the street. So I couldn't imagine her being able to understand, or, more important, accept the truth about me. I needn't have worried. I put off telling her until one day when she called, I was feeling so overwhelmed that I just had to let it all out. Although we had never been able to express our emotions openly before, I found myself crying as I recounted everything that had led to my discovery. My sister listened quietly. When I had finished she said, "I'm only sorry you didn't feel comfortable enough to tell me at the beginning so that you wouldn't have had to go through so much pain alone."

My older brother, though he tends to hide his feelings, was equally supportive. "You're my sister," he said simply when I told him. "Nothing can change that." Then, kind of gruffly, because he wasn't comfortable voicing his feelings, he said, "I love you."

Both my brother and sister were concerned about my husband, who has been like their brother for so many years. "You're both special people," my sister said, "I don't want to see either of you hurt, but you are different. I want you both to be happy."

When I told my sister-in-law about me, she said, "I love you and would like you to continue to be my sister-in-law but even if your marriage doesn't work out, I'd like you to continue to be my friend."

For me, the greatest moment of acceptance came when I broached the subject of going to the gay parade with my mother. I had hesitated because she was visiting with my aunt Gertie, whom I hadn't told.

"Aunt Gertie knows," my mom said. "I told her, and we'd love to go."

Both women, one sixty-nine and the other seventy-nine, came with me to the parade. We all marched carrying signs. Theirs read: PROUD OF MY GAY DAUGHTER and PROUD OF MY GAY NIECE. Mine read: PROUD OF MY STRAIGHT MOM AND AUNT.

My mother and my aunt were awed by the thousands upon thousands of marchers: young and old, men and women, doctors, lawyers, teachers, mechanics, productive members of society. "These people aren't monsters. Just people like us," my mother said.

PART THREE

Selfhood

9

Sexual Intimacy

I HAD SPENT MONTHS searching for information: reading, questioning, feeling completely disassociated and isolated. And then I met a woman and we connected. We talked for hours and hours over pasta and bread sticks in a small village café. Neither of us wanted to say good-bye when it was time to part. A few days later we went for a walk along the shorefront and talked some more. The third time we saw each other we came together, and I knew that I was a sexual human being.

Whether women were able to come together at once, or whether tremendous fears and insecurities dogged their attempts and delayed their sexual coming of age for years made no difference. What I learned as I interviewed women from across the country was that their first physically intimate relationships with other women were almost identical. They spoke of an immediate sense of well-being and rightness that came over them. They felt a new freedom when they connected with that other woman. Those who considered themselves heterosexual for most of their lives equated their first same-sex experience to an adolescence they now realized they had missed. I could identify with them.

While the women described sex with their husbands in mechanical terms, they spoke about their lovemaking with other women as being emotional, passionate, and all-inclusive. They reported a loss of the inhibitions that had been associated with their heterosexual relationships. They reported new feelings of acceptance and completeness.

Riva sums up her feelings: "With a man, I always felt that the physical aspect was expected. With a woman, there was a much richer and fuller kind of relationship. The physical aspect was just a component and not the totality of it."

While some women described their first same-sex experience in intimate sexual detail, for others the coming together was child-like and innocent.

MARGARET

Shortly after she married, Margaret was working in an office. "Carolyn walked in and I saw her. I would say the weather changed in my whole body. I don't even know what season it was. It looked like springtime; she looked like springtime. There could have been a snowstorm, but I doubt it. A part of me held in reserve suddenly woke up. It was a full-blown crush on sight. Everything at once . . . I felt enthralled. I didn't know what she was about. Nothing. All these things about love at first sight. I didn't think I was in love. I didn't know what I was. There was such a strong attraction. My eyes were truly riveted to her. And I thought: 'This is a momentary thing. She'll go away and I'll never see her again.'

"In the beginning, I thought I was being unfaithful to my husband, but I really didn't have much of a marriage to preserve. I had realized that and tried to work on it with him. I thought we should go for marriage counseling. He refused. I asked him if the sexual part of our relationship was important enough to save, and he said it was fine the way it was. It was diminishing. He had become impotent, tired, disinterested.

"I felt very uncomfortable and I wanted to straighten it out because I felt responsibility for him and the union, but he wasn't willing. I tried again, and when he refused, I said, 'The sexual part of our marriage is coming to an end. If you won't come to counseling with me, then I can't sleep with you.' And he said that was okay with him.

"After that I had more energy to be free in my sexuality.

"It got to be that Carolyn became more and more affectionate in a natural, loving, wonderful way, decent and normal. I felt my reaction was not normal. I brought my feelings to her attention with apologies, while we were driving together, certain I was going to get over it. But in the meantime, I told her, it would be a good idea if she wasn't so affectionate.

"Carolyn said to me, 'I have similar feelings.' When she said that, I thought my car had gone into a 180 degree spin. I was overwhelmed. It made me feel very sexual for the first time in my life. And very appealing and attractive. I felt I had come home. I felt wonderfully alive."

Shortly after their conversation in the car, the two women were watching television. "I remember Carolyn saying, 'I would really like to kiss you.' I remember looking straight ahead and saying, 'Why don't you?' Then I wondered who had said that. Was that me? And I turned toward her and she kissed me. Very sweetly, very lovingly, very softly, very wonderfully. A six-dimensional kiss for me. Everything rolled into one. I didn't know what it meant or what you call it, but it was just so wonderful for me. It was a very mild, young, innocent, beautiful kiss."

That was not the beginning of their physical relationship, however. Neither woman could deal with the demands that her feelings were making on the other, nor with what she was feeling physically. For more than five years they fought, alternately breaking off communication, then reuniting.

"I behaved like I was twelve years old," says Margaret. "I was very unsure of myself, very bashful, very backward. I needed to be egged on and encouraged and I perceived Carolyn as behaving like a woman of the world. Sexy, alluring, sure of herself.

"I was so shy the first time we went to bed together. We planned on having some sort of sex, but we didn't know what. I lay down beside Carolyn and she said, 'Do you want to take your shoes off? How about your coat?' I behaved very jerky every step of the way. Almost like I didn't understand the English language."

"I didn't see myself as worldly," Carolyn said. "Neither of us quite understood what was going on or what we were getting involved in."

Eventually Carolyn divorced her husband, not because of her sexuality, but because he was abusive; though Margaret remained in her marriage, she never came out to her husband and neither woman has come out to her children. Now in their early sixties, the two women are still in a loving relationship, and Carolyn says, "Looking at Margaret still brings the same rush of joy."

According to Shere Hite, for generations "female sexuality has been seen essentially as a response to male sexuality and intercourse. There has rarely been any acknowledgment that female sexuality might have a complex nature of its own which would be more than just the logical counterpart of (what we think of as) male sexuality."

In the fifties, women were given little or no sex information. Boys at least had all sorts of ego-enhancing appellations for their penises, from given names to titles such as "The Monster" and "Mr. Wonderful," whereas girls simply referred to their genitals as "down there" or "privates."

Dalma Heyn writes in *The Erotic Silence of the American Wife*, "Daughters do not hear a great deal about sexual pleasure, from their mothers or anyone else—and how can silence beget anything but more silence? With no expression of girls' erotic feelings, no discourse of pleasure and desire passed from mother to daughter, no narratives of a girl's coming into sexual awareness, there exists no language for them in which to speak about their own experience. And because they do not speak, it is easy to assume girls' desire does not exist—for why wouldn't they say so, if it did?"

If women were given any sexual information, they were taught that after marriage, their sexual pleasure *should* come from their husband's penis. This frequently did not happen, yet silence kept each woman believing that this sexual inadequacy was hers alone.

Sexual surveys such as *The Hite Report* have done much to dispel this myth, as have sex counselors or experts like Betty Dodson, author of *Sex for One*. Dodson finds that while women are now willing to talk about their sexual fears and hangups, men are less open. "Somehow men were supposed to have gained enough sexual expertise to teach women about sex. But having to project a masculine image at all times kept them from learning. If you already know all the answers, you can't ask questions."

Women are attracted to women for all the same reasons that men are. As Nancy Friday, in *Women on Top*, explains, "There is something uniquely satisfying in a woman's body that cannot be had with a man. As sexually exciting and elegant as a male body may be, it lacks the obvious physical attributes of our first source of love, mother. It isn't just the breasts, it's the texture of the skin, the smell, the whole mysterious aura of that first body we lay against, which fed, warmed, and overwhelmed us with its power. . . . How could any of us, male or female, forget that relationship?

"Whatever sexual pleasure women may find with a man, they cannot get this primitive physicality with him . . . even the most tender of men cannot offer the unique satisfaction found in a woman's body."

Psychotherapist Hedda Begelman says, "Women have always been nurturers. When women connect with one another, they have a chance to know what it is like to *be* nurtured. They learn that making love is more than sexual intercourse. Their new knowledge is frightening to men like Freud, who have taken it upon themselves to tell women how they are 'supposed to' feel."

Women had been led by Freudian theory to believe that orgasms caused by clitoral stimulation were adolescent and that, upon puberty, when they began having intercourse with men, vaginal orgasms would naturally replace clitoral ones. Before Shere Hite's *The Hite Report* came out and dispelled this belief, women believed that if this did not happen, they were at fault, either being immature or needing to resolve sexual conflicts.

In the early 1990s, *Sex in America,* a survey designed by academics at the University of Chicago's National Opinion Research Center, questioned 3,432 men and women and found that while 75 percent of American men experience orgasm every time they have intercourse, only 29 percent of American women experience orgasm. If intercourse were the only "natural form of sex," the percentages of orgasms for men and women ought to be more equal.

RENEE

By the time Renee was twenty-three, she had had four children. While she had no idea of her true sexual identity when she married, she knew that sex wasn't one of the things she married for.

"But," Renee says, "I thought I could put up with it because I wanted a normal life."

Renee's husband made many sexual demands on her and she soon discovered that "when I am pregnant, I could say no to him. When I was nursing I could say no too. That's why I have so many kids."

There was very little to their relationship, but the routines and responsibilities of the household and young family kept the couple too busy for the first few years for them to realize this. It was only after she started therapy to trace the source of her unhappiness that Renee was able to identify herself as an MWLW.

Coitus has been set up to be the norm and, as most therapists would have us believe, any deviation from it is a sign of sexual dysfunction and, as such, abnormal. What is deceptive is trying to limit physical relations between humans to intercourse alone. Women who are with other women know that having intercourse and making love are not necessarily synonymous. When women connect, because there is no need to culminate their lovemaking with the physical act of male penetration, there is more of an equality.

LYNN

"Men have always been conditioned to define themselves more through how much they make and what they do for a living; relationships are not *sooo* terribly important to them, not like to a woman.

"I had an affair with a man and I didn't feel I had to leave my marriage. But when I was with *her*, it was just so synchronized.

"When I was dating her, I didn't have to say to myself, 'Is she going to call tomorrow?' She called tomorrow. With her I didn't have to wonder, 'Are we talking too much?' With a guy, I always wondered. With her I felt so much more welcome. My body wasn't an issue. With guys it was 'Am I skinny enough?' With her I didn't worry. I always felt welcome. I felt like it was just right. I didn't feel lacking or wanting. I felt she intuitively understood me much better than men did.

"And I also had no power struggle with her because she was a woman. With men I'd get into, 'What do you mean by that? Are you trying to put me down?' I became more defensive with men, feeling I'd have to explain myself more to be understood. I didn't have those issues with her. I felt more loved, more safe, more comfortable.

"Maybe it was my own issues with men. Men need you to take care of them emotionally. They feel very entitled to many things from women. To talk first, to talk most, their day is harder than your day, what they go through is harder than what you go through. You do all this nurturing for men. We do it, and we do it so naturally that we don't even know we do it, so when you're with a woman who's been taught to nurture, it was interesting to get that nurturing back. Not that I did anything differently. I did the same thing I did with men, but I got so much more back. So it felt so much more complete."

LOIS

"Trying to understand and communicate with a man is so much work. I think it's a genetic thing, like men have selective vision. When women are fixing a meal together they just go out there and do it and they work side by side. They put something in a pan and someone stirs it and someone puts a lid on, kind of like a ballet. When you're in the kitchen with a man, you're each just trying to stay out of each other's way. Women just fit. The steps work out. . . .

"I have a lot of lesbian friends, but it never even entered my mind that I would ever be that way," Lois, thirty-seven, married for five years, and positive about her heterosexual orientation, says. "Initially, when we first got married, there was definitely sexual attraction between my husband and me. We had a great sex life. But the longer we were married, the more and more infrequent it became. . . ."

For years Lois had traveled on the road with her husband and fellow entertainers. Because of a change in her status to manager, Lois felt cut off from him and the other men who had been her friends.

"The feeling of isolation I had grew so strong," she says, "that I turned to another woman on tour for friendship. She was vivacious, energetic, and intellectual and all those wonderful words.

She'd had a history as a lesbian but she wasn't the one who initiated our relationship. I was.

"It started as a friendly relationship between us and then it became more emotional. Then physical things were happening with me.

"I know if it was strictly sex I needed, I certainly could have gotten that from my husband. No. That wasn't the reason I turned to her. Emotionally I had a need that was not being filled. Things were evolving with my husband and me and not in a good direction.

"Sexually, everything with her felt right from the start. Wonderful and right. I don't know what came first, if it was that emotionally I was not getting what I needed from my husband so I went someplace else, or if it was because there was so much great energy coming from her that I was drawn like a magnet.

"Ever since I'd been with her . . . the pleasure [with my husband] definitely seemed to wane in comparison. My body didn't respond the same way. I was definitely more excited with her and it was more from touch. The feeling of her skin was better than the feeling of his skin. The way he touched me was not the same.

"Making love with my husband became really stilted. It was almost like I would see how long I could hold my breath and hope that it would get over soon. With her if it went on for hours, that was terrific with me."

The fallacy that a woman cannot be made love to without a man is shared by educated and uneducated people alike. Dr. David Reuben, the author of *Everything You Always Wanted to Know About Sex but Were Afraid to Ask*, in response to the question "What do female homosexuals do?" quips, "One vagina plus another vagina equals zero." Contrast this sexist response with that of Dr. Earle M. Marsh, assistant clinical professor of obstetrics and gynecology at the University of California Medical Center. At a 1968 series of lectures on sex, Dr. Marsh was quoted as saying: "It's too bad that every male cannot have instruction from a female homosexual prior to marriage. Only a female homosexual really knows how to make love to a woman. We, as men, are kind of duds along those lines."

One woman and her female friend had been physically intimate for several years. When I asked her if she ever experienced feelings of guilt or betrayal toward her husband while with her friend, she was surprised. "Neither of us has a penis, so we're not really having sex."

As Hite wrote, ". . . the role of women in sex, as in every other aspect of life, has been to serve the needs of others—men and children. And just as women did not recognize their oppression in a general sense until recently, just so sexual slavery has been an almost unconscious way of life for most women . . . our model of sex and physical relations is *culturally* (not biologically) defined, and can be redefined—or undefined. We need not continue to have only one model of physical relations—foreplay, penetration, intercourse, and ejaculation."

HELENE

"It wasn't until ten years after I started having affairs with men that I fell in love with my best friend. I realize now I was seeking intimacy. With men there had always been a challenge and a thrill but intimacy and romance were lacking.

"When I fell in love with my best friend, I suddenly realized that love and sex could be very much the same. Loving her made me want to love and have sex all in one and I realized that maybe that's what passion is. It supersedes everything. It was the first time I felt love and sex were entwined."

SHARI

"In the context of marriage, having an affair with a man is very different than an affair with a woman. Having an affair with a man is seeking something outside the marriage that should be obtained within the marriage. Having an affair with a woman is seeking something outside the marriage that could never be obtained within a marriage.

"The first time I held my special friend's hand was a sexual as well as an emotional experience. So was the first time I hugged her. That felt wonderful and true—like a dream coming to life. Skipping to the more intense stuff—clothes off, skin to skin, sucking her breast—felt amazing, mind-blowing, and so incredibly natural.

"The first time I put my hand between her legs I was so

shocked, all I could say was 'Oh, my God.' I was totally stunned at the warmth and wetness and softness between the sturdiness of her legs. The simultaneous thought was that I had actually touched heaven and the sea/origin of all life. Metaphysical concepts turned real in my hand.

"I was totally blown away. When she briefly licked me between my legs, the warmth and softness of her breath caught me so off guard that I could hardly talk. What I did manage to tell her—between gasps—was that this was like starting to pass through the gates of paradise. I couldn't pass all the way through, because if I did, I might never come back, meaning there would be nothing that could hold me to my family."

Long before she had her first experience with a woman, Shari's sex life with her husband had become intermittent. "It had become such a rare event that we actually forgot about it. From time to time we wondered why, but it didn't feel like an especially serious problem.

"As soon as I came out, I had an amazing surge of sexual energy and an intense desire to solidify our bond as a couple. So we started having sex again—maybe once a week or every two weeks—and it was more intense and pleasurable than I recalled it having been for a long time.

"As the months passed, the frequency has again dwindled. . . . Eddie is concerned that we might never have it again. I told him that over the years, my feelings about sex have changed so that now it's primarily an act of emotional bonding.

"While I try to help him to see that it is not a matter of personal rejection, I'm sure it has pretty much the same effect on him. In some ways it's a relief not to be active sexually with him, because I feel there are many ways to bond with him on an emotional level. However, I'm also fearful that he will emotionally move away from me because sex is currently not a part of our bonding."

BARBARA

"I believed that our society equates sex with marriage. The benefits of being in a marriage—legal rights, medical and insurance plans—are rewards for having legal sex. And I believed that even if I wasn't interested in sex, I didn't have the right to say no when my husband approached me.

"Still, I was shocked when I realized I was a lesbian. I certainly didn't know when I married. I knew I wasn't very interested in sex, but I thought I just had a low sex drive."

"I began doing different things to avoid sex with my husband: claiming headaches, creating additional periods or pretending they had lengthened, falling asleep on the couch rather than going into the bedroom.

"By the time I found out about myself, we had settled into a celibate marriage."

While some marriages become celibate at the time of the woman's announcement, often celibacy comes about, as it did in Barbara's marriage, before the woman actually identifies herself. In other marriages, while the sexual component is still in evidence, eventually it dwindles.

Barbara is not the only woman who has taken the path of a sexless marriage. Many heterosexual marriages continue long after the sexual component is gone.

On June 25, 1990, in a column called "Sex and Marriage," Ann Landers printed a letter from a woman in her late fifties who said that she and her husband had given up sex while in their forties and were content and happily married. They wondered if they were "oddballs." She asked, "How many other married couples live together happily without sex?" Ms. Landers conducted a poll and received over thirty-five thousand pieces of mail on that subject in two weeks. Landers found the following: "More than 65% of the couples over 60 years of age who wrote, and 75% of the couples over 70, have little or no sex and they don't miss it."

According to Landers's mail, "Men of all ages are far more interested in sex than women and an amazing number of women in all age groups consider sex a duty or a nuisance. They pretend to enjoy it and fake orgasms to keep their men happy. Some couples gave up on sex in their early 30s while others were still enjoying it in their 80s."

Diana Waltz, author of *Celibate Wives*, has found that the reasons for celibate marriages range from infidelity, boredom, loss of respect, alcoholism, illness, spiritual growth, and verbal abuse to simply incompatible sex drives.

As women grow more sexually astute, they are beginning to question the quality of their marital sex lives. Self-help books on improving marriages flood the market. Articles on making marriages work appear regularly in women's magazines. Some downplay sex, telling couples that all they need to do is lower their sexual expectations. Others offer suggestions for refining their sexual techniques.

DOROTHY

Dorothy, believing she had a low sex drive, never questioned her sexuality—until she fell in love with her friend. Because her love was not returned, and her friend was gone, all that remained for her was a haunting question: "Am I a lesbian?"

Searching for a confidante, Dorothy eventually met Tanya at a center for gays and lesbians. As a young girl in Russia, Tanya had had a physical relationship with a close girlfriend. Yet when she grew up, she married twice, wanting and trying to fit, not able to accept the fact that she preferred women.

Dorothy smiles. "We exchanged stories immediately. We spent a day walking in the park. Then we went up to her apartment to hear some tapes. When it was time for me to go, she gave me a hug good-bye. From somewhere deep inside my body a huge sigh escaped and I felt a sudden discharge between my legs. Confused, I stepped away and looked at her. Then, awkwardly, I came closer for another hug. The same thing happened.

"I walked downstairs bewildered, wondering about the wetness in my panties, eager to see Tanya again. I had been married for twenty-two years and had never experienced anything like this before.

"The following week she invited me over for the evening. I felt like a little kid getting ready for a party. I told my husband I was going to see my new friend, never realizing that she would be much more to me when I left her apartment later that evening.

"We sat and talked. Each time one of us shifted positions, our bodies came nearer. But we didn't touch. Then she got up and leaned against the back of a chair. I leaned against the piano facing her. We smiled at each other. She took my hands in hers and pulled me into her arms. Our lips touched. She cupped my face in her hands and whispered, 'When the time is right, I want to make love to you.'

"My legs turned to rubber and I held on to her so I wouldn't fall. 'The time is right,' I said. 'It's right . . . but I don't know what to do.'

"Tanya said, 'Do anything that you'd like to do.'

"I touched her face, running my fingers across her cheekbones and over her eyes, her lips. My fingers tingled. It felt like electricity jumping from her to me. I put my hand against her back, and timidly inched my fingers under her sweater. Her skin was so warm and soft and smooth.

"The two of us being together, what we were doing, it all seemed so natural. She led me to her bedroom and made love to me while I lay there touching her face, her breasts, her back and saying over and over again, 'Oh, my God, oh, my God. Thank you, thank you.' "

There is a scene from Fanny Flagg's *Fried Green Tomatoes* where the women have brought mirrors to class to study their private parts. Tawana is so uncomfortable, she can't look at her own body. Unfortunately, many women have been socialized to feel shame and embarrassment in regard to their bodies. When women experience physical intimacy with other women, however, they become freer and more comfortable with their bodies and are able to reexamine their old negative feelings and to form more positive attitudes toward themselves. Some women report that the initial experience of being with a woman, and the comfort level with their own bodies derived from it, stimulates their marital sex life.

ANGELA

Angela, strongly tied to her Italian roots, says, "For years I felt like I was going through the motions sexually. I wanted kids. After the first, I had no interest. I liked and cared about my husband, but we didn't have an emotional sharing. Men are raised not to express their feelings. Women are taught to be more expressive and more emotional, so I turned to women. I always turned to them emotionally. I always told my best friends more, much more than I did my husband, because he's not a feedback person. I can connect with women emotionally in a much more satisfying way than I can with men.

"When I started loving women, I began to look in the mirror and began to like myself. I guess I felt since I wasn't a size six and I didn't look like the women in magazines, I must not be beautiful. But somehow, when I connected my sexuality with women, I began to feel beautiful from the inside out.

"Once I took the pressure off myself and allowed me to love me, I felt more beautiful, sensual, and sexual than I ever had in my life. Because I feel better about me, I feel better about being physical with my husband.

"I enjoy sex with my husband much more since I discovered I love women."

Even those men willing to read marriage manuals about how to please their wives have difficulty understanding that it is the total psychological situation that many women react to. While men often see hugging as a precursor to sexual intercourse, often, between women, there is much hugging, touching, and kissing outside a sexual scenario as well as within one. Tenderness, nurturing, and caring are part of an intimate life that goes on all the time, not just when it's time to go to bed.

ELLEN

"With my husband, Dave, intercourse was never anything special, but not boring. He got off and that was fine with me. After a while we realized I could get off better on top, so we did that regularly. And I usually came that way too, but I never compared it to coming through masturbation. I have multiple orgasms in masturbation. Also, after he would come he would stop and that would leave me wanting more. I usually finished in the shower or tub.

"I don't think that before I met *her* I was aware that something was missing in my marriage. But once it happened I knew. It was the passion, tenderness, and softness of another woman."

Still, while some MWLW were, or became, completely turned off by male bodies, Ellen, who identifies herself as a lesbian, continues to have a sexual relationship with her husband.

She says, "I have always liked Dave's cock. Somehow we discovered anal intercourse. I am most satisfied when I give myself to him this way. To his way of thinking, no change has taken place since I have been involved with women. Actually there is one change. We have never done oral sex where he goes down on me. Now that I've been with women, this will never happen. That is reserved for women only."

GLENDA

Having been sexually indoctrinated in our heterosexual society, a small minority of women, coming together with another woman for the first time, remembered feeling great stress. Glenda, like other women, had spent her life judging her body against those she saw on billboards and in magazines. She says, "I was not young anymore. I was fifty-three. I was just so nervous about, 'Would she like me? Was my body going to be pleasing to her?'"

A highly successful executive in the corporate world, Glenda was a woman who needed total control in every aspect of her life, in the workplace and in bed as well.

Glenda says, "Actually, I was totally bewildered about the love aspect that grew out of our relationship because I had never thought beyond the physical.

"For many years, I never really thought about anything more than hugging and kissing another woman. I could imagine more, but it was not important. Then, two years ago, the desire to have an experience became very intense. Still, I don't think I would have had the nerve to go looking for another woman if I hadn't met my lover.

"We met at a twelve-step program. I had shared some of my feelings. We began to talk. It was very strange. A friendship didn't really have time to build up, but we had something in common. We were both married and in the same state of needing to have this experience. We were both conscious of each other's sexual inclinations, so from the beginning it was like a flirtatious friendship.

"We talked and I invited her to my office and we had dinner out and I began to realize that I was trying to impress her and there was an attraction. I think it began more as an experiment. I urged her on by asking her where the relationship was going. She looked at me like I was crazy.

"It took months. We were both shy. She finally just came over, took me in her arms, and kissed me. We began doing natural things, touching, caressing. We ended up in the bedroom.

"I remember saying, 'This feels so good, it can't be wrong.' I wanted to tell the whole world. I was so pleased, proud. I finally had found the courage to do something for myself. I experienced myself. I grew up.

"The first time we were together my lover had a tremendously natural orgasm," Glenda says. "I was very hot, but it didn't happen for me for the first couple of months because I am a control freak. I was aroused but I was afraid to let go. I could satisfy my lover but I couldn't let anybody make me vulnerable. Then she told me I was a fantastic lover. After that it got easier for me to let go.

"Still," Glenda confides, "when the first time was over, I cried. It was such a relief. It was so beautiful. I think it was the emotional thing of being with someone I trusted so much. It was a whole package, not just the physical thing I had thought it would be."

ELLIE

An account executive, Ellie met her first lover while working on a large ad campaign. For her the experience was completely absorbing, and for the first time in her life she opened herself up completely. "We worked on a project together. There was an emotional draw. Although we didn't have much in common, I found myself attracted to her in a way I had never felt before. I found myself making excuses to call her after we had finished the project. I began to obsess about her, and attributed it to wanting some sort of a kick. I invited her to join me for dinner.

"When we finally got together, I knew it was not a kick. I didn't want to stop. I knew there was more to this. I became a lunatic; I was crazed. After we slept together I felt like I was on another planet. I couldn't concentrate. I'd find myself reading the same line over and over because nothing would sink in. I had to summon every ounce of concentration to work, to listen to someone, to do anything. Either I wanted to be with her or I wanted to be alone. I felt like I was on another planet or I felt like I was an alien who had dropped on this planet. I had no idea what was going on around me. It was incredible. I found myself walking miles in the freezing cold, just totally lost all track of time. It was pretty intense.

"We saw each other the following weekend. This went on for a while. After four or five weeks she called me and told me she thought she was falling in love with me. 'No,' I told her, frightened. 'We're both having an infatuation but it's not love. It can't be. It has nothing to do with that.'

"I was a mess, a total wreck. I, of course, could not tell anyone about this. No one knew at all. I'd go away with my family on weekends and wait until my husband was out of the house so I could sneak a call to her. I'd be afraid he'd look at the bill and ask who I was calling. I became terrified of everything and the big thing was having no people to talk to. I started to retreat from people. My friends would call me for dinner and I'd think of an excuse not to join them. How could I sit and pretend I was having an intimate conversation when this was what my life was totally about now?"

FRAN

Now sixty, Fran was married for seventeen years and had two children before realizing her love of women. In retrospect, she realizes she had not been in love with her husband, "But I would never have known, as I didn't know about my sexuality and my sensuality. I certainly did not know what being in love was. I would have assumed that I thought that I loved him. I still certainly care for him at this time in my life. My relationship with my husband is null and void seventeen years already. But my caring for the person is still there.

"I've done my homework and I'm able to identify now that I have feelings of anger . . . of growing up in a time when he was supposed to teach me and he didn't. I was told, 'He will show you.' And I'm certainly talking about sex. 'He will give you what you're supposed to have.' He was supposed to be the sexual one, the aggressive one. What I'm angry about is that he didn't fill that role. It wasn't his fault either. We had both been duped."

Fran and her family had moved to Israel. Her best friend, Rifka, was living in the United States. Their friendship continued through letter writing. "The connection was always there," Fran says. "The caring was always there and I didn't know that more was involved or that I could even be more involved with another human being. I was a married woman. When I talk about my relationship with Rifka, and going outside my marriage, I had to deal with the right and wrong of it and the morality.

"But what happened was, once I gave myself permission to be physically sexual with her, I was free. I never felt freer in my life. I never felt more like a woman. Everything changed. Before, I had no femininity, no sexuality, no sense of who I was. It wasn't the thought of being in love with her, it was the act of allowing myself physically to love her, and even then I wasn't aware that I wasn't experiencing the best of what could be there for me, and I'm referring to an orgasm.

"I had been married for more than fourteen years and never experienced an orgasm with my husband. I didn't have an orgasm when I first came in contact with Rifka either. Sexually, I thought I was doing what I was supposed to do, until she told me, 'No, there's more for you. You're settling.' The exciting thing was not only to be in on it but to have it and the it was totally for me.

"I was still married at this time, visiting back and forth. It was very difficult." Yet, Fran, like the majority of women interviewed, spoke of experiencing an immediate feeling of rightness and well-being.

Fran was nearly forty before she divorced her husband to live in domestic partnership with her best friend, Rifka. The women have now been together for almost twenty years.

Regardless of whether marriages continued or ended after the revelations, very rarely did the women blame their husbands for their turning to women. They realized that not only they, but the men as well, had been raised with and given false information about sexuality.

Men were told that a man is not "a man" unless he wants intercourse and so, maintaining an erection during sex became the focus for many men. This forced the timing and sequence of events to revolve around the erection, eliminating the possibility of more spontaneous feelings and actions. While it was known that women could masturbate to orgasm clitorally, they were told that the right way to orgasm was only from vaginal penetration by the penis. When this did not work, they were told they were to blame. Men felt that there was something wrong with them or their penis if the woman didn't orgasm. According to Hite, these oppressive expectations have led to needless suffering.

While the sexual difficulties a couple experiences are not always due to the wife's revelation, her discovery may suddenly become the husband's convenient answer for all the couple's old and unresolved sexual problems. And conversely, it is these same unresolved problems that often lead a woman to discover her true sexual preference in the first place.

TAMI

"My marriage was more of a friendship. He was ten years older than I was. I let him take care of me. He was very gentle, a good father. We had a house in the suburbs. We were very traditional. He went out to work, I raised the children. I was very unhappy but didn't know why. No matter what he would do, I was unhappy. We had no sex life whatsoever. He had a real big problem. To this day I don't know why. But I'm grateful that he had a problem, because I didn't have to act on it.

"He'd say, 'It's me, not you.' There were times I wondered if he was a latent homosexual. I don't think he could have acted on it. He's very homophobic. He has a sister who has been gay since she was a young teenager. He didn't talk to her for a year.

"I watched my sister-in-law's gender preference grow. I was very interested in her sexuality, but I didn't understand why."

When Tami began work, a coworker came in and she felt a sudden connection with the other woman. A year and a half later they became lovers. Then Tami realized why she had identified so strongly with her sister-in-law.

MIRIAM

"Marriage started out okay, not because I was attracted to him, but because he was able to turn me on. But it was really all wrong. I never looked at him and said, 'God, this is someone whose body I desire.' I had sexual feelings and enjoyed doing sexual things and having orgasms, but I had never had a desire to really stimulate a man, to stimulate his organs, to reach out and touch them. I thought that was normal, the way women were, the low sex drive.

I was aware that I had feelings of sexual pleasure in myself but I didn't see anything odd about my lack of sexual desire for him. I understood that men were more mechanistic, into fondling genitals, and women were into tenderness, that this was normal."

Before they were engaged, Miriam says, "The only reason I had sex with him was because I was a horny thing and he was a horny thing and he knew how to turn me on. I was also tired of him nagging me and I decided what am I protecting here? What is virginity anyway? It all went sour before we got engaged.

"At that point there got to be an unwritten rule about the nature of our commitment. That was that sex was not going to be a make-or-break issue for our relationship. The commitment was not based on sex. Sex was just not that important, and we kept hoping it would get better. There was lots wrong with our sexual connection. It wasn't connected with his emotions. It always felt very mechanical to me; press this button, wiggle this knob."

BETTY

"I was never really in love with my husband. I was twenty-three years old. Everyone else had already married and had a first baby and was working on a second. We were great pals and good friends so we figured, 'Let's do this.' "

Betty has since divorced her husband but says, "We're still on friendly terms because of our son. But we went and fucked up a very good friendship. After we were finally separated permanently, we started becoming friends again because we didn't have unrealistic demands on each other any longer."

Betty's discovery came as an evolutionary process after her divorce. "As a teenager, my girlfriends were more important to me than boyfriends, but for certain occasions you needed a date, so I had one. I didn't know anything about gay people. After my marriage broke up, I still wanted to have sex but I didn't want involvement. That was in the early seventies, when swinging was a big thing. I tried it. At first it was with men that I was getting my sexual needs taken care of, but then I started getting closer to women, and I realized, for the first time, I was really enjoying sex and in a very short period of time men were pushed aside."

CHERRY

"I grew up in a rigid Protestant, Waspy suburban family with fifties and sixties Anita Bryant–type values. The only thing I ever heard about homosexuality was that I'd never have to worry about it. It didn't apply to me.

"In high school, other girls called me a 'dyke' or 'lez' if I didn't have a boyfriend. It sounded like the most dirty, low-life thing in the world. I proved I could date boys just like them, but I never felt bad about the feelings I had toward girlfriends, even though they were unreturned. I wanted to hug, hold hands, snuggle, wrestle, massage, etc. Sex was not on my mind. Just affection in a situation where I didn't have to worry that sex was expected, as it would be with a guy."

Married for two years, Cherry says, "I married the man who I could 'tolerate' most sex-wise, but I am failing at forcing myself to be straight.

"I have remained in my marriage because I love my husband as a person and also because I want to have a child. We went to a marriage counselor, but she focused on our individual wants and needs, which made us pull away from each other, so we stopped going. There is a lot of stress on my husband, Burt, since I don't satisfy him sexually and he doesn't satisfy me.

"We have talked about it [my feelings for women] extensively, but whenever we talk it into the ground I get stressed. I like things better when they are quiet and mellow. I got him *The Other Side of the Closet*, but the book stressed him out because every couple he read about either broke up or had affairs. So I avoid the subject with him as much as possible and try to concentrate on being friends.

"Burt considered my unresponsiveness to be a result of neglect I received from my parents, and a couple of date-rape experiences as a teen. He thought if he were gentle and not forceful, he could make me enjoy sex. I felt if I forced myself and put a lot of effort into it, I could make myself like it. But I didn't know that my mind was going to continue to rebel. I expected when we got married that he would just do what he wanted in bed and that I could get away with just lying there until it was over. It became more and more clear to me that I couldn't do this for the rest of my life, but we continue to look for new, creative ways to make it different and tolerable for me.

"We have compromised on one time per month, and we both masturbate. We fight about that because he feels he has to do it because he can't control the urge and I feel I should be able to do it because he doesn't satisfy me. We compromise by doing it only when the other isn't around and not letting the other know about it.

"I feel the only way I can have a sex life with him for good is if I can also find some enjoyment on the side, including an occasional experience with a woman if that turns out to be what I like."

Cherry, fearful, has yet to act upon her feelings for women.

CARMEN

"My husband has always known everything about me. He was obviously quite present throughout my struggles with our sexual relationship and he was aware of the confusion I experienced and the longing and frustration I felt. He was surprisingly supportive of my mental exploration of homosexuality; I'm afraid he found the idea a bit of a turn-on, but rather than getting perturbed about that, I chose to focus instead on his cooperative attitude and necessary flexibility. When I finally came to the long-awaited, life-affirming conclusion of my own lesbianism a year and a half ago, he shared my joy and elation as a true friend would.

"However, since my relationship with my woman has become so all-encompassing and intense, more powerful than my husband or even she and I could have anticipated, his supportiveness has, not surprisingly, become tainted with hurt feelings, jealousy, anger, resentment, and concerns about issues of practicality like management of time, money, and energy resources.

"Before, sex was about his power and his pleasure and his entitlement, at my expense—a constant source of pain throughout our marriage. Once I claimed my own sexuality, I was able to forgive him these hurts and discover a sense of peace and self-acceptance and sexual enlightenment I hadn't known before.

"So far, he tells me the lack of sex in the marriage is not a problem, saying if it ever becomes a problem, we will deal with it then. Because I prefer to avoid that problem, and because I do love my husband dearly, I have occasional and minimal sexual contact with him. Because I now enjoy a sense of peace and self-knowledge, I no longer feel forced, and I no longer feel powerless and angry. Happily, he is extremely considerate and giving. Our occasional sexual encounters usually involve unadorned mutual manual contact; aside from these encounters, though, we regularly express our love for each other, as close friends do, through caring embraces and playful touches."

While current television shows and magazines have lifted some of the negativity associated with lesbianism and the word is becoming heard more often, women who love women have always been around. In the early 1900s, Vita Sackville-West, a well-known English writer, and wife and mother, began a passionate love affair with another woman. "Her marriage not only survived infidelity, sexual incompatibility and long absences, but it became stronger and finer as a result." According to Nigel Nicolson, the son who found West's autobiographic journal after her death, while his father sought diversion with other men, his mother found her passion with women. For West and her husband, devoted to each other, marriage and sex were separate things and being in love with someone of the same gender had little to do with the felicity of their marriage. "They achieved their ideal companionship only after a long struggle . . . but once achieved it was unalterable and lifelong, and they made of it . . . the strangest and most successful union that two gifted people have ever enjoyed."

Little did I know when I realized my sexuality that everything I went through would be more about my long struggle toward self-hood and a successful union than about having a same-gender sexual preference. It would be about discovering who and what I am, and being honest with myself and with those who matter most to me. It would be about having the courage to go beyond the limited place society had dictated was mine and reaching a new level of growth and understanding. And it would be about being able to reconstruct my marriage in a realistic light.

By reexamining feelings and attitudes instilled in me since childhood, and understanding society's motives behind them, I was able to break through the silence that had kept me from being able to acknowledge my own needs as a woman.

Recently, having freed myself of the embarrassment, shame, and discomfort I was taught to feel in regard to my body, I was able to take off my clothes, and, in the moonlight, with the exuberance of a child, roll naked down a grassy hill covered with sparkling dew.

My journey to selfhood has not been an easy one. Yet I would gladly go through the same pain and suffering all over again to be able to reach my new beginning.

10

New Beginnings

THE ADMISSION of my true sexual identity was the beginning of a journey fraught with agony, isolation, pain, and panic. Not only did I have to live with the knowledge that I had violated one of society's imposed social mores, but I now felt forced to live a deceitful existence within my marriage as well.

Having been taught the value of honesty and openness, I desperately wanted to tell my husband why I felt unable to meet his needs. Having also been taught not to hurt others, I initially chose silence instead to shield him from any additional suffering. The internal conflict I lived with is one that most MWLW have to resolve in order to live a full life instead of a double one.

Often people ask, "Why couldn't you just keep your sexual identity to yourself?" While some women can and do, I felt as though I was on an emotional roller coaster and saw coming out as something I had little choice about. I felt as though it was a life-or-death situation, a fight for my sanity. I was feeling invisible, like part of myself was dying, because no one knew who I was. I would run to women's bars, not to drink, not to talk to anyone in particular, but to sit in a place where others would know I was a gay woman. Once I came out to my family and friends, the desperate need to run disappeared.

JACKIE

"I'm basically an honest person, and although I have a rule that I would never lie to my husband, I told him half-truths. I don't have a moral compunction against lying, but I have a terrible memory so I don't lie because I can fuck myself up. These half-truths were getting to me and I didn't like living two lives, the life with my family, which I loved and never thought of leaving, and the life with my lover, who I loved but couldn't share with anyone."

GRACIE

"At first I didn't feel guilt. It didn't feel like I was even cheating. I loved somebody and it felt like there couldn't possibly be anything wrong with loving somebody the way I loved her. I still feel that loving somebody is not a bad thing. Later on I did feel guilt, not so much for what I was doing—actually it wasn't really guilt. It was fear, I guess, that I was going to hurt him. That the knowledge was going to hurt or destroy him or my children."

DIANNA

Women are often brought up to believe that conflict is terrible and must be avoided at all costs. Still, some confront their internal conflict by coming out. Dianna, forty, the mother of a five-year-old, is in a committed relationship with another woman, yet feels strongly about remaining in her marriage. She felt the only way to deal with her dual identity was by being open and honest about it and she told her husband about herself.

"My husband has been everything," Dianna says. "He's been furious, he's been suicidal, he's felt totally betrayed. But I guess still, for him, there is enough in the relationship and there is enough we have created together that makes it worth it for him to hang in. He struggles and he certainly knows there are huge areas, emotionally especially, where he cannot meet me.

"I used to be bitchy. I used to feel so deprived, so hungry, so needy. In some ways I think it's almost easier for him now because I'm getting my needs met."

□ □ □ □

While I am very fortunate to have the support of my family, for many, the coming-out process is often fraught with pain, rejection, and disappointment. Coming out often involves the loss of family and friends: the loss of their approval, love, and understanding, and might also involve the loss of children's respect.

Women who choose to remain in their marriages are often accused of "taking the easy way out." Yet remaining is often more difficult. The MWLW who is hiding her identity from her husband and yet has a need to be with women faces the possibility of accidental or deliberate exposure. One woman said she had heard of several cases where women had been blackmailed.

Most women, whether they are out or not, deal with feelings of guilt and anxiety whenever they take time from their husbands and children for themselves. This is especially true if they choose to spend that time with a lover. One woman said, "I look forward to being with my woman friend and going away with her and we have a wonderful time whenever we're together, but I find myself getting irritable and starting arguments, especially when it's time to return home. I hadn't been aware that I was doing this and that it had become a pattern until my lover brought it to my attention. I realize now that I feel so torn, wanting to be with her—I truly feel freer to be me when I'm with her and we have so much fun together—yet I also feel, at the same time, that I am supposed to be responsible and be with my family. Maybe it sounds crazy, but creating friction before we part must be my way of separating myself from her to be able to go back to my family."

When a woman feels obligated to spend time with her husband rather than with her lover, she also suffers the same irritability. Additional tension arises if the other woman is a single lesbian who wants her to leave her husband when she'd rather not have to choose. As one woman put it for many, "It's so hard to be everything for everyone."

Those women who had come out to their husbands and then decided to separate also faced a multitude of uncertainties. For some, depression and sadness followed the dissolution even though that's what they thought they wanted. Fear of finality made one woman unable to sell the house she had shared with her husband. One, missing her husband, kept coming up with excuses to go back to her house until he finally said, "You don't need excuses to come to see me," and they cried together. Another talked of going home to bring the kids for a visit and seeing her ex-husband helping his new girlfriend with laundry and shopping, things she'd always wanted him to do with her. Although these women were happy with their lovers, and it would have made no difference in their decision to leave, the pain was there nonetheless. What added to their sadness was their inability to share these particular feelings with lovers who might not understand.

MWLW are often ostracized by both the straight and gay communities. While we are used to seeing women hugging and kissing and dancing together in our society, in many people's minds the idea of women being truly intimate with each other upsets the "natural order," procreation being the one acceptable end to sexual function. Consequently, in the heterosexual community, a woman having an affair with a woman is viewed as a perversion. Yet, having an extramarital affair with a man is accepted as nearly normal.

In the lesbian community, there is resentment against those women who are a part of "the other world." One woman, aware of her lesbianism since the age of nine, said, "You [MWLW] know what it's like to feel normal, to feel fully accepted. I never felt that acceptance."

FELICE

Felice, the mother of four, felt excluded from the lesbian community because "the only lesbians I know have no children. They're not married and that's a whole different world. I was out with my friend one day, and it was the only time I ever wanted to knock her on her butt. There was a woman with three little kids, and Luz looks at me and says, 'Oh, there's another breeder.' I was devastated. I finally said, 'I take great offense at that word.' "

It is often difficult for a childless lesbian to understand the primal connection and protective instincts a mother feels for her children. "I think it was Luz's own stuff," Felice says. "Envy, sorrow at never having been a mother. Then she admitted to me, 'One of the things that attracted me to you was that you had these children and you seemed to be so good at it.' "

□ □ □ □

As human beings we continually struggle, torn by wanting to be who we really are and wanting to be who we feel we are supposed to be. We live with different degrees of repression. We often fake what we don't feel, say yes when we want to say no, pretend we don't care when we do. Every life is filled with these conflicts, but as the disparity grows between who we realize we are and the role we have played, the tension can become unbearable.

According to psychotherapist Hedda Begelman, director of the Gay and Lesbian Counselling Center of Long Island, "Should the woman be involved at the moment, not just with the thought that 'I love women,' but that 'I am in love with a particular woman,' the stress is multiplied even more. And leaving any marriage is not necessarily the easy way out. There are stresses involved with leaving: having children to deal with, going back and forth, having to keep a relationship with an ex-husband because there are children involved, and having to go through his anger. Having to go through all of the things you have to go through because you're a lesbian adds to the stress."

Psychotherapist Gwenn A. Nusbaum, former clinical director of Identity House, a Manhattan-based peer-counseling organization serving the lesbian, gay, bisexual, and transgender community, says, "Fear of expressing true sexuality keeps many people trapped, as does fear of being who they really are. Unfortunately, much of the fear is understandable. The American culture is basically a heterosexual one, dictating rules and values as to what types of attachments are right and which are wrong. A married woman tends to be perceived as correct and is often envied. A single woman or one involved in same-sexed attachments is often seen as strange or abnormal.

"Consider the Moral Majority and the repressive, dangerous factions around. When you talk about lesbians and gays, you are often talking about a hotbed of political activity fraught with hatred and fear. Individuals who are uninformed or may experience homosexual desires of their own, may use morality as a way to ward off fears connected with being more open to homosexual choices."

Simone de Beauvoir points out in her book *The Second Sex*, that among women artists and writers there are many lesbians. Their sexuality is not the source of their creative energy, but, absorbed in their work, they do not want to waste time playing a feminine role or struggling with men.

In previous centuries women had been hospitalized for various mental illnesses known as "hysteria" or "madness." Their "symptoms" often were a strong independent streak or, according to Phyllis Chesler's *Women and Madness*, "sexual disinterest in their husbands." Today the rates for depression are three times higher for women than for men. And again, in evaluating the mental health of women of any age group, it's important to consider societal factors and cultural expectations.

Many of the MWLW I interviewed experienced some form of depression during their discovery period. For the first year and a half or two of my discovery I cried more than I ever had in my lifetime. The women I had confided in needed only ask "How are you," and the floodgates would open. My therapist would look at me and I'd grab a handful of tissues. I'd go to a consciousness-raising group and, regardless of the topic, tears would flow.

My tears were for many things—the void I felt at the loss of my best friend, the isolation my silence condemned me to, my own internalized homophobia. While I had always rationally been able to accept people who were different, now I was one of them. I felt like an outcast. My beliefs had proven to be false. After twenty-five years of marriage I had betrayed my husband and children. I was living a lie.

Things I had always been able to talk about intellectually and with detachment now became emotionally charged. I felt like a giant balloon stretched to capacity with only a tiny hole from which to squeeze the pain that was threatening to make me explode. Until my worlds came together, I walked a line between the two. In one, my feelings were impenetrable and I was able to function as I always had before, family and old friends none the wiser. In my new world my pain could not be held in check.

At the most extreme level, some MWLW, like their counterparts during the nineteenth century, were committed by their families when their same-sex predilections were discovered.

ALICE

Alice, the mother of three small children, needed a vacation and went away with her best friend. "I didn't know about myself, but when my friend found a waiter and didn't come back to the room that night, I was distraught. I wanted to be with her and I wanted her to want to be with me. When we drove home, I got hysterical. I said, 'I wanted to spend the weekend with you.' She said, 'Do you know what that means? Are you a lesbian?' It had never crossed my mind. I had never thought about it. I said, 'I love you very much.' And she said, 'This could never be.'

"When you're Jewish, you're taught you go to school, listen to the teacher, get married, have children. Nowhere are you taught you might love a woman, but when I read *The Well of Loneliness*, I knew it was me. I became so distraught that I tried to kill myself—twice."

Alice was committed to a mental institution. She decided she didn't want to die and from the facility called the lesbian hotline for help. "I was thirty-nine and had never seen a lesbian. Nanette walked in and she was just a person. Eventually we fell in love. When I left the hospital she came to live with my family. I didn't tell my husband about us but I told my parents. They were grateful that I was no longer suicidal and accepted her as my friend."

LEAH

Leah was also committed to a mental hospital, but not because she tried to commit suicide. "My family found out I was having an affair with another woman when I was seventeen. They had me committed. I was given shock treatments. When I tried to escape, I was doped so badly that I was almost a vegetable. After seeing what they had done to me in the hospital, my same brother who had had me committed fought to have me released." Terrified of being locked away again, Leah sought safety in a heterosexual marriage and has remained there, silently and unhappily, ever since.

As women, we learn that our sexuality should be hidden, that it is dangerous or shameful. By announcing a same-gender attraction, a woman reveals not only her sexuality, but her rejection of the heterosexual model. While the media has made lesbianism "chic" of late, social mores have always shunned the openly sexual woman, consigning her the title of prostitute, whore, tease, or "bad girl." And so just coming out can risk the consequence of social ostracism and rejection. For the MWLW already dealing with internalized homophobia, this anxiety may be overwhelming.

RIFKA

Rifka believes that it was the humiliation of realizing her same-gender sexuality as well as a lifetime of bottled-up feelings that brought about her illness.

"I had left my marriage and my family for my best friend, Fran," Rifka says. "Still, I couldn't admit to being a lesbian. The shame and embarrassment at the thought of being one was totally overwhelming. I had always been a health food person, a physical educator, and a health educator, and after Fran and I had been together a year and a half, I came down with Crohn's disease. I was very sick, hospitalized for twenty-one days, and suddenly, like a spiritual transformation, I knew that only if I really changed my life would I come out of this. I began to come out, fully come out every day.

"I got rid of the feelings that I had bottled up for so many years . . . childhood and everything else, and freeing myself to be a lesbian, I got rid of all that shit too. Understanding what Crohn's was for me, self-subordination, it just clicked. I've never had another incident and very few people are ever cured from it."

JOYCE

Joyce, who has been married for fifteen years, says, "I had a problem with sex in my marriage since my son was born. I nursed him for a long time and any interest in sex with my husband went away. When my sexual feelings came back, they had nothing to do with men. I attended church and I began to notice that if a woman stood near me, I had a sexual response. I think it was preverbal. There were no words for it.

"I went to a peer counseling center and started going to a

coming-out group. It was very painful thinking about separating from my husband. I really care about him a lot. Although I don't have sexual feelings for him, he's one of my best friends.

"I stopped going to the counseling center and started focusing my energy on my marriage instead. I told my husband about my feelings and initially he didn't think it was so threatening. He accepted what I told him, but he tried to understand it in terms of something that could be changed.

"We've been in therapy together for over a year, and have done a fair amount of work, but my sexual feelings for him are still not there. I've been sick so much this year. The conflict of really trying to make things work with him and really wanting to be with a woman is making me sick, and I just suddenly got it. My insides and my outsides are not in alignment.

"Last year there was guilt and suffering at the thought that maybe I was making the choice for my own pleasure, but now I understand that it's nonnegotiable, and the way things have come to be. I don't feel much guilt now. I feel like my molecules changed and I've become a different person."

It wasn't until the middle of the nineteenth century that psychologists, intent upon establishing psychology as a science, chose to make homosexuality the object of a systematic study.

Methodical identification of people on the basis of same-sex relations had not been contemplated until sexologists first used the term *lesbian* in 1869. Prior to that, while same-sex eroticism and relationships have existed in every known culture, there was no concept of "the homosexual" as a particular kind of person. Homosexuality was a practice, not an identity.

In the creation of their new discipline of "sexology," psychologists chose to make homosexuality a categorical entity rather than a term that covers a widely diverse range of individuals. For this purpose, says Beverly Burch, author of *Intimate Terms*, lesbians and gay men, noted primarily for their lack of heterosexuality, became "the Other." Their differences with respect to each other, and the internal differences within each group, were not considered.

When the word *homosexual* was coined, *heterosexual* was also coined so as to be able to differentiate the "normal" from the "deviant."

In conjunction with the establishment of this new discipline of "sexology," the category of lesbian, also called a sexual invert, was formulated. Some described a sexual invert—taken from the word *inversion*—as one who is attracted to one's own sex rather than to the opposite sex. Some used it to mean having the stereotypical characteristics of the other sex—effeminacy in the male and masculine strengths in the female. Neither group would include the majority of male homosexuals and lesbians, who do not show these traits. The terms *inversion* and *invert* have acquired a negative connotation and are not commonly used today.

Lillian Faderman, in *Odd Girls and Twilight Lovers: A History of Lesbian Life in Twentieth-Century America*, says, "It was to a large extent the work of the sexologists, which was disseminated slowly to the layman, but finally became part of popular wisdom after World War I, that accounts for the altered views of women's intimacy with each other. It may be said that sexologists changed the course of same-sex relationships not only because they cast suspicion on romantic friendships, but also because they helped make possible the establishment of lesbian communities through their theories, which separated off the lesbian from the rest of womankind and presented new concepts to describe certain feelings and preferences that had before been within the spectrum of 'normal' female experiences."

Since psychologists now depicted the lesbian as abnormal or sick, or men trapped in women's bodies, the taboo on a woman recognizing her love for another woman was increased tenfold. Fearful that her feelings were now unnatural, she might force herself to repress them, spend her life hiding "in the closet," or leading a double life.

However, according to Faderman, "Experiences that are within the realm of the socially acceptable during one era may be considered sick or dangerous or antisocial during another—and in a brief space of time, attitudes may shift once again, and yet again.

"The period of World War II and the years immediately after illustrate such astonishingly rapid shifts. . . . In the 1930s—an era when America needed fewer workers, the lesbian (a woman who needed to work and had no interest in making a man happy) was an antisocial being. During the war years that followed, when women had to learn to do without men . . . and when female labor—in the factories, in the military, everywhere—was vital to the functioning of America, female independence and love between women were understood and undisturbed and even protected. After the war, when the surviving men returned to their jobs and the homes that women needed to make for them so that the country could return to "normalcy," love between women and female independence were suddenly nothing but manifestations of illness, and a woman who dared to proclaim herself a lesbian was considered a borderline psychotic. Nothing need have changed in the quality of the woman's desires for her to have metamorphosed socially from a monster to a hero to a sicko."

SHIRLEY

"Even though we're located geographically in one of the most lesbian-active and lesbian-friendly areas in the United States, I worry about how well my son will handle me being out in a small town," explains Shirley, who, with her husband, is redefining her marriage in the hopes that they can stay together. "I worry about the effect on our marriage: How much of my needs can I serve and our needs as well? How about my husband's needs? It's a continual balancing act, and the thing that most often tips my emotional balance is sorting out feelings that are indicators that I need to pay more attention to my family from the feelings that are unhealthy, unnecessary guilt.

"There's the irrational guilt: 'Why didn't I figure myself out before I got married and spare everyone this trauma? Why must I follow my needs instead of being a saint and subjugating them to the good of the family?' I can know all of the 'right' answers to these questions, and still spend time feeling like a shit.

"Then there is the anxiety. Will my needs eventually come into such conflict with my family's needs that there will be loss of love and mutual respect? Or a loss of the family? Will I never be able to have a complete, long-term relationship with a woman because she can't handle me being married?

"Despite the fear and guilt and anxiety, I've never been happier in my life. I am so elated that I have found me and that me feels wonderful to be. I feel charged—physically, mentally, emotionally, and spiritually—which is good, because all these aspects of me have been working overtime in overdrive since I came out—and I need every bit of energy replenishment I can get."

JULIA

Julia, who chose to remain in her marriage while she has maintained a longterm relationship with Tillie, says, "It drove me crazy. I had to lie a lot. I was lying so much, I began not to know what the truth was. But I did it. I'm glad I did it. I don't regret it. I took care of my children and then I went out for the evening. I definitely had feelings of anxiety. Wherever I went, I thought my husband would walk in. I worried if I was at a dance or in a bar or with a lot of lesbians. As the years rolled on I became less concerned. I didn't want my children to know. I felt guilty and inappropriate, but as time went on I became more sure of myself and I realized that what was going on for me was that I was thoroughly and very much in love."

JEAN

Jean remembers the isolation both she and her lover felt when they first realized they were gay over thirty years ago. "We didn't know there was anyone else around like us until we saw the movie *The Killing of Sister George*. We saw women relating to each other, socializing together, going places together. We planned a trip to England.

"Then we saw a TV program on gay men and lesbians. They mentioned an organization called the Daughters of Bilitis, and we realized we didn't have to go to England to meet other women like us. We called and couldn't wait to go. I remember we had to go up a very long staircase and it was hard for me because I'd just had surgery. My lover said, 'Are you sure you want to go?' and I said, 'Yes,' pulling myself up by the banister one step at a time. We actually saw other women like us. It was such a thrill and I haven't lost that thrill. Every time I go someplace where there is a group of lesbians, I still get a shiver or a thrill."

LENA

"It was a dirty trick heaven played on me," says Lena. "If I had known about my true sexuality, I would not have suffered physically, emotionally, and spiritually as much as I did. But because I believe in my faith, I believe that there is a reason for all this, that the time for it to be revealed was that time, for particular people, for a certain reason. I left the Salvation Army because they have definite thoughts against homosexuality of any kind. I joined River City Metropolitan Community Church, which reaches out to lesbians and gays and all people. My husband and all of the family belongs.

"This revelation has brought me more clarity and a lot of suffering. Pain is there because I want to be able to eat, sleep, and breathe and enjoy my life. Pain becasue I live in a society that won't let me do that. Pain because every two steps that I make in progress as an individual, I'm still black, I'm still poor, and I'm still stigmatized. That's where the pain is. The pain is saying I'm doing something strange or unusual with my life because I want to share all that I have with another woman. Pain because society says, 'No, you must choose.' My God didn't say I had to choose. And society says I have to."

GWYN

"Most of my exposure to religion came from accompanying my good friends to their church and synagogue services and experiencing their different religious practices with their families in their homes. I realized as a young child that my own religious views flew in the face of traditional religions as I was coming to understand them. While I considered myself an extremely spiritual individual, I found myself objecting to the exclusionism and judgmental attitudes I heard expressed in places of worship. I searched for many years as a young adult for a church or religion where I could feel comfortable, where my views would be affirmed or at least tolerated.

"About five years ago I discovered a Unitarian Universalist fellowship that is now my home. Homosexuality is acknowledged and accepted as a matter of official policy, but of course many individual members are still close-minded or inadequately enlightened.

"I believe if it were not for the critical, judgmental influence of traditional, conservative, organized religion, I would have achieved a healthy understanding of myself and realized true happiness much earlier in life.

"The morality stuff came from sources external to me; even before I understood my own gayness, I opposed mainstream society's judgmental attitudes toward gays and other oppressed groups. I didn't buy the package of close-mindedness and bigotry that was presented to me, but I still found myself victimized by it. Once I finally felt strong and healthy enough to reject these dangerous external voices, I experienced intense elation at the freedom and beauty of finally knowing and accepting and loving my lesbian self."

SONIA

For Sonia, it wasn't her religious upbringing but a sudden awareness of what lay in store for her that helped her to come to terms with who she was.

"I was in this incredible hell. I felt disassociated, losing weight, all these horrible things. I was upstate with my kids and we were playing on the bed and I remember, in the past, thinking, 'This is absolutely it. This is as good as it gets. I will never love anybody in my life as much as I love my children. I know I don't love my husband and haven't loved him in a really long time. This is what it's all about.'

"Something about that made me sad and disturbed me. What I was afraid of was similar to what happened to me when I was growing up. My parents didn't have the best marriage, and what happens is parents put so many expectations on their children. I was so afraid of doing that. My kids are the great love in my life, and fifteen years from now they'll be grown up and be their own people and what will I be left with? I'm going to be sitting in a rocking chair with my husband and we're going to have absolutely nothing and that scared me, absolutely scared me.

"What am I going to want my kids to give back to me? What will I demand of them? What rightfully should they give to me? I can't expect them to fill this emptiness in me.

"Then, after Janie and I got together, I was playing with my kids and I came to the realization that I really did love her. Before that I was in complete, total denial. I wanted to see her. I was obsessed, but I was in total denial about my sexuality, about loving her, about what this really meant. I couldn't deal with this at all. When I realized that, it was like a weight lifted off. All of a sudden I was in touch with my emotions and I could see much clearer than I could before. It was a turning point for me."

When a woman discovers her true sexual identity, all of her senses are shaken up. Unquestioned teachings of her church and family—deeply instilled issues of morality and her sense of right and wrong—become suspect. She questions her previously held belief system. While she might try to deny the existence of her new identity, the passion, pain, and utter confusion she experiences during her journey serve as catalysts that bring other feelings to the surface. Some women likened their evolution to having gained a third dimension.

Unfortunately, many people go through their entire lives never having experienced passion of any kind, or the turbulent emotions that accompany it, and so it is almost impossible for them to comprehend what the MWLW is going through. When *Bridges of Madison County* came out, an enormous part of the public embraced the book, and then the movie that followed, for just this reason. They were able to identify with, and live vicariously through, two individuals very much like themselves. And, at last, they were able to taste and to feel the passion they had never personally experienced.

SARAH

When Sarah was in her late thirties, she met Dotty, the woman who became her life-long lover. Sarah and her husband had stopped living together intimately, as man and wife, sometime before that. She had anticipated divorcing her husband, but his diminishing eyesight made her change her plans. Instead, Dotty moved in with Sarah's family. They told outsiders that Dotty was just staying with the family while she attended college—she remained for about thirty years.

Now seventy, Sarah explains, "It almost sounds like a menage à trois, but it wasn't although there were times when she and I would gang up on Bill and times when they would gang up on me. My daughter [in high school at the time] and a lot of friends knew our situation, but not the local friends."

Dotty became ill and spent the last eighteen months of her life in and out of the hospital. "When she checked in, I was referred to as her friend," Sarah says. "I finally got sick of that and told the social worker on the unit, the director of nurses, and the doctor. Our relationship was not talked about, but it was pretty much an open secret. The hospital staff were very supportive. They never made us feel we were out of the ordinary and did as much for us as they did for anyone else.

"Dotty was standing after having been on a respirator for about seven weeks. A nurse was bustling around and all of a sudden she turned around and put her hands on her hips and said, 'So how long have you been together?' Now, Dotty was an intensely private person. She didn't discuss her personal affairs with anyone and was always circumspect about everything. I said, 'Twenty-nine years.' It felt good to be able to say that.

"Even when Dotty died, people didn't know. We were very fortunate. When she was in the hospital, we met a young woman, Molly, who was in training to become a minister. It turned out she was a lesbian, so Dotty asked her to say a few words at her funeral."

Sarah says, "Dotty was a very traditional person, so I don't know how she ever got mixed up with me. I was her first, last, and only experience. She was a churchgoer and played the organ and the church had been supportive during her illness, although they didn't know about her. She felt we had to do the traditional thing at the funeral, but she did ask the young woman we had met to say a few words, and Molly was very discreet. She spoke words that only those of us who were in the know were able to understand."

Still, Sarah says, "If I came out with my secret, my church would treat me with a cold shoulder. I haven't been there since Dotty died because of my anger. There would be snickering and laughing in my community and I have a grandson in high school and another one starting next year. I wouldn't want to do that to them. It makes me angry that it has to be like this."

After Dotty died, loneliness brought Sarah out of her retirement and she returned to her field of social work.

Sarah says, "One of our social workers said that one teenage boy had come out to him and he wanted to know if we knew of any gay or lesbian social workers to whom we might refer the boy. I sat there silently. And so did the other social worker I knew was gay. I felt like I was really letting down people who needed my help. I felt this shit had to stop. So I went to my boss and told him, 'I feel like shit and I'm getting angrier and angrier.' That's what I told my boss. It's bad enough when young people have to keep secrets, but when you've had to keep secrets for as long as I have, thirty years, you just get angrier and angrier. I said, 'You can do anything with it [this information] you want to.' He was accepting.

"I'm trying more and more to come out and to be as honest as I can.

"It's a hard life. People don't deliberately go out and stick their heads in a meat grinder because that's a pleasure to them. They go out and face this life because that's who they are."

The MWLW who had reached the point of being comfortable with themselves said the process of working through their identity issues had given them new insight, strength, awareness, and confidence. While these women had always been dutiful daughters and responsible wives and mothers, few had felt like real people in their own right. Now they began to take control of their lives, accepting responsibility for their own emotional, physical, and, in some cases, financial well-being. The compulsion to fit some norm, or to expect their families to do so, disappeared. The metamorphosis freed and opened them to a kind of love that is unrestricted by society's demands or controls. They spoke with pride of the women they were becoming.

Two years ago, my husband and I attended a fiftieth birthday party for Jeff, one of our oldest friends. Before we were married, we had often group-dated with Jeff and his wife Sherry and five other couples. Sherry had lovingly created a collage of memories spanning Jeff's high school years and on through the present, and his oldest friends had been asked to prepare small anecdotes about Jeff.

I watched as Sherry and Jeff stood arm in arm, listening to the stories. She looking up to him lovingly, and suddenly my eyes filled with tears and I had to leave the room. This simple scene had stirred painful reminders of the times my husband and I had experienced similar closeness at joyous occasions years ago.

It took me some time before I learned that while we have changed and might never again share the picture-perfect relationship we once thought we had, we can appreciate ourselves for the new and honest understanding we have of each other.

Dealing with weddings, anniversaries, funerals—any rite of passage—can be awkward for everyone involved. Families can be at a loss as to how to conduct themselves. Should they pretend they had forgotten the anniversary and avoid any mention of it? This was the issue my husband and I faced as our thirtieth anniversary, the first after my announcement, neared. My children, and my sister and brother-in-law who live nearby, were at a loss as to how to conduct themselves. Should they avoid any mention of our anniversary, pretend they had forgotten it? My husband was all in favor of that. I myself was at a loss as to how to treat it. At first I also thought forgetting it would be best. Then the reality came to me. Through good and bad, my husband and I had weathered these years together. We went through job losses, moves, family illnesses, and deaths, and we raised two wonderful kids. In the process, we just happened to grow separately rather than as a couple.

While this anniversary was not the typical expression shared between two people "in love," for me it represented hurdles we had come through together, and the caring we had for each other, and the new friendship we had established, regardless of the other issues. It was a landmark occasion and deserved not to be ignored.

I asked the family to join us for dinner at our favorite restaurant. Around the table, I could feel everyone's apprehension, my husband's included, until I verbalized what everyone had been afraid to say. I lifted my glass and acknowledged how difficult the last year had been for all of us. I made a toast recognizing my husband, then our children and other family members. I acknowledged their love for me and for my husband and appreciated their support through our difficulties without having taken sides or chosen abandonment, the easy way out. There was an audible sigh of relief. The discomfort and the tension left, and we had a very special evening.

Appendix

Where to Turn for Help and Information

UNTIL RECENTLY, books with lesbian themes have been
published primarily by small presses. For the general public, chances of buying a book from one of the large chain bookstores in which a lesbian was realistically portrayed was slim. Except for the books of Rita Mae Brown, Lisa Alther's *Other Women*,
Margaret Erhart's *Unusual Company*, and biographies about celebrated women who loved women such as Vita Sackville-West,
Virginia Woolf, and Eleanor Roosevelt, there was little chance of
finding books with lesbian content.

Now, however, large publishing houses, realizing the growing
need for, interest in, and marketability of lesbian and gay literature, are adding these writings to their lists. Likewise, major chain
bookstores, recognizing the lucrative lesbian market, are beginning to carry books that at one time could be found only in new
age or women's (also called feminist) bookstores.

Women's bookstores, generally community-minded, are good
places to pick up information on and become familiar with
women's activities and groups available in the community. To find
out where these stores are, you can contact *The Feminist Bookstore
News*, P.O. Box 882554, San Francisco CA 94188; 1–415–626–
1556. It has a list of almost two hundred feminist and general
interest bookstores across the country.

If you live in a remote area and cannot find a woman's bookstore, *Womankind Books* (5 Kivy Street, Huntington Station, NY

11746), a mail-order bookstore in existence since 1979, offers a catalogue of lesbian books and videos. Their mailings are discreet and charge orders do not itemize the titles of books ordered. Their telephone number is 1–516–427–1289.

Another national publication that lists resources, publications, organizations, religious associations, health services, support groups, and more is the *Gayellow Pages*. It is carried at most bookstores dealing with lesbian and gay issues. Their mailing address is P.O. Box 533, Village Station, New York NY 10014–0533.

For women in their earliest phases of discovery, even making a long distance phone call to a bookstore or a resource center can be difficult. There is the fear of having to answer questions if a spouse sees an unusual number on the phone bill. While I do not advocate deception, the aim of this book is to help women in distress. One way to enable them to understand themselves is by giving them access to as much information as possible. With this in mind, I will share what others have told me has worked for them.

A long-distance operator can tell you how much a specific phone call will be. Then, armed with the necessary amount of coins, you can make your call anonymously from a pay phone. When calling to order books or literature, ask if discreet wrappings are used before you place your order. If payment must be sent in advance, money orders (available at banks and post offices) can be purchased so as to avoid a record of the purchase in your checkbook or on your credit card.

For those afraid of having literature sent to their homes, post office boxes are available for minimal rates. You may pay cash in advance for your box and use any pseudonym you choose.

MWLW use a multitude of schemes to afford them the protection they feel they need when they visit a therapist, attend a support group or rap session, or meet and talk with other MWLW. Pretexts range from registering for classes whose hours coincide with actual meetings, to keeping car trunks filled with packages so that a woman can produce a bag or two and say she has been shopping.

Whether you are looking for help, guidance, advice, assistance, information, or just some comfort, there *are* places you can turn. The first place to look is your local phone directory.

The New York City telephone book, for example, lists several lesbian support services in the business section of the White Pages, including the *Lesbian and Gay Community Services Center* 1–212–620–7310. A base for almost four hundred community groups, the center fulfills social, emotional, cultural, spiritual, and political needs for the nearly five thousand people who come through their doors each week. They have a national directory with which to assist long-distance callers in finding their nearest sources of help. They will also refer callers to places like New York's Identity House, which offers a walk-in center for one-on-one peer counseling or short-term referral for therapy for the lesbian, gay, and bisexual community. The ID House also offers workshops, including discussion groups for women in transition, a women's coming-out group, a talk-and-listen rap group, and a rap group for women over forty. The *Lesbian Herstory Archives*, 1–718–768–3953, located in Brooklyn, New York, houses the world's largest collection of materials by and about lesbians, including books, unpublished papers, newsletters, photographs, slides, periodicals, tapes, videos, films, subject and organization files, reference tools, artwork, calendars, manuscripts, music, and clothing. Volunteer staffers are available to assist long-distance researchers and guests alike.

Not every city or small community phone book lists the kinds of lesbian services offered in New York. But resources can still be located. Professional groups such as the Family Services League, the National Association for Social Workers, the Society for Clinical Social Work, and the Organization of Gay and Lesbian Health Care Workers may have access to the information you need, or can help you to locate individuals or groups who deal with gender-related issues.

Any listing that begins with "Women" such as the Women's Counseling or the Women's Health Care Services are good sources. Psychological or psychotherapy services are also places to try. Another good source is NOW, the National Organization for Women, at 1–202–331–0066. NOW has a lesbian rights director who can assist you in finding nearby support services, or you might try your local chapter. Local YWCAs are another source for gathering information on woman-related issues. PFLAG (Parents and Friends of Lesbians and Gays), a national organization with local chapters, is a self-help group for parents and friends who are trying to understand their children's homosexuality or who have accepted and are trying to help other parents do the same. The national headquarters is: Parents FLAG, P.O. Box 27605, Washington, D.C. 20038.

It may take many phone calls before you find the kind of help you are looking for. Another option for finding help if you live in an area where the phone book doesn't have the listings is the AIDS hotline. AIDS hotlines have become information centers for the lesbian as well as the gay community. Generally, they are staffed by volunteers who are sensitive to lesbian needs, and will direct you to available services and support groups.

Colleges and universities are other places you can gather information. Most now offer women's studies programs and many have women's centers, where literature on topics of interest to women is disseminated. College bookstores offer additional reading material.

The Metropolitan Community Church and the Unitarian Church have a history of social activism and can also be turned to. Other places to search for literature that might be of help to women in transition are alternative or new age learning centers. These are places that openminded people frequent. Information on these centers can generally be picked up in health food stores.

Several women have told me that they found others like themselves by placing ads in alternative newspapers. If you choose to follow this route, use a post office box number for your own protection. Have people write you there and give you their phone numbers or addresses. If you do arrange to meet, choose a well-populated diner or restaurant for your first meeting.

If your city or town does not have the center or services you are looking for, you might try establishing a support group yourself. Remember, as lonely as you are and as frightened as you may be about exposing yourself, you are not alone. There are other women like you looking for you to talk to.

Notes

INTRODUCTION

p. xix According to *The Hite Report* . . . Shere Hite, *The Hite Report* (New York: Macmillian, 1976).

p. xix Consequently, it is understandable . . . Amity Pierce Buxton, *The Other Side of the Closet* (Santa Monica, Cal.: IBS Press, 1991), p. xiv.

p. xxi Because the subject of lesbianism . . . *Statistical Abstracts of the United States* (U.S. Department of Commerce, Bureau of the Census, Washington, D.C., 1996), p. 105.

p. xxii According to Carol Botwin's book . . . Carol Botwin, *Tempted Women* (New York: William Morrow & Co., 1994).

p. xxiii Other current books such as . . . Dalma Heyn, *The Erotic Silence of the American Wife* (New York: Random House, 1992).

p. xxiii Other current books such as . . . Sonya Friedman, *Secret Loves* (New York: Crown, 1994).

CHAPTER 1 **Awakening**

p. 8 Whether or not Roberta would . . . Arlene DiMarco, telephone interview, December 12, 1993.

CHAPTER 2 **What Am I?**

p. 25 Of the forty-five participants . . . Eli Coleman, "The Married Lesbian," *Marriage and Family Review*, Vol. 14, No. 3/4, 1989, p. 121.

p. 26 Amity Pierce Buxton, Ph.D., writes . . . Buxton, *The Other Side*, p. xiv.

p. 27 In the seventeenth and eighteenth . . . Lillian Faderman, *Surpassing the Love of Men* (New York: William Morrow & Co., Inc., 1981), p. 16.

p. 27 Mark DeWolfe Howe, the . . . Faderman, *Surpassing*, p. 190.

p. 27 According to Faderman, "What surprised . . ." Faderman, *Surpassing*, p. 16.

p. 28 "If she dressed in clothes . . ." Faderman, *Surpassing*, p. 17.

p. 29 females who attended college . . . Lillian Faderman, *Odd Girls and Twilight Lovers* (New York: Penguin, 1991), p. 12–14.

p. 29 "Lesbian interaction, however, is . . ." Tikva Frymer-Kensky, "Sex and Sexuality," *The Anchor Bible Dictionary*, Vol. 5, David Noel Freedman (ed.), (New York: Doubleday, 1992), pp. 1144–1146. Typographical error in the source. The passage referenced is actually Leviticus 20:13.

p. 29 " 'The act,' he says, 'is . . .' " Faderman, *Odd Girls*, p. 34.

p. 30 Aristotle then used this female . . . Shari L. Thurer, *The Myths of Motherhood* (New York: Houghton Mifflin Company, 1994).

p. 30 beyond all of the aspects symbolizing . . . Hite, *Hite Report*, p. 151.

p. 30 In the 1930s, writer . . . Margaret Mitchell, *Gone With the Wind* (New York: Macmillan, 1936).

p. 30 In her earliest book, *Lost* . . . Margaret Mitchell, *Lost Laysen* (New York: Scribner's, 1996). Recently found and published.

p. 30 in the heterosexual United States . . . Nancy Marvel, "The Case for Feminist Celibacy," *The Feminist* (pamphlet), New York, 1971.

p. 31 "Lesbians were forced to submit . . ." Chandler Burr, "Homosexuality and Biology," *The Atlantic*, March 1993, Vol. 271, No. 3, p. 48.

p. 31 "In 1974, the American Psychiatric . . ." Buxton, *The Other Side*, p. xv.

p. 32 "The origins of human sexuality . . ." Dean Hamer and Peter Copeland, *The Science of Desire: The Search for the Gay Gene and the Biology of Behavior* (New York: Simon & Schuster, 1994), p. 20.

p. 32 "The homosexual, on the other . . ." Del Martin and Phyllis Lyon, *Lesbian Woman* (New York: Bantam, 1972), p. 74.

p. 32 "In females, the female structures . . ." Burr, "Homosexuality," p. 60.

p. 32 He says, "We didn't isolate . . ." Hamer and Copeland, *The Science of Desire*, p. 147.

p. 33 "A complicating factor was that . . ." Hamer and Copeland, *The Science of Desire*, p. 146.

p. 33 "Research on the population percentages . . ." Burr, "Homosexuality," p. 168.

p. 33 "They move among straight, bisexual . . ." Burr, "Homosexuality," p. 169.

p. 33 It's pretty much a phenomenon . . .' " Burr, "Homosexuality," p. 169.

p. 34 She adds, "I think few . . ." Burr, "Homosexuality," p. 171.

p. 34 She says, "If a genetic . . ." Telephone interview with Gwenn A. Nusbaum, November 15, 1993.

p. 34 "It seems to me," she concludes . . . Arnie Schwartz, "Surpassing the Odds," *10 Percent Stonewell 25*, June 1994, pp. 66–70.

p. 35 **"Others may feel that being . . ."** Beverly Burch, *On Intimate Terms* (Champaign, Ill.: University of Illinois Press, 1993).

p. 36 **"People may be attracted to . . ."** Anastasia Toufexis, "Bisexuality: What Is It?" *Time*, August 17, 1992, pp. 49–51.

p. 36 **Also, since it is possible . . .** June M. Reinisch and Ruth Beasley, *The Kinsey Institute New Report on Sex* (New York: St. Martin's Press, 1990), p. 143.

p. 37 **"We may resist new scientific . . ."** Masters, Virginia Johnson, "Tangled Lives," *Mirabella*, February 1994, p. 147.

p. 42 **"Bisexuals, who do not fit . . ."** Martin S. Weinberg, Colin J. Williams, and Douglas W. Pryor, *Dual Attraction: Understanding Bisexuality* (New York: Oxford University Press, 1994), preface.

p. 43 **"They insist that bisexuality is . . ."** Toufexis, "Bisexuality," pp. 49–51.

p. 43 **"Instead of connecting sexuality with . . ."** Weinberg, Williams, Pryor, *Dual Attraction.*

p. 43 **"Gender, not sexuality, is the . . ."** Weinberg, Williams, Pryor, *Dual Attraction:*, p. 49.

CHAPTER 3 **What Now?**

p. 49 **"Because the child's first intense emotional/libidinal . . ."** Eileen Starzecpyzel, "The Persephone Complex," *Lesbian Psychologies* (Champaign, Ill.: University of Illinois Press, 1987), p. 264.

p. 50 **"Because a man's masculinity is . . ."** Starzecpyzel, "The Persephone Complex," p. 264.

p. 50 **"A girl's relation to him is . . ."** Burch, *On Intimate Terms*, p. 27.

p. 50 **"The traditional explanation of lesbianism . . ."** Burch, *On Intimate Terms*, p. 26.

p. 50 **"Finally, the circumstances of life . . ."** Burch, *On Intimate Terms*, p. 27.

p. 50 **"because the psychic love affair . . ."** Burch, *On Intimate Terms*, p. 26.

p. 51 **This often leads to low . . .** Sue Vargo, "The Effects of Women's Socialization on Lesbian Couples," *Lesbian Psychologies* (Champaign, Ill.: University of Illinois Press, 1987), p. 163.

p. 51 **Having been brought up to . . .** Colette Dowling, *The Cinderella Complex* (New York: Pocket Books, 1981), p. 50.

p. 51 **In the latest backlash against . . .** Naomi Wolf, *Fire with Fire* (New York: Random House, 1993), pp. 70–71.

p. 53 **"It is only the women . . ."** DiMarco telephone interview.

p. 56 **"I observe in my practice . . ."** Starzecpyzel, "The Persephone Complex," p. 263.

p. 56 **"Until he gains a wife/mother . . ."** Starzecpyzel, "The Persephone Complex," p. 265.

pp. 56–57 **"The loss of and longing . . ."** Starzecpyzel, "The Persephone Complex," p. 265.

p. 58 While the paternal seduction is . . . Starzecpyzel, "The Persephone Complex," pp. 265–281.

p. 59 "Being a lesbian is one . . ." Interview with Hedda Begelman, September 22, 1993.

p. 62 once an internal frame of . . . Eli Coleman, "The Married Lesbian," *Marriage and Family Review*, Vol. 14, No. 3/4, 1989, pp. 119–135.

p. 63 She adds, however, that "whether . . ." Begelman interview.

p. 64 In *Codependent No More*, Melody . . . Melody Beattie, *Codependent No More* (San Francisco: Harper and Row, 1987), p. 89.

CHAPTER 4 **Do I Tell My Husband or Not?**

p. 73 "The very term 'sexual orientation' . . ." Chandler Burr, "Homosexuality and Biology," *Atlantic Monthly*, March 1993, Vol. 271, No. 3, p. 48.

p. 74 "More than ninety percent have . . ." Margaret Nichols, "Lesbian Sexuality: Issues and Developing Theory," *Lesbian Psychologies*, (Champaign, Ill.: University of Illinois Press, 1987), p. 106.

CHAPTER 5 **The Reality of Marriage**

p. 88 "These marriages were described as . . ." Barbara Seaman, *Free and Female* (New York: Fawcett Crest, 1972), p. 205.

p. 88 "Not marrying could easily mean . . ." The Radical Therapist Collective, ed., "Brainwashing and Women," *The Radical Therapist* (New York: Ballantine, 1971), p. 123.

p. 88 One woman explained. "If a . . ." Seaman, *Free and Female*, pp. 210–211.

p. 92 "They were invited to the . . ." Blanche Wiesen Cook, *Eleanor Roosevelt* (New York: Viking, 1992), p. 14.

p. 92 *Portrait of a Marriage*, written by . . . Nigel Nicolson, *Portrait of a Marriage* (New York: Atheneum, 1980), pp. 105–106.

p. 97 "the average income of women . . ." Dalma Heyn, *The Erotic Silence of the American Wife* (New York: Turtle Bay, 1992), p. 261.

p. 97 "In the year before a separation . . ." Tom Biracree and Nancy Biracree, *Almanac of the American People* (New York: Facts on File, 1988), p. 203.

p. 97 While the standard of living . . . Biracree, *Almanac*, p. 203.

p. 101 "In this context, divorce might . . ." Catherine Whitney, *Uncommon Lives* (New York: New American Library, 1990), pp. 11–12.

p. 103 For some women, this requires . . . Friedman, *Secret Loves*, p. 205.

CHAPTER 6 **The Husbands**

p. 121 "You are likely to gain the approval . . ." Robert T. Michael, John H. Gagnon, Edward O. Laumann, and Gina Kolata, *Sex in America: A Definitive Survey* (Boston: Little, Brown & Company, 1994), p. 113.

p. 121 "About a third have sex . . ." Michael, Gagnon, et al, *Sex in America*, p. 214.

p. 121 "In the last few years . . ." William H. Masters, Virginia E. Johnson, and Robert C. Kolodny, *Masters and Johnson on Sex and Human Loving* (Boston: Little, Brown & Company, 1988), p. 392.

p. 122 "for people who get no . . ." Masters, Johnson, et al. *Masters and Johnson on Sex*, p. 392.

p. 122 Only 1 percent said sex. Biracree, *Almanac*, p. 167.

CHAPTER 7 **What Do the Kids Think?**

p. 129 "If children feel loved and . . ." Phone interview with Lois Wadas, Sunday, January 19, 1997.

p. 131 "There is evidence, in fact . . ." Reinisch and Beasley, *The Kinsey Institute New Report*, p. 141.

p. 131 These children were "no more . . ." Laura Benkov, *Reinventing the Family* (New York: Crown, 1994), p. 62.

p. 131 Because today's gay father or mother . . . William A. Henry III, "Gay Parents: Under Fire and on the Rise," *Time*, September 20, 1993.

p. 131 "The Bank Street study tapped . . ." Benkov, *Reinventing*, p. 207.

p. 131 "But many children—even those . . ." Benkov, *Reinventing*, pp. 198, 199.

p. 137 While one study done by . . . Linda Garnets and Douglas C. Kimmel, eds., *Psychological Perspectives on Lesbian and Gay Male Experience* (New York: Columbia University Press, 1993), p. 258.

p. 137 Another study on mental health . . . Garnets and Kimmel, *Psychological Perspectives*, p. 258.

p. 143 According to Laura Benkov . . . Benkov, *Reinventing*, p. 202.

p. 145 "Although there is little stigma . . ." Dr. Lee Salk, *Familyhood* (New York: Simon & Schuster, 1992), p. 94.

p. 145 "In particular, if the parents . . ." Paul Bohannan, *All the Happy Families* (New York: McGraw-Hill, 1985), p. 128.

CHAPTER 8 **Coming Out to Friends and Family**

p. 154 "For a mother, a daughter's . . ." Sherry Zitter, "Coming Out to Mom," *Lesbian Psychologies* (Champaign, Ill.: University of Illinois Press, 1987), p. 193.

p. 154 "From a family systems perspective . . ." Zitter, "Coming Out," p. 193.

p. 155 "This myth, which runs deep . . ." Vargo, "Effects of Women's Socialization," p. 165.

p. 164 "His reaction to her coming out . . ." Zitter, "Coming Out," p. 183.

CHAPTER 9 **Sexual Intimacy**

p. 174 "There has rarely been any acknowledgment . . ." Hite, *The Hite Report*, p. xi.

p. 174 "And because they do not speak . . ." Heyn, *The Erotic Silence*, p. 70.

p. 174 "If you already know all . . ." Betty Dodson, *Sex for One* (New York: Crown, 1987), p. 108.

p. 175 "Whatever sexual pleasure women may . . ." Nancy Friday, *Women on Top* (New York: Pocket Star Books, 1991), p. 236.

p. 175 "They learn that making love . . ." Interview with Hedda Begelman, September 22, 1993.

p. 175 "Their new knowledge is frightening . . ." Begelman interview.

p. 175 Before Shere Hite's *The Hite* . . . Hite, *The Hite Report*, p. 154.

p. 175 In the early 1990s . . . University of Chicago's National Opinion Research Center, "Sex in America," *U.S. News and World Report*, October 17, 1994, Vol. 117, No. 15, pp. 74–81.

p. 178 "Only a female homosexual really . . ." Martin and Lyon, *Lesbian Woman*, p. 57.

p. 179 "We need not continue to . . ." Hite, *The Hite Report*, p. 297.

p. 181 She asked, "How many other . . ." Ann Landers, "Bed and bored: Giving up sex," *Daily News*, June 25, 1990.

p. 181 reasons for celibate marriages range . . . Joan Avna and Diana Waltz, *Celibate Wives* (Los Angeles: Lowell House, 1992), pp. 4, 5.

p. 183 There is a scene . . . Fanny Flagg, *Fried Green Tomatoes* (New York: McGraw-Hill, 1988).

p. 189 According to Hite, these oppressive . . . Hite, *The Hite Report*, p. 217.

CHAPTER 10   **New Beginnings**

p. 199 "Having to go through all . . ." Begelman interview. September 22, 1993.

p. 199 "Individuals who are uninformed . . ." Telephone interview with Gwenn A. Nusbaum, November 15, 1993.

p. 199 Their sexuality is not the . . . Simone de Beauvior, *The Second Sex* (New York: Vintage Books, 1989), p. 411.

p. 200 And again, in evaluating the . . . Phyllis Chesler, *Women and Madness* (New York: Doubleday, 1972), p. 5.

p. 203 Their differences with respect to . . . Burch, *On Intimate Terms*, pp. 18, 19.

p. 204 The terms *inversion* and *invert* . . . Wayne R. Dynes, ed., *Encyclopedia of Homosexuality*, Vol. 1, 1990, p. 610.

p. 204 "It may be said that sexologists . . ." Lillian Faderman, *Odd Girls*, p. 35.

p. 204 Since psychologists now depicted . . . Faderman, *Odd Girls*, p. 3.

p. 205 "Nothing need have changed in . . ." Faderman, *Odd Girls*, p. 119.

Bibliography

Abbott, Deborah, and Ellen Farmer. *From Wedded Wife to Lesbian Life*. Freedom California: The Crossing Press, 1995.

Alther, Lisa, *Other Women*. New York: Signet, 1984.

Aona, Joan, and Diana Waltz. *Celibate Wives*. Chicago: Contemporary Books, 1992.

Barrett, Martha Barron. *Invisible Lives*. New York: William Morrow & Co., 1989.

Beattie, Melody. *Codependent No More*. San Francisco: Harper and Row, 1987.

Benkov, Laura. *Reinventing the Family*. New York: Crown, 1994.

Biracree, Tom, and Nancy Biracree. *Almanac of the American People*. New York: Facts on File, 1988.

Bohannan, Paul. *All the Happy Families*. New York: McGraw-Hill, 1985.

Boston Lesbian Psychologies Collective, ed. *Lesbian Psychologies*. Champaign, Ill.: University of Illinois Press, 1987.

Botwin, Carol. *Tempted Women*. New York: William Morrow & Co., 1994.

Braverman, Lois. "Chasing Rainbows." *Networker*, July/August 1995.

Brown, Rita Mae. *Rubyfruit Jungle*. New York: Bantam, 1977.

Brown, Rita Mae. *Venus Envy*. New York: Bantam, 1993.

Burr, Chandler. *A Separate Creation: The Search for the Biological Origins of Sexual Orientation*. New York: Hyperion, 1963.

Buxton, Amity Pierce. *The Other Side of the Closet*. Santa Monica, Cal.: IBS Press, Inc., 1991.

Burch, Beverly. *On Intimate Terms*. Champaign, Ill.: University of Illinois Press, 1993.

Burr, Chandler. "Homosexuality and Biology." *The Atlantic*, Vol. 271, No. 3, March 1993.

Chesler, Phyllis. *Women and Madness*. Garden City: Doubleday, 1972.

Chodorow, Nancy. *The Reproduction of Mothering: Psychoanalysis and the Sociology of Gender.* Berkeley, Cal.: University of California Press, 1978.

Clarke, Donald. *Loving Someone Gay.* Berkeley, Cal.: Celestial Arts, 1987.

Coleman, Eli. "The Married Lesbian." *Marriage and Family Review*, Vol. 14, No. 3/4, 1989.

Cook, Blanche Wiesen. *Eleanor Roosevelt.* New York: Viking Penguin, 1992.

Corley, Rip. *The Final Closet, the Gay Parents' Guide for Coming Out to Their Children*, Miami Fla.: Editech Press, 1990.

Cunningham, Amy. "The Good, the Bad, and the Phony: Why Women Smile." *Lears*, March 1993.

Cunningham, Amy. "Married Sex." *McCalls*, May 1993.

Curb, Rosemary, and Nancy Manahan, eds. *Lesbian Nuns Breaking Silence.* Tallahassee, Fla.: The Naiad Press, 1985.

de Beauvoir, Simone. *The Second Sex.* New York: Vintage Books, 1989.

Dodson, Betty. *Sex for One: The Joy of Selfloving.* New York: Crown, 1987.

Doup, Liz. "When Love and Marriage Don't Go Together," *The Washington Post*, February 8, 1993.

Dowling, Colette. *The Cinderella Complex.* New York: Pocket Books, 1981.

Elmer-Dewitt, Philip. "Sex in America," *Time*, October 17, 1994, Vol. 144, No. 16.

Dymes, Wayne R., ed. *Encyclopedia of Homosexuality.* New York: Garland Press, 1990.

Erhart, Margaret. *Unusual Company.* New York: New American Library, 1987.

Faderman, Lillian. *Odd Girls and Twilight Lovers: A History of Lesbian Life in Twentieth Century America.* New York: Penguin Books, 1991.

Faderman, Lillian. *Surpassing the Love of Men.* New York: William Morrow & Co., 1981.

Fairchild, Betty, and Nancy Hayward. *Now That You Know.* Orlando, Fla.: Harvest/HBJ, 1989.

Flagg, Fanny. *Fried Green Tomatoes*, New York, McGraw-Hill, 1988.

Friedman, Sonya. *Secret Loves.* New York: Crown, 1994.

Friday, Nancy. *My Mother My Self.* New York: Dell, 1977.

Friday, Nancy. *My Secret Garden.* New York: Pocket Books, 1973.

Frymer-Kensky, Tikva, "Sex and Sexuality," *The Anchor Bible Dictionary*, Vol. 5, David Noel Freedman, ed. New York: Doubleday, 1992.

Garber, Marjorie. *Vice Versa: Bisexuality and the Eroticism of Everyday Life.* New York: Simon & Schuster, 1995.

Garnets, Linda D., and Douglas C. Kimmel, eds. *Psychological Perspectives on Lesbian & Gay Male Experiences.* New York: Columbia University Press, 1993.

Hamer, Dean, and Peter Copeland. *The Science of Desire: The Search for the Gay Gene and Biology of Behavior.* New York: Simon & Schuster, 1994.

Heyn, Dalma. *The Erotic Silence of the American Wife.* New York: Turtle Bay, 1992.

Hite, Shere. *The Hite Report.* New York: Macmillian, 1976.

Hite, Shere. *Women and Love.* New York: St. Martin's Press, 1987.

Hite, Shere. *Women as Revolutionary Agents of Change.* Madison, Wisc.: The University of Wisconsin Press, 1993.

Hollis, Judi. *Fat Is a Family Affair*. San Francisco: Harper/Hagelden, 1986.

Johnson, Sonia. *Wild Fire Igniting*. Albuquerque, N.M.: Wild Fire Press, 1991.

Johnson, Sonia. *Ship That Sailed into the Living Room*. Albuquerque, N.M.: Wild Fire Press, 1991.

Jong, Erica. *Fear of Flying*. New York: Penguin Books, 1973.

Kelly, Janis. "Sister Love: An Exploration of the Need for Homosexual Experiences." *The Family Coordinator*, Vol. 21, No. 4, October 1972.

Kinsey, Alfred C. *Sexual Behavior in the Human Female*. New York: Pocket Books, 1965.

Loulan, Jo Ann. *Lesbian Passion: Loving Ourselves and Each Other*. San Francisco: Spinsters, 1987.

Martin, Del, and Phyllis Lyon. *Lesbian Woman*. New York: Bantam, 1972.

Marvel, Nancy. "The Case for Feminist Celibacy." *The Feminist*. New York, 1971.

Masters, William H., and Virginia E. Johnson. *Human Sexual Inadequacy*. New York: Little, Brown & Company, 1970.

Masters, William H., Virginia E. Johnson, and Robert C. Kolodny. *Masters and Johnson on Sex and Human Loving*. Boston: Little, Brown & Company, 1988.

Michael, Robert T., John H. Gagnon, Edward O. Laumann, and Gina Kolata. *Sex in America: A Definitive Survey*. Boston: Little, Brown & Company, 1994.

Muller, Ann. *Parents Matter: Parents' Relationships With Lesbian Daughters and Gay Sons*. Tallahassee, Fla.: Naiad Press, 1987.

Nicolson, Nigel. *Portrait of a Marriage*. New York: Atheneum, 1980.

Penelope, Julia. *Call Me Lesbian*. Freedom, California: The Crossing Press, 1992.

Pomeroy, Sarah. *Goddesses, Whores, Wives and Slaves*. New York: Schocken Books, 1975.

Price, Deb, and Joyce Murdoch. *And Say Hi to Joyce*. New York: Doubleday, 1995.

Rafkin, Louis. *Different Mothers: Sons and Daughters of Lesbians Talk About Their Lives*. Pittsburgh: Cleis Press, 1990.

Reinisch, June M., and Ruth Beasley. *The Kinsey Institute New Report on Sex*. New York: St. Martin's Press, 1990.

Reuben, David. *Everything You Always Wanted to Know About Sex But Were Afraid to Ask*. New York: David McKay, 1969.

Rosen, Judith. "Women's Bookstores: 20 Years and Thriving." *Publishers Weekly*, Vol. 239, No. 22, May 11, 1992.

Russianoff, Penelope. *When Am I Going to Be Happy*. New York: Bantam, 1988.

Salk, Dr. Lee. *Familyhood*. New York: Simon & Schuster, 1992.

Scarf, Maggie. *Unfinished Business*. New York: Ballantine, 1980.

Schrof, Joannie M., and Betsy Wagner. "Sex in America," *U.S. News and World Report*, Vol. 117, No. 15, October 17, 1994.

Schwartz, Arnie. "Surpassing the Odds," *10 Percent Stonewall 25*, June 1994.

Seaman, Barbara. *Free and Female*. New York: Fawcett Crest, 1972.

Sutphen, Dick. *Reinventing Yourself: A Metaphysical Self-Renewal System*. Malibu, Cal.: Valley of the Sun Publishing, 1993.

Tannahill, Reay. *Sex in History*. Lanham, Md.: Scarborough House, 1992.

Toufexis, Anastasia. "Bisexuality: What Is It?" *Time*, Vol. 140, No. 7, August 17, 1992.

Walters, Marianne, Betty Carter, Peggy Papp, and Olga Silverstein. *The Invisible Web, Gender Patters in Family Relationships.* New York: The Guildford Press, 1988.

Weil, Bonnie Eaker. *Adultery: The Forgivable Sin.* New York: Carol Publishing Group, 1993.

Weinberg, Martin S., Colin J. Williams, and Douglas W. Pryor. *Dual Attraction.* New York: Oxford University Press, 1994.

Welsh, Patrick. "Gays in School." *The Washington Post*, March 4, 1990.

Whitney, Catherine. *Uncommon Lives: Gay Men & Straight Women.* New York: New American Library, 1990.

Winterson, Jeanette. *Written on the Body.* New York: Knopf, 1993.

Woodman, Sue. "For the City's Lesbians, the Political and Social Climate Has Never Been So Conducive to Coming Out. Why, Then, Is the Decision Still So Wrenching?" *New York Woman*, February 1990.

Acknowledgments

I WISH TO THANK all of the following people: the courageous women who entrusted me with their secrets—speaking to you was an enriching experience; the women who called but were too frightened to follow through with interviews—your fear and silence kept me focused on the importance of the book; the husbands and children who came forward—I applaud you for your openness and honesty and for choosing paths of understanding and acceptance rather than rejection and anger.

Thank you: to the International Women's Writing Guild and my Guild sisters, who believed in me and encouraged me to keep on when I faltered, and especially to Liz Alshire, Guild member and teacher, who taught me the "nuts and bolts" of writing a book; to the Greater New York Mensa Writers' SIG, especially Ed Pell, Bruce Kent, and Ian Randal Strock, your critiques forged the direction that *Married Women Who Love Women* would take; to the Second Thursday Networking Group and to Doris, who understood the importance of this book and insisted that I spend my time writing it rather than working on her committee; to my cronies from Stoney and to Connie Kurtz and Ruth Berman for teaching me to "make my own kind of music."

Special thanks: to Toni, who started me on my journey; to Becca Ritchie, who encouraged me from the beginning and who offered clear-headed advice as well; to reference librarian Susan Levy of the Grand Army Plaza branch of the Brooklyn Public

Library for being so accommodating; to Rita Montana, who was never too busy to listen when I needed to vent; to Henny Weiss, whose spelling abilities I availed myself of when my children were unavailable; to CeCe, a stranger who opened her home to me so that women in her area could tell me their stories; and to the numerous other women who touched my life along the way.

I am indebted to Jeanne Ferg, my friend the poet, who offered this simple counsel, "The more you talk about this subject, the less frightening it will become," and whose favorite expression, "Use it and defuse it," was, in part, responsible for the birth of this book.

In addition to being blessed with special friends, I am blessed with a special family. I thank them all: my dad, Robert Wagner, who taught me, "If you have a mouth to ask directions, you'll never be lost"; my mom, Bobbe Wagner, whose voice I'd hear saying, "It doesn't pay to be lazy," whenever I looked for short-cuts or wanted to procrastinate; my brother, Sam, for his tremendous praise after reading my synopsis and for saying, before he had, "It doesn't make any difference, you're my sister and I love you"; and my sister, Melody, who said, "I'm only sorry I didn't know sooner so I could have been there for you when you were going through the pain."

My very special thanks and love go to: my son, Ian, whose invaluable critiques, editorial expertise, and spelling prowess moved my early drafts along; my daughter, Laurie, who transcribed hours of tapes for me and served as my grammar consultant and number two spell checker; and my husband, Noel, who said, "I'm not comfortable with this book but I know how strongly you feel about it so I'd never ask you not to do it."

Special thanks also to Carol Mann, my agent, and Betsy Lerner, my editor at Doubleday. This book would not have been possible without you.